A History of Italian
Fascist Culture, 1922–1943

A History of Italian Fascist Culture, 1922–1943

A LESSANDRA T ARQUINI

Translated by Marissa Gemma

THE UNIVERSITY OF WISCONSIN PRESS

Publication of this book has been made possible, in part,
through support from the George L. Mosse Program in History at the University of
Wisconsin–Madison and the Hebrew University of Jerusalem.

GLM

GEORGE L.
MOSSE
PROGRAM IN HISTORY

The University of Wisconsin Press
728 State Street, Suite 443
Madison, Wisconsin 53706
uwpress.wisc.edu

Gray's Inn House, 127 Clerkenwell Road
London EC1R 5DB, United Kingdom
eurospanbookstore.com

Printed in the United States of America
This book may be available in a digital edition.

Library of Congress Cataloging-in-Publication Data
Names: Tarquini, Alessandra, author. | Gemma, Marissa, translator.
Title: A history of Italian fascist culture, 1922–1943 / Alessandra Tarquini ;
translated by Marissa Gemma.
Other titles: Storia della cultura fascista. English |
George L. Mosse series in the history of European culture, sexuality, and ideas.
Description: Madison, Wisconsin : The University of Wisconsin Press, [2022] |
Series: George L. Mosse series in the history of European culture, sexuality, and ideas |
Originally published in Italian as Storia della cultura fascista, © 2011
by Società editrice il Mulino | Includes bibliographical references and index.
Identifiers: LCCN 2021028485 | ISBN 9780299336202 (hardcover)
Subjects: LCSH: Fascism and culture—Italy—History—20th century. |
Fascism—Italy—History—20th century. | Italy—Cultural policy—History—20th century. |
Italy—Intellectual life—20th century.
Classification: LCC DG571 .T34813 2022 | DDC 320.53/30945—dc23
LC record available at https://lccn.loc.gov/2021028485

CONTENTS

PREFACE TO THE
ENGLISH-LANGUAGE EDITION

This edition is based on the second Italian edition of *Storia della cultura fascista*, which was published in 2016.

I would like to thank Ugo Berti for suggesting that I write this book and for very often being right during our conversations. I am particularly grateful to Emilio Gentile: while I was writing this book I had the good fortune of discussing most of the ideas in it with him, and he offered invaluable feedback on the draft manuscript. For their critiques and encouragement I'd like to thank my friends Francesco Benigno, Igor Mineo, and Michele Surdi, who read unpublished drafts of this book, sometimes more than once. I'm also pleased to thank Paolo Acanfora, Pierluigi Allotti, Donatello Aramini, Stefania Bartoloni, Maddalena Carli, Angelo Gaudio, Vincenzo Lavenia, Igor Mineo, Alessio Ponzio, Gianluca Scroccu, Alfonso Venturini, and Maurizio Zinni for their help and references. Finally, to Francesca Rosa, Alessandra Staderini, Daniela Tarquini, and Annamaria Trama, thank you, as always.

This book is dedicated to the memory of my mother, the first antifascist I encountered.

A History of Italian
Fascist Culture, 1922–1943

Introduction

In the opening lines of the book *La cultura fascista* (Fascist culture), published by the National Fascist Party for its political training courses aimed at young people, one reads that "a culture is a concept of life," "a manifestation of social, spiritual, and historical action," and not "an individual way of being," "an intellectual adornment or private matter of contemplation." Culture is, in essence, an activity that "create[s] a public."[1]

These passages are just one instance of the many writings in which the fascists displayed their belief that the existence of the Italian people had meaning only within the framework of the regime's aims and activities. Convinced that politics constituted "the essential part of every event" and that "each individual's freest gestures and most intimate thoughts" would gain "concrete meaning" only if they were "directly traceable back to a political value," the fascists celebrated the primacy of politics over all other forms of modern life.[2] They believed that culture was an instrument for creating the new civilization that had been born when they seized power in October 1922.

This way of understanding culture was a manifestation of fascism's totalitarian nature, as I try to emphasize in this brief history of fascist culture—a history that does not undertake a wholesale summary of Italian culture in the years between the two world wars. The following pages, in fact, dwell only on the most important forms of the regime's culture, those that directly reflect its actions, leaving out cultural phenomena that, despite having enormous salience for the history of twentieth-century Italy (and in some cases for twentieth-century history *tout court*), are not clearly linked to the politics of fascism.

In the chapters that follow, we shall analyze the fascist cultural universe, characterizing the regime's *cultural politics*, its *forms of knowledge*, and its *ideology*. The term *cultural politics* refers primarily to the activities of the National Fascist Party (Partito nazionale fascista, or PNF) and the government, and allows us to characterize the ruling class's decisions, from the creation of new institutions (like the Istituto nazionale fascista di cultura, the National Institute of Fascist Culture, founded in 1925) to the handling of traditional governmental functions (like education policy). The phrase *forms of knowledge*, in turn, refers to the contributions intellectuals and artists made to fascism. In this case, we will attempt to understand whether there was such a thing as a fascist literature, a fascist architecture, a fascist philosophy, and so on, and in what sense it is possible to identify them. And, finally, *ideology*, which is the expression of political myths, that is, of images, words, and beliefs capable of supplying a group with a sense of action—so argued Georges Sorel, the theorist of revolutionary syndicalism who first studied myths as a means of analyzing modern politics.

In reality, this distinction between *cultural politics*, *forms of knowledge*, and *ideology* has a purely expository purpose: it allows us to select certain aspects of a seemingly inexhaustible topic, like a regime's culture during a given period of history. In practice, from 1922 to 1943 cultural politics, ideology, and the works of artists and intellectuals arose together to produce fascist culture. For example, the Mussolini Forum, built in Rome between 1927 and 1933 by the architect Enrico Del Debbio, was a complex of buildings that testified to the presence of a fascist architecture and as such is undoubtedly a cultural expression of the '30s. At the same time, though, it is an example of the cultural politics of the Fascist Party (and especially of the fascist youth organization that it had built). It is also the expression of an ideology rooted in the omnipresent myth of Mussolini, to whom a marble obelisk 62 feet high was dedicated at the entrance to the grounds, bearing the inscription "Mussolini Dux." A similar example can be found in the Scuola di mistica (the School of Fascist Mysticism), founded in 1931 at the National Institute of Fascist Culture in Milan to train young people in the cult of Il Duce. Here, too, we see the regime's political culture giving rise to a new institution; the fruits of an ideology founded on the myth of Mussolini; and the concrete actions of the historians, philosophers, and legal scholars who taught at the school from 1931 until 1943 and made their own contributions to the elaboration and diffusion of fascist culture.

This book is divided into seven chapters. In chapter 1, we will examine scholarship on fascist culture from the postwar period until today. My goal is to explain why this aspect of the history of fascism, which has by now become something of a historiographical trend, received no attention from Italian intellectuals until the 1970s, since the majority of these scholars were convinced up to that point that the fascist regime had been incapable of giving voice to a culture of its own. Between the 1970s and early 2000s, historians effectively overturned their own rulings, shifting from denying the existence of fascist culture to reconstructing its many and diverse facets, and considering them not only important but actually essential for understanding fascism as a whole. In chapter 2 we will reconstruct the cultural politics of the 1920s through the government and the Party's key initiatives. In chapter 3 we will consider the contributions of the intellectuals and artists who were the main proponents of fascist culture during this period, with an eye to the diverse trends and groups that played a starring role on the Italian cultural scene. Chapter 4 is dedicated to fascist ideology: its myths, theorists, and the primary characteristics that distinguish it from other twentieth-century political ideologies. Chapter 5 analyzes the cultural politics of the '30s, summarizing the government's and the Party's activities in a few key areas: youth culture, schooling, women's lives, and popular culture. In chapter 6 we will examine the literati, philosophers, scientists, and architects who represented fascist culture until the end of the 1930s, and in chapter 7 we will study a few particularly significant undertakings from the 1940s.

In reconstructing this history of fascist culture, we have tried to bear in mind Benedetto Croce's well-known dictum "All history is contemporary history," and thus all historiographical problems arise from questions that are alive and well in the mind of the historian.[3] However remote the facts in question may be, Croce wrote in 1938, history is always related to a current situation, such that, in turning their gaze to the past, historians respond to problems raised by their own intelligence, curiosity, or daily life. In effect, Croce's definition may be so frequently cited in the introductions to books of history because authors feel the need to remind the reader that they are conscious of the historical and thus partial nature of the questions they seek to answer. The question that this book attempts to answer, within the scope of its inquiry, was born of the desire to understand why men and women of culture dedicated their time, creativity, and labor to the service of the fascist regime.

It is a sad question, just as the answer offered here is sad. There are no heroes, no victories, no redemption, and above all the story does not end with the triumph of good over evil. There are intellectuals, artists, and politicians who built a violent dictatorship, believing in politics as one believes in a religion, envisioning a life of integrity and absolutism, and ensuring the vitality of a totalitarian regime. Studying the writings and works of these men and women means asking oneself if what we call "culture"—through which we have the pleasure of reading about, listening to, and understanding the stories of others—is the same thing that they believed in, those who spent their lives in a totalitarian regime and didn't have, or couldn't find, the possibility of living differently. It means taking history seriously, and not getting used to the violence of power.

1

The Historiographical Debate
from 1945 to Today

The First Studies of Fascist Culture

The first studies of fascist culture appeared immediately after the end of World War II, a time when the historiographical debate about fascism was being shaped by the political battle that had just ended. The discussion among historians unfolded, at that time, among proponents of three interpretations: one liberal, one radical, and one Marxist—all given voice by political cultures or individual scholars linked to the world of antifascism.[1] Following in the footsteps of Benedetto Croce, liberal intellectuals viewed fascism as the symptom of a moral disease that had exploded in the first half of the twentieth century with the spread of irrationalism in European culture and society. Fascism, in their view, was the simple but brutal product of a bad phase of history. By contrast, the democrats and radicals, following the example of the antifascist intellectual Piero Gobetti, did not believe that the phenomenon of fascism was confined to the first half of the twentieth century. Instead, they saw fascism as "the autobiography of the Italian nation"—that is, the result of long-standing, unresolved issues and of an economic and political development unlike that of other European nations. For these scholars, fascism had no original traits *per se* but rather showed signs of resembling earlier regimes that, like fascism, had expressed the anomalies of Italian history. Socialists and communists, finally, identified fascism with the eruption of reactionary forces against the rise of the proletariat. But in their eyes, too, fascism had invented nothing. As a manifestation of class conflict, it merely expressed a stage in the struggle between capital and the power of the labor movement.

What these three extremely different interpretations shared was a lack of reflection on the unique characteristics of fascism, which came to be described as a regime capable of imposing its domination on the Italian people through violence and terror, and thus deserving of condemnation and contempt—but not of particularly detailed historiographical analyses, since it lacked any kind of originality. Indeed, scholars with diverse worldviews and training agreed that fascism had no ideology, as Norberto Bobbio asserted. At the end of World War II, Bobbio began associating with the Action Party (Partito d'azione), which had been secretly founded in 1942 as a continuation of the liberal-socialist movement Justice and Freedom (Giustizia e Libertà). In his own telling, and according to what he wrote over the course of his long scholarly career, Bobbio represented those democratic and antifascist intellectuals who, immediately after the war, understood their role as scholars as a mission to be fulfilled. That mission was to fight against any form of subordination to a party or a state, whether fascist or Soviet, the latter serving as a point of reference for much of the Italian left at the height of the Cold War.

In the early 1950s Bobbio claimed that fascism had not been able to produce any culture whatsoever, and that even a man like Giovanni Gentile, minister of public education in Mussolini's first government, "when writing as a fascist became bloated and rhetorical, using flowery prose to fill a conceptual void."[2] He would reiterate these opinions in the years that followed, as he did in 1973, arguing that "the quintessential fascist intellectuals were for the most part two-bit intellectuals,"[3] and that fascism as a movement had been "antidemocratic, antisocialist, anti-Bolshevik, antiparliamentarian, antiliberal—anti-everything," rooted in activism and irrationalism.[4]

In forming these views, Bobbio was influenced by Gaetano Salvemini, Carlo Rosselli, and above all Benedetto Croce and Piero Gobetti. From studying Croce he developed the conviction that the theoretical foundations of fascism were irrationalism and activism, which had developed as a moral disease in early twentieth-century Europe.[5] From Gobetti, on the other hand, he adopted the idea of Italy as separate and distinct from the rest of the civilized modern world. This Italy was rhetorical, backward, illiberal, and petit bourgeois; Gentile was its authoritative exegete, and fascism one of its most consequential products.[6] Thus reconciling Croce's liberal interpretation with Gobetti's radical-democratic one, Bobbio defined culture as the result of freedom of thought, the exercise of criticism, and the rational analysis of existence. Accordingly, fascist intellectuals, who renounced their independence and served the interests of politics, could not be considered true scholars, but merely "two-bit" intellectuals. In keeping with this notion of culture, fascism in Bobbio's view was nothing more than a period of crisis in the history of Europe and Italy.

This position was born of the necessity of hiding a past that was difficult to comprehend. Recognizing the existence of fascist culture would have required Bobbio and the many other scholars who expressed similar views to explain why Italian intellectuals had offered their talents to the totalitarian regime. They would have had to explain how their generation had become democratic and antifascist despite having never publicly dissented in any way during the regime's years in power—indeed despite, in some cases, having played public roles in the regime, teaching in universities, writing for fascist newspapers, and generally functioning as the Italian cultural elite. They did not explain this, choosing instead to whitewash "the specific characteristics of the fascist experience,"[7] to "de-fascistize" it, albeit unintentionally. They thereby erased the attributes that had constituted the regime's historical specificity, denying that it had ever had a culture, an ideology, a ruling class, a totalitarian nature, or its own individuality.[8]

Unlike Bobbio, Eugenio Garin, who at that time was one of the most prominent leftist scholars affiliated with the Communist Party, argued that Italian culture in the years between the two wars was a topic worthy of attention. For this reason he gave it pride of place in his 1955 *Cronache di filosofia italiana* (Chronicles of Italian philosophy). Garin thought that, after an initial phase in which Gentile had played a decisive role in fascist culture, the regime had revealed its true reactionary and conservative colors with the Lateran Treaty of 1929. The treaty showed that it had chosen to reconcile with the Catholics, who had always been hostile to Gentile and other proponents of modern philosophy. In short, Garin was convinced that fascist culture was a reactionary culture with Catholic and spiritualist roots.[9]

If Croce and Gobetti were key reference points for Bobbio as he formulated his historiographical judgments about fascism, Garin was influenced by the communist intellectual Antonio Gramsci—and, to a lesser extent, by Croce as well. From Gramsci, who died in prison in 1937 after writing *The Prison Notebooks* (published posthumously between 1947 and 1951), Garin derived the belief that ideologies are not simple superstructures of economic life, as a certain strain of Marxist orthodoxy claimed, but rather contain their own intrinsic value. Garin further argued, again following Gramsci, that ideologies are not born from the development of coherent concepts—they are not ideas born of other ideas—but rather result from a cultural and political battle to transform everyday life. In this sense, Garin thought that the Italian cultural tradition ought to be reimagined as the history of intellectual groups "not isolated in their ideas and writings, but rather seen in relation to the forces currently operating" and expressing their own worldview.[10] These reflections lent themselves nicely to the idea of philosophy as historical knowledge that Garin had adapted from Croce. As he acknowledged many times, Garin admired the idealist philosopher's willingness to measure himself against the practical problems of his own time, and he endorsed the notion that the process of producing ideas is always connected to the way sociopolitical life unfolds.

Now, neither Croce nor Gramsci had ever claimed that the regime had a culture of its own. In 1924 the communist leader had declared the cultural artifacts of fascism "plaything[s] for the Fascist Youth."[11] His reflections on ideologies as everyday realities, and on the relationship between intellectuals and political power—born as they were of the exigencies of being a communist leader and a Marxist theorist—had not led him to an understanding of fascism as a revolutionary phenomenon with a unique culture distinct from its predecessor.[12] For Gramsci, fascism was the most obvious symptom of the liberal ruling class's failure to rise to the challenges of mass society. From his place of captivity within the regime's prisons, Gramsci saw fascism as a reactionary phenomenon, to be studied as one studies an adversary who has won a battle.

Though he was not a Marxist, as Garin developed these arguments, he (like many intellectuals of his generation) approached Gramsci's thought as a tool for building a new civic consciousness that could fuel Italy's recovery from fascism. This is why he drew closer to the politics of Palmiro Togliatti, who had begun trying to rebuild the Italian Communist Party as soon as World War II ended, ultimately transforming it from a small, Leninist faction in the 1920s into a new national party for the masses.[13] As we can see, then, the first studies of fascist culture were produced in leftist circles, by antifascist leaders with democratic, socialist, and communist leanings—all of whom nevertheless denied the very existence of the subject in question.

The view among Catholics was no different: the majority of Catholic intellectuals declared themselves in agreement with Bobbio's interpretation and agreed without hesitation that there had been no such thing as a fascist culture, given that "the doctrine of fascism was but the mask or costume assumed on various occasions to hide how things really were." Such was the opinion of the literary critic Carlo Bo. In his youth, Bo had contributed to a range of fascist magazines, like *Rivoluzione* (Revolution) and *Primato* (Primacy), and later he became an authoritative Catholic scholar. For Bo, "the history of fascism was nothing more than a series of improvised motifs, the fruits of journalistic labor in the best case, given that they derived from the study of specific situations." He was convinced that, in seeking to define fascist ideology, scholars would realize that "it never existed."[14] Two years later, in a collection of essays, a range of Catholic scholars highlighted how difficult it was to identify the substance of fascist doctrine.[15]

The only exception to this decidedly uniform historiographical land-scape was Augusto Del Noce. Right after the war, the Catholic philosopher wrote that fascism had "deep roots in the habits of modern spirituality," thus declaring his agreement with Croce.[16] For Croce, the defining characteristic of fascist thought and culture was activism. However, for Del Noce, activism was not to be mistaken for "a spirit of indoctrination, simple-mindedness, or coarseness," because, quite to the contrary, "it had refined, cultured, and classically European roots."[17] In the years that followed, he deepened these reflections, arguing that the origin of fascist culture could be found in Gen-tile's philosophy, and that the fascists had understood politics not as an instrument for transforming the world but rather as a religious faith—and therefore as something to be lived whole-heartedly and absolutely.[18] From the early 1970s onward, repeating what he had argued for more than three decades, Del Noce insisted that fascism was not a "reactionary" political phenomenon—that is, it was not born out of a reaction to modernity. It had come not from a clash between the Catholics and the conservative forces united against progress, as Garin believed; nor was it an anticultural regime, as Bobbio thought. In Del Noce's opinion, fascism was born as "an error of modern culture," not "an error against culture."[19] In fact, he was convinced that alongside secular modernity had arisen an absolutist notion of politics that, in attempting to replace God, believed it was possible to attain happiness and free mankind from suffering. For Del Noce, all revolutionary thought represented an attempt to create a secular religion, from which it followed that totalitarian regimes, like the fascist one, represented the apotheosis of modernity, its logical extreme.

This interpretation flew in the face of the prevailing ideas of the period, dominated by the works of Marxist scholarship that were among the first to systematically take up the history of fascism.

Marxist Historiography

From the end of World War II until the 1980s, with a few key exceptions, Marxist scholars portrayed fascism as a counterrevolutionary political phenomenon, created by the bourgeoisie's reaction against the proletariat's power. Hence, they denied that it had a specific identity of its own, viewing it rather as the epiphenomenon of class struggle. Moreover, most scholars with communist leanings accepted the orthodox Marxist understanding of ideologies as superstructural manifestations of economic relationships between social classes—in other words, as outcroppings of structural problems, with no intrinsic value of their own. Believing that the ruling class's ideas are the dominant ideas of every age, and thus that a society's ruling class is at the same time its spiritual center, Marxist scholars assigned the term *ideology* to the amalgam of cultural artifacts produced by the social class in power at a given moment, which put forth a distorted image of reality to justify its own existence.

From this premise arose several arguments of enormous import for thinking about culture and, by extension, about fascist culture. In particular, it produced a view of the history of culture as a history of false representations of reality, representations produced by the economic and political landscape in which they developed; and thus the conviction arose that it was not necessary to study the content of ideology, but rather its means of dominance. Convinced that it was their calling to debunk prejudices, mythologies, and superstitions in order to lead historiography toward a higher plane of knowledge and consciousness, Marxist scholars shared this goal with liberals and scholars of various orientations, who likewise trusted in progress and in the possibility of using reason to shed light on the workings of oppression.

In point of fact, looking closely at this portrait of Marxist postwar culture, one can discern at least two main lines of research among the many studies it produced: one linked to Gramsci and Togliatti, and another that can be traced back to experiences of communism that spread through the West, especially after 1968, as demonstrated by the works of the Hungarian philosopher György Lukács and the Italian literary critic Alberto Asor Rosa, two figures who nonetheless differed starkly from one another.

In *The Destruction of Reason*, Lukács chronicled the history of German philosophy from Schelling to the rise of nationalism, persuaded as he was that European culture's most significant trait at that time was the affirmation of irrationalism—and thus, according to Lukács, of a bourgeois, reactionary line of thought developed in Germany during the nineteenth and twentieth centuries.[20] Irrationalism, which Lukács described as the result of an inevitable trajectory—the offspring of a social and political process—expressed itself through various philosophies that prepared the cultural way for National Socialism, from Schopenhauer to Weber, and from Kierkegaard to Nietzsche. Nietzsche, in particular, was in Lukács's eyes primarily responsible for imagining an imperialist Germany; he was the philosopher who best represented "the permanent interests of the reactionary bourgeoisie," and thus the spiritual father of National Socialism.

Paradoxical as it may seem, Lukács's arguments and conclusions about the origins of National Socialist culture were indistinguishable from those of liberals, who considered fascism to be the product of irrationalism and militarism. Bobbio acknowledged as much in 1976, reviewing Lukács's book and highlighting the commonalities between his own argument about the incoherence of fascist culture and the Hungarian philosopher's reflections.[21] Indeed, it is possible to discern a broad convergence among Marxist scholars and liberal-democratic authors of that time on the topic of the irrationalist nature of fascism, which symbolized for all of them the final chapter of a crisis that had begun in the latter half of the nineteenth century. As Mario Isnenghi explained in 1979, this was no "happy outcome." They began as "militant antifascists, perhaps Marxists," only to "find themselves once again Croceans—a revived Croceanism, and a leftist one at that."[22]

In 1965, in *Scrittori e popolo* (published in English as *The Writer and the People*), Alberto Asor Rosa recounted a history of Italian literature in which he identified a common thread running through the cultures of the

Risorgimento, fascism, and post-fascism. With the "national question" re-
solved, many Italian intellectuals had begun to occupy themselves with the
peasant masses, turning their attention to a populace excluded from the
construction of Italian national unity and now seen as the guardians of strong
values. From that point on, pitting the popular masses against the ruling
classes, conservative and progressive Italian literati alike wrote in the name
of and in defense of the people. And so, according to Asor Rosa, "while in
the twentieth century Europe produced the last great flowering of a bourgeois literature ferociously critical and destructive of the world that produced
it, Italy continued to produce generations of intellectuals naively credulous
about the socially regenerative function of art and poetry."[23] From Alfredo
Oriani to Giovanni Pascoli, from Enrico Corradini to Gaetano Salvemini,
from Massimo Bontempelli to Pier Paolo Pasolini, the populism Asor Rosa
described was the product of a petit bourgeois, anticlassist culture that created a nebulous, mythical image of the people, instead of understanding
the masses as a social class with all the trappings of such. We can see this
in the fascist writer Curzio Suckert—republican, interventionist, Garibal-
dian, syndicalist revolutionary, and *squadrista* (i.e., a member of the fascist
action squads)—who was one of the many fascists who exalted the people
as pure power.[24] In short, just like late nineteenth-century progressives, fascist writers associated "the people" with good values and engaged with the
social world around them by advocating for the creation of a national popular state.

In 1975, in the fourth volume of the *Storia d'Italia* (History of Italy) published by Einaudi, Asor Rosa devoted over three hundred pages to fascist
culture, claiming that it had been "the accumulation of unsatisfied ambi-
tions and delusions, a reactionary, counterreformist, multi-headed mix-
ture of Voce-anism, Prezzolinismo, Papinismo, Sofficismo, Gentilianesimo,
Futurism, Sorelism, D'Annunzianism, ruralism"—the "cesspit, in short" into
which all the "archaic, backward, provincial, schizophrenic aspects of pos-
tunification Italian culture" flowed together.[25] In this essay, Asor Rosa also
identified links between prefascist literature and that of the '20s and '30s,
showing that "all or nearly all of the premises of the various intellectual
forces that together sustained fascism" subsisted in Italian culture, and that
it was possible to discern a "a perfect continuity ... between the unfolding of national issues from the beginning of the century to 1922–23."[26] Yet,

diverging from his claims in *Scrittori e popolo*, in this 1975 essay Asor Rosa emphasized that Italian culture had registered those events "as a crisis of civilization and therefore, however painful, inevitable."[27] Fascist writers, poets, journalists, and novelists had continued to tell the story of an archaic and provincial Italian culture, as Italian intellectuals had done at the beginning of the century, when the long crisis resulting in fascism had begun—and therefore they had borne witness to the end of a civilization that had been unable to rise from its own ashes. Thus, while in *Scrittori e popolo* Asor Rosa had pointed to the populism of Italian intellectuals as the principal feature of the nation's culture from the Risorgimento to fascism—thereby proposing a critical reflection on modern literature that included the fascists' contribution—in the pages of Einaudi's *Storia d'Italia*, he described fascism as the expression of a backward and reactionary culture that had developed at the end of the nineteenth century.

Yet, as we noted above, in the early 1970s Marxist historians who had absorbed the *Lezioni sul fascismo* (*Lectures on Fascism*) Togliatti gave in Moscow in early 1935 were beginning to put forth arguments of a very different nature. In Togliatti's lectures, published in 1970, the secretary of the Italian Communist Party invites his listeners to grasp the unique qualities of the fascist dictatorship. The lectures eschew generalizations, and Togliatti does not restrict his view of the regime to seeing it as one of many manifestations of the battle between capital and the forces of the workers' movement. Instead, he dwells at length on fascism's structural elements, defining it as "a reactionary regime of the masses," and, therefore, a dictatorship wholly different from the nineteenth-century authoritarian regimes. In Togliatti's opinion, fascism had given shape to a modern political system, "a wholly reactionary system" that was decentralized, furnished with a reactionary bourgeois ideology rooted in nationalism and pro-Catholicism, and capable of "hold[ing] together the petty bourgeois strata."[28] To be clear, this argument was not a reflection on fascism's ideas, which for Togliatti held no interest, but rather on culture as an instrument wielded by political powers to mobilize the popular masses. On this topic the party secretary was clear: "I warn you against the tendency to regard fascist ideology as something that is solidly formed, complete, homogeneous. Nothing more closely resembles a chameleon than fascist ideology."[29] In this sense, Togliatti took a page from Gramsci's book, and from the entire Marxist tradition, seemingly giving no credence to the hypothesis that fascism had expressed a culture of its own, distinct from that which had preceded it.[30]

Togliatti's work heavily influenced the thinking of Italian historians close to the Communist Party, who grappled with the subject of fascism in the 1970s. Convinced that the liberal understanding of culture offered insufficient explanation for two decades of fascism,[31] communist historians acknowledged that fascism was "the only period in the history of unified Italy in which intellectuals' support for the ruling classes" was the norm.[32] In effect, as Giuseppe Vacca wrote, aside from the few "who stayed with or went to the opposition, and the very few who emigrated or went to prison, the vast majority of intellectuals cooperated in building the regime."[33] This understanding prompted an inquiry into how the status of people of culture had changed under fascism, compared with their status in liberal Italy, and thus how fascist political power had made use of Italian intellectuals—questions that were subsequently taken up by Luisa Mangoni, Eugenio Garin, and Gabriele Turi.

In 1974 Luisa Mangoni published *L'interventismo della cultura* (The interventionism of culture), the first history of Italian intellectuals from the Italo-Turkish War to World War II. Explicitly citing Togliatti's lectures and Garin's *Cronache di filosofia italiana*, Mangoni argued that to understand Italian culture between the two wars, one had to study the marriage of fascism and nationalism and see it as the bourgeoisie's attempt to "reorganize" after liberal Italy's crisis, to "reconstruct the State's instruments of control and power."[34] She too contended that nationalism was the principal ingredient of fascist culture: "it was no accident," she wrote, citing Togliatti, "that [Alfredo] Rocco, a nationalist, was the legislator of this dictatorship—no accident that [Giuseppe] Bottai, also a nationalist, was one of its greatest figures."[35] In Mangoni's view, such nationalist figures were the most authoritative exponents of moderate fascism, which had the firm support of the Catholics. Indeed, like Togliatti and Garin, Mangoni thought that the alliance between the fascists and the Catholics had expressed the fascist regime's true nature, and that the Lateran Treaty of 1929 had "signified the substitution of Catholicism for idealism as the regime's dominant culture."[36] Consistent with this line of reasoning, she too believed that Gentile and his students were not true representatives of fascist culture, a role played instead by the young people who came of age during the Ventennio (the twenty-odd years of the fascist regime in Italy) and by the anti-idealist philosophers of the

1930s. For Mangoni too, therefore, the cultural universe of fascism had been absorbed on the one hand by nationalism—which had taken shape as a political movement long before 1929—and on the other by Catholic intellectuals, who in their own right gave voice to a culture that could not be straightforwardly reduced to political ideology.[37]

It was also in 1974, in *Intellettuali italiani del XX secolo* (Twentieth-century Italian intellectuals), that Garin reaffirmed his assessment from two decades before, writing that fascist ideology took shape as a hodgepodge of "heterogeneous, eclectic, utilitarian" elements, and thus as an extremely complex phenomenon that was practically impossible to define—a collection of elements that harked back to spiritualism, the last century's crises of positivism, and the worst parts of Italian culture. Reconciling Gobettian themes with Togliatti's lectures, Garin believed that three kinds of intellectuals lived under the "reactionary" regime: first, the antifascists forced to dissemble to survive under a dictatorial government, the so-called Nicodemites, who, like the followers of Protestantism in the seventeenth century, hid their faith to escape Catholic persecution; second, the naive fascists, who sought to change the regime from the inside and did not recognize their own impotence; and, last, the youths who quickly understood antifascism's *raison d'être* and could be considered proto-antifascists. In a country of slaves and courtesans, turned fascist because it had been indelibly marked by a counterreformist culture—a country that had not known modernity because it had not been able to overcome its own congenital political immaturity, and thus could not consider itself entirely civilized—Garin believed that there had been no true fascist intellectuals: that is, no men of culture who consciously and independently declared themselves fascists, who conducted research, wrote, published, and taught in Italian universities because they were stalwart supporters of the totalitarian regime.[38] The debate was characterized by, on the one hand, authoritative pronouncements from Mangoni, for whom fascism expressed nationalist and Catholic culture, and, on the other, from Garin, who in the mid-1970s had landed upon an even more drastic interpretation, one that denied the existence of any kind of fascist culture, thus coming closer to what Bobbio had been arguing for some time. In this context, Gabriele Turi's work represented a genuine novelty.

In 1980 Turi published *Il fascismo e il consenso degli intellettuali* (Fascism and the consent of intellectuals), which examined various cultural institutions in order to show that high culture, too, had undergone fascism's influence. For example, contrary to the rather widespread opinion that the *Enciclopedia italiana* (Italian encyclopedia) had maintained a certain degree of independence because it was edited by Giovanni Gentile—that is, by a philosopher who many believed had not been fascist—Turi studied entries related to politics and confirmed, in his words, "beyond the shadow of a doubt the presence of not only a fascist ideology, but also a fascist culture, through which the regime attempted to give itself historical legitimacy."[39] He was convinced, in fact, that fascism had been able to bring together "threads of the liberal bourgeoisie" in a "*koiné*" that, though it had availed itself of diverse materials, had been no less "homogeneous in terms of goals . . . and in the continuous interchange between culture and ideology."[40] For this reason he argued that studying how fascism had succeeded in influencing intellectuals, and thus analyzing the conditioning work undertaken by a myriad of cultural institutions, could reveal the extent of Italian society's consent during the regime. And the very presence of a vast institutional apparatus demonstrated, in his view, the difficulty of expressing any kind of thought truly free from politics.

Despite these novel considerations, Turi did not set out to analyze fascist culture. In fact, in his work in the early '80s, on the one hand he clearly posited the existence of an ideology and a culture that had influenced Italian intellectuals through the institutions created by the regime; and, on the other hand, he gave a cursory description of this culture, as if it were unimportant to understand what it was made of, imagining continuity between "the class characteristics of bourgeois culture before and during fascism."[41]

By the early 1980s, then, these were the key debates and positions among communist scholars. It was only in 1989, after the fall of the Berlin Wall, that Marxist historiography changed its reading of the history of fascist culture, finally accommodating what was being written in Italy and abroad, where a different perspective had been taking hold since the early 1960s.

The Contributions of European and American Scholars

From the early 1960s on, European and American scholars of diverse training and ideological positions took up the issue of culture between the two world wars, arguing that understanding this culture was essential to any wholesale understanding of the phenomenon of fascism.

In 1963, with his imposing *Der Faschismus in seiner Epoche* (published in English as *Three Faces of Fascism*), the German scholar Ernst Nolte inaugurated a new phase of study, examining l'Action française, National Socialism, and Italian fascism and developing an argument that he would return to over the course of his long scholarly career. He argued that these three political moments stemmed from the European bourgeoisie's fears in the face of the Bolshevik Revolution and gave voice to a reaction at once conservative and modern: conservative because it sought to counter the communists' attempts to rebel against the existing order; modern because it was bourgeois and revolutionary, and therefore the offspring of a tradition that had opposed the *ancien régime* since the French Revolution, invoking a notion of liberty as freedom from a system of traditional values. The hearth gods of this tradition were Nietzsche and Marx, and therefore it could not wholly identify with conservative ideas developed in nineteenth-century Europe.[42] To understand this tradition, Nolte argued, it was necessary to take it seriously and to let "Hitler and Mussolini speak," even when "they had nothing original to say."[43]

Like Nolte, the Israeli historian Zeev Sternhell thought that it was possible to identify a typology of commonalities among these diverse political moments. In his contribution to a 1976 collection by prominent American and European historians, and in his many works over the following years, Sternhell argued that a prototype of fascism had arisen from the encounter between anti-Marxist socialism and nationalism in late nineteenth-century France and then spread through Europe in the twentieth century.[44] Thus, while for Nolte fascist thought derived from Nietzsche's and Marx's philosophies, for Sternhell it stemmed from a reaction to the Enlightenment and from the encounter of nationalism and socialist antimaterialist thought, found first and foremost among the revolutionary syndicalists of the late nineteenth century. In his opinion, in fact, fascism was a political phenomenon equipped with its own revolutionary ideology, no less coherent than liberalism or Marxism, which had given voice to the desire to create a new civilization and a new man. Sternhell argued that fascism had been able to answer the questions posed by mass society at the beginning of the century: "what's the relationship between the individual and the collective?" "what constitutes a nation? ... the free choice of individuals or a people's history, religion, and culture?"[45] Sternhell, like Nolte and like Del Noce in Italy, was among the first to view fascism as the political offspring of modernity.

In America during the same period, A. James Gregor, Edward Tannenbaum, and Philip Cannistraro studied key moments and features of fascist
culture, using a different methodological approach that partially confirmed
Nolte's and Sternhell's findings. In 1969 Gregor, an American historian, published *The Ideology of Fascism*, whose first volume was devoted to this topic.[46]
Among his primary sources were the works of Giovanni Gentile, who in
his opinion had provided the regime with "its most coherent and defensible
normative rationale," and those of intellectuals like Julius Evola, Sergio Panunzio, and Carlo Costamagna.[47] Gregor did not stop at positing the existence of fascist ideology, however, but shed light on its various components.
In his study he synthesized the debate about the nature of the state and the
issues that dominated political culture in the '20s and '30s—and in this way
he articulated the positions expressed by fascist intellectuals, demonstrating both their debt to the broad trends of European thought and the relative
coherence of fascist ideology. Tannenbaum and Cannistraro also devoted
themselves to investigating the political culture between the world wars. Tannenbaum examined education, artistic movements, and propaganda, arguing that fascist culture *per se* had not existed.[48] Cannistraro, on the other
hand, examined the Ministry of Popular Culture, created in 1937.[49] His goal
was to show how, in a political climate of constant conflict between modern
and traditional factions, the regime had generated consent from its ideological foundation of nationalism and, in the end, its efforts to fully integrate its citizens into a unified national life. To achieve these ends, fascism
had taken two different tacks: on the one hand, bringing the masses closer to
culture through theater, radio, and cinema, and, on the other, forcing intellectuals "to serve the political and social interests of fascism."[50] As we can
see, like Mangoni and Turi in those years, Cannistraro saw fascist culture as
an instrument for creating consent, controlling intellectuals, and mobilizing
the popular masses, even if, unlike those scholars, he believed that fascism
had been able to elicit robust and widespread consent.

This approach to studying fascist culture was superseded by the works
of George L. Mosse, whose contributions effected a true transformation in
fascist historiography and, more broadly, in research on nineteenth- and
twentieth-century culture.[51] In the early 1960s Mosse was already arguing that millions of people had seen in fascism a solution to the crises of
modernity, and therefore the end of the modern person's alienation via their

reintegration into a national collectivity, capable of providing a new sense of belonging.[52] Since then he had seen fascism and National Socialism as the products of revolutionary cultural and political currents. In fact, contrary to what Lukács and Croce had argued, Mosse claimed that the irrationalism of the late nineteenth century had given rise not to a reactionary or conservative climate, nor to a degeneration or involution of European culture, but rather to a revolutionary ideology that was entirely consistent with the trends that had preceded it. "Fascism," he wrote, "was the climax of many habits of mind which grew up after the age of romanticism."[53]

Building on these initial and influential ideas, in the late '60s Mosse enriched his understanding of the workings of culture by studying the relationship between popular ideas and politics, influenced by the anthropology of Claude Levi-Strauss and the philosophy of Ernst Cassirer. Thus equipped with a sense of the term *culture* quite similar to that developed by modern anthropology, in which culture represents a heterogeneous collection of the customs, beliefs, attitudes, values, ideals, and habits people acquire as members of society,[54] Mosse posed the question of how a given cultural system related to a given ideology, developing the concept of the "new politics." In 1975, in *The Nationalization of the Masses*, he argued that the "new politics" was a nationalist lay religion born of the culture of secularization. To escape the suffering inflicted by industrialization, urbanization, and the erosion of Christian values, in a world grown unfamiliar because ever more alienating and standardized, the "new politics," like all religions, expressed itself through a liturgy, which was accompanied by an apparatus of myth, ritual, and symbol. In this sense, its most original trait was that it was an attitude rather than a system—a frame for the national cult rather than a political ideology. "Its rites and liturgies," Mosse wrote in this vein, "were central, an integral part of a political theory which was not dependent on the appeal of the written word."[55] Studying fascist culture thus meant trying to understand how that culture had expressed itself in politics, not identifying a coherent, codified ideology.

The Nationalization of the Masses influenced generations of scholars of cultural studies and offered the most convincing refutation yet of liberal and Marxist approaches to fascist culture—the former denying its very existence and the latter focusing on intellectuals' role in managing power and propaganda. Mosse questioned the oversimplified schema that identified culture with propaganda, and the conviction that leaders manipulated their followers. In his opinion, instead, the new politics as a religion—that is, as a belief system capable of offering everyone who practiced it a sense of belonging and salvation—engaged both the ruling elites and the popular masses. In this respect, Mosse was deeply skeptical of the assumption that "the leader mobilized the masses via propaganda and terror." "The term 'propaganda,' always used in this context," he wrote in 1980, "leads to a misunderstanding of the fascist cults and their essentially organic and religious nature. In times of crisis they provided many millions of people with a more meaningful involvement than representative parliamentary government."[56]

Mosse's work was concerned with attitudes toward politics in the modern age. As such, it deliberately ignored legislative acts, institutions, organizations, and ideologies. Sternhell noted as much, arguing that in the great German historian's works there was an imbalance between fascism's symbolic aspects—that is, the myths, rituals, and religious forms of politics— and its ideas.[57] Emilio Gentile further emphasized this point, claiming that "the rationality of fascist culture was politically efficacious not only because it fascinated the masses with myths, symbols, and rites, but also because it associated itself with the rationality of the organization and the institution, becoming party and regime. . . . Without the rationality of the organization and the institution, without being party or regime, without becoming the ideology of a modern state," Gentile added, "fascism would have remained on the margins of politics and history, confined between the camps of intellectual snobbery."[58] And indeed, if we want to study the fascist regime's cultural institutions or the internal political conflicts that erupted about the "fascization" of culture, we will find no answers in Mosse's work, which cannot help us grasp the internal battles of a regime that became totalitarian because it knew how to achieve its plans for domination. Paradoxically, then, one of the great scholars of the cultural politics of totalitarianism contributed to rendering the image of the totalitarian regime murkier by inaugurating a line of research that has in recent years produced somewhat debatable results.

The New Italian Historiography

Italian historians began to address the subject of fascist culture in the latter half of the 1960s, when Luisa Mangoni, Emilio Gentile, Alberto Asor Rosa,

Mario Isnenghi, Gabriele Turi, and Piergiorgio Zunino published some of their most important works. Some of these works we have already encountered in the preceding pages, while others shall be examined shortly. But first we must emphasize the importance of Renzo De Felice, whose work provoked a wide-ranging debate among scholars and the public. De Felice played a unique role among historians of fascism, attracting international attention to his work and shaping Italian cultural life for over thirty years.[59]

De Felice authored numerous studies of the Ventennio's key personalities, aspects, and episodes, most importantly a monumental biography of Mussolini, which told the history of fascism through the life of its leader. In these works De Felice took on issues that would become central to subsequent analyses of the regime and its culture. He claimed that fascism was a novel modern phenomenon, born, like its leader, of the political culture of the left, and in this sense quite distinct from National Socialism and traditional forms of authoritarianism. He believed that fascism was a product of the Great War, limited to Europe between the two world wars, and capable of manifesting a strong push toward modernizing society, culture, and the economy—and of responding to the middle class's demands. Accordingly, he believed that, despite the differences among its various factions, and the presence of an internal dialectic between the revolutionary wing and the conservative one tied to the old liberal regime, fascism had succeeded at generating a form of mass consent that reached its apogee in 1936, with the Italo-Ethiopian War and the declaration of empire. He argued as much in the fourth volume of his biography, *Mussolini il Duce: Gli anni del consenso* (The years of consent), spanning the period 1929–1936.[60] Developing these claims in that volume, he highlighted the need "to place the culture of the period of the regime in the context of the fascist political system, of its ability to *isolate* and *settle* . . . the questions of society of that time, and, therefore, to socialize its intellectuals."[61] This approach made it necessary to study intellectuals' behavior toward the regime.[62] Such an effort, however, was complicated by the fact that "a political system of the authoritative type," like the fascist one, had "among its most exasperating quirks that of monitoring, limiting, and outright impeding . . . intellectual activity."[63] In light of this, in addition to examining Giovanni Gentile's oeuvre at length (and referencing Del Noce),[64] De Felice called for a distinction: most of the time, Italian intellectuals acted "in accordance with the social world in which they moved and in which they were fully integrated"; in fact, very often, by virtue of being intellectuals, they had accentuated "these communities' dominant behaviors. They were, therefore, very often fascists, card-carrying members of the National Fascist Party, who supplied the party with a great number of officials, especially provincial officials, and a few central ones as well." High culture was another matter, according to De Felice, for in that sphere there were prominent figures who kept a certain distance from the regime, at times expressing their frustration. Until 1935, the pressure the regime exerted on high culture was tolerable—so much so that nonconformist magazines like *Solaria, Il Saggiatore,* and *Civiltà moderna* could survive. "This was not insignificant, from a cultural and personal point of view, even if," he noted, "none of these magazines could strictly speaking be seen as part of a political opposition."[65]

In the mid-1980s De Felice's thinking about the relationship between politics and intellectuals shifted. Fascism's galvanization of all arenas of Italian culture then seemed to him aimed not merely at shaping national trends but at creating a new civilization, as demonstrated by the work of Giuseppe Bottai, "who mostly strongly advocated for the necessity of operating at all levels of culture, including at the highest levels of research."[66] The belief that fascism had extended its sphere of influence to all sectors of Italian society, rather than being simply a tool used by the regime to mobilize the popular masses, had required a change of perspective. Starting in 1981, in fact, De Felice had begun to modify his views, emphasizing the regime's totalitarian nature, all the while acknowledging Emilio Gentile's influence on his thinking.[67]

Gentile had published *The Origins of Fascist Ideology* in 1975 and since then had assiduously investigated this topic, all the while deploying a consistent methodological approach. In his work, indeed, he had always maintained that it was important not to separate the regime's cultural forms from political history; instead, it was necessary to connect fascism's ideological traits to the social forces that composed it, "to the political action that it undertakes, to the organizations and institutions it produces, which are also, in a sense, the expression of its ideology, its vision of man and politics."[68] Consistent with this approach, Gentile argued that fascist ideology could not be understood as the mechanistic translation of a conceptual model, and therefore could not be analyzed as if it were a political theory; rather, it had to be examined by reconstructing the organizational aspects of the Party's initiatives, its institutional aspects related to the government and the regime's activities, and its truly cultural aspects, insofar as they expressed a single phenomenon. Thus, in *The Origins of Fascist Ideology*, Gentile analyzed Mussolini's thought, the key contributions of the theorists of fascism, and the problems that intellectuals and politicians grappled with between 1919 and 1925. From this emerged a detailed portrait of fascist ideology, described as a new synthesis of political thought, born of the national radicalism that had developed at the beginning of the century and was nurtured by the Great War's new mythologies. This was a new nonideological ideology, which refuted the primacy of reason in history and traditional categories of political thought, and which understood politics as a totalizing force by which man could transform himself—an ideology that, at bottom, was "the most complete rationalization of the totalitarian State."[69] In this monograph, then, Gentile began the examination of totalitarianism to which he would devote himself over the following years.

In *The Italian Road to Totalitarianism*, Gentile asserted that fascism, as a manifestation of revolutionary nationalism, was the first mass movement to come to power under a liberal democracy; the first party equipped to explicitly assert the will to organize the nation, imposing the primacy of politics upon the life of individuals and the masses; the first totalitarian state.[70] Faced with the criticism of those who accepted Hannah Arendt's assertion that fascism had not been a totalitarian regime because, unlike National Socialism and Stalinism, it had not achieved its totalitarian aspirations, Gentile argued that totalitarianism is always imperfect—that it is a continuous experiment, a dynamic process aimed at institutionalizing the principle of permanent revolution.

This definition commanded the attention of students of fascist culture for two reasons: first, because it claimed that one of the totalitarian regime's characteristics was the primacy of politics above all other facets of individual and social life; and, second, because it tackled head-on the problem of modernity in fascism, as Gentile demonstrated in *The Sacralization of Politics in Fascist Italy*, published in 1996.[71] This book's central argument is that a key feature of modernity is the transfer of the sacred from the sphere of religion to that of politics, and that fascism, as a modern, revolutionary political phenomenon and totalitarian experiment, was a political religion that gave shape to the mythologies, rituals, and symbols that rendered the state sacred, "and assigned it the primary educational task of transforming the mentality, the character, and the customs of the Italians. The aim was to create a 'new man,' a believer in and an observant member of the cult of Fascism."[72]

As we noted at the beginning of this chapter, the scholars who made the most significant contributions to our understanding of fascist culture, starting in the late 1970s, were Mario Isnenghi and Piergiorgio Zunino. Their work prompted a critical reflection on Italian historiography with antifascist lineage, which more often than not had shown itself to be narrow-minded and incapable of opening up new horizons of research. In 1979 Isnenghi painted a grim picture of Italian historians along these lines, observing that "entire generations of postfascist intellectuals had tried to solve the problem of their relationship to the past by simply denying that fascism had any cultural coherence. This gave rise to an image of fascist Italy as an empty church, with no religion and no believers, whose false priests had failed to connect with their congregations except through rites of cloying and bloated demagoguery. This complete and utter denial of the object of study, this repression of the very idea of a fascist culture, created a vast field of the unsaid." In his opinion, in fact, historians had not explained "the historiographical puzzle of the mass consent" that fascism had managed to elicit, which again raised the problem of "understanding how the fascist State had connected itself to society, and, vice versa, to what degree a fascist civil society" had contained "the structures of the regime's apparatus."[73]

In his *L'ideologia del fascismo* (The ideology of fascism), Piergiorgio Zunino also took up the question of how civil society related to the state, observing that the majority of Italian scholars considered the state to be the fascist regime's most representative form, while believing that civil society had succeeded at maintaining its independence from fascism. It was precisely this assumption that made it so difficult to study ideology, a phenomenon that by definition constitutes the channel through which politics interfaces with society.[74]

In reality, however, Zunino's monograph did not offer a political history of fascist ideology. It aimed instead to tell a history of ideas, tracing the currents of thought that legitimated the dominant coalition during the Ventennio, providing a sense of national identity, giving the people social cohesion, and turning the nation into a bearer of values.[75] In his book, Zunino analyzed fascist ideology's most significant myths, noting the presence of certain contradictions: traditionalism against modernism, pragmatism against subtle ethics, state control against liberalism, ruralism against industrialism. Confronting the oppositions typical of fascist ideology, in marked contrast to what others had written, Zunino described an important problem. "That which appears most singular," he wrote, "was not their presence so much as the fact that not very many, if any, of these *cleavages* were bridged over the course of the Ventennio—and yet neither did they deepen or widen enough to compromise the soundness of the fascist ship."[76] When it came to "the great circle traced by fascist power, the many and various forces animating Italian society" that were "on the inside, not the outside,"[77] Zunino argued, "that which united nonetheless seems to outweigh that which divided."[78] In the mid-1980s, this work did not receive the appreciation it deserved: historians continued to argue that the presence of conflicts, debates, and diverse political currents and cultural products precluded one from identifying a unique fascist culture, ideology, and politics.

Two examples will suffice to prove this point. The first is the work of Guido Quazza, who in 1985 proved himself faithful to the idea he first articulated in the 1970s: namely, that fascism had influenced culture without, however, managing to produce anything of significance.[79] The second is a collection of essays called *Cultura e fascismo* (Culture and fascism), published in 1996. In the preface to this volume, Enrico Ghidetti claimed that there had been no fascist culture, which meant that "the only possible historiographical approach ... could be to identify a series of lines of research destined never to meet"; "that Julius Evola's trajectory at the margins of the regime ... will never encounter the project of a politics of the arts pursued in vain by Ardengo Soffici"; that "fascist Italian studies was an antifascist enclave because it was led by [Arnaldo] Momigliano, [Luigi] Russo, and [Natalino] Sapegno, who all arrived at antifascism"; that the theater and cinema, "in spite of the efforts to organize mass culture," had produced a "substantially negative" balance, given that "the creation of the Academy of Drama [Accademia d'arte drammatica] and Cinecittà had not meant the birth of fascist theater or fascist cinema, not because the regime's bureaucracy lacked a broad, long-range vision, but rather because of the difficulty of transmitting a credible cultural message except via the indecorous and dead-end road of propaganda."[80] These conclusions disregard the findings of Italian and international historiography, including the ample and indeed nearly redundant historiographical work of recent years.

The Debate at the Turn of the Twenty-First Century

Over the past few decades, historians have reversed their earlier assessments. From completely repressing the idea of fascist culture's existence, they have gone on to reconstruct its many and diverse features, considering them essential to an overall understanding of fascism. Thus, fascist culture has gone from a being relatively marginal field of study to one of the most frequently studied topics among scholars of fascism. How did this happen? Why do a majority of scholars now believe not only that the regime had its own culture but also that it was one of the reasons for its success?

Broadly speaking, the new scholarship was affected by a change underway in historiography as a whole, a consequence of the crisis in Marxist thought that emerged in the 1970s. Today it is hard to find a historian who understands culture in a strictly doctrinaire sense, as an instrument for indoctrinating and mobilizing the popular masses into class struggle; and work that frames fascism's cultural products as either false representations of reality or simple demagogic promises meets with less and less acceptance. The decline of Marxism was coupled with the twilight of structuralism, the other major wave of thought that defined the work of many European and American historians in the 1950s and 1960s, engaged as they were in studying societies as complex and generally stable systems. Contrary to this trend, which gave pride of place to structures, models, quantitative analysis, and the *longue durée*, in the 1980s historians once more began to tell the story of history, as Lawrence Stone observed in 1979. The English historian noted that after twenty years of structuralism, historiography reassumed its original role: recounting "the particular and the specific rather than the collective and statistical."[81] In effect, the crisis of Marxism and the decline of structuralism opened up new pathways of research.

Starting in the early 1980s, as the ideological conflict of the Cold War subsided, historians demonstrated a special sensitivity to "representation." And since culture in a broad sense—more so than society, economics, and politics—lends itself to being described via a worldview, since it is itself at bottom an expression of a worldview, cultural studies gained and still claims a wide audience. In the scholarship on fascism, this is clearly evident in the rediscovery of George Mosse's works.

As it happens, the scholarly landscape is diverse, and in European and American scholarship we must distinguish at least three different research approaches: cultural studies work, scholarship on totalitarianism and political religions, and efforts to identify a generic fascism.[82] In the first category we can locate scholarship on the aesthetic dimension of fascist culture, among which we must refer to the works of Jeffrey T. Schnapp, Mabel Berezin, and Simonetta Falasca-Zamponi. In 1996 Schnapp argued that the regime's grand cultural maneuverings were a tool for covering over the inconsistency of its ideology.[83] That same year he distilled this claim, writing that when it came to political ideas, fascism remained "a paradoxical creature . . . unable definitively to resolve the question of its identity by recourse to the utopias of theory and technology," a regime that "sought answers to its identity crisis in the domain of culture."[84]

Mabel Berezin based her 1997 interpretation of fascist political culture on official celebrations: memorials for fallen soldiers, rallies organized on the occasion of Mussolini's visits to young recruits, and ceremonies to inaugurate new monuments. Berezin, like Schnapp, held that fascism had no cultural politics animated by ideology. Fascism's cohesiveness, in her opinion, was expressed not on an ideological level, but rather in style and in its emphasis on action. In this sense, fascism repudiated speech and substituted emotion and feeling for rational discourse, since performance was considered much more important than the coherence of its ideological expressions.[85]

Also writing in 1997, Simonetta Falasca-Zamponi examined the symbolic language of fascism, as articulated via images, writing, and speeches.[86] Starting from Walter Benjamin's concept of the "aestheticization of politics," she studied exhibitions put on by the fascists to mark the anniversaries of important events, focusing in particular on the cult of Mussolini. In her interpretation, the recurrence of Mussolini's image in the regime's iconography fueled the myth of his omnipresence. Using the head of state's writings and speeches as primary sources for her research, Falasca-Zamponi studied fascism as a *discourse* and that discourse as a *text*.

As we can see, by considering culture as a world apart, these writers came to conclusions analogous to those of historians who denied the very existence of fascist culture. This may seem paradoxical, but upon reflection it is easy to understand. Against a backdrop of historiographical interpretations based on materialist philosophy (according to which history is the history of class struggle) or on pragmatism (for which history is the expression of humanity's opportunism), some scholars chose to reconstruct history using the tools of anthropology, aesthetics, or linguistics, without examining the meaning and political weight of individual forms, thus running the risk of seeing them vanish into thin air and transforming all cultures into systems of representation. Thus, for example, in Falasca-Zamponi's book, Mussolini's writings appear untethered from the context in which they were produced, independent of the intentions that animated them, the political meanings they had, and the culture and ideology in which they were produced.[87]

It is also true that, in recent years, many scholars have conceived of politics as an ensemble of institutional processes or of measurable "facts" that have no commerce with culture—and of culture as a sphere unto itself, independent from politics. This is why more recent cultural studies work has denied the very existence of fascist ideology—that is, of a phenomenon that is by definition the by-product of an encounter between culture and politics. In this vein, Sergio Luzzatto defined "the political and cultural machine during the fascist period" as "a bazaar in which compromises were traded: where party leaders, ministerial inspectors, successful artists and writers, worthless hacks, industrialists engaged in printing and cinema, and university professors all laboriously attempted to reconcile the imperatives of power, the market and the enticement of fantasy."[88] Convinced that fascist ideology had absolutely no substance, Luzzatto claimed that the categories of scholarship on fascism had changed because studies of ideology had given way to those of political culture, as evidenced by the works of Emilio Gentile.

In reality, however, Gentile's claims were far from postulating an opposition between ideology and culture. In his works, which were emblematic of that second approach to studying fascist culture, the Italian historian noted that the concept of the "aestheticization of politics" developed by Benjamin (and adopted by many others) could be misleading to the extent that it led one to neglect another, more important, characteristic of fascism: namely, the "politicization of aesthetics." This is why he stressed that an overemphasis on the aestheticization of politics could lead to an aestheticization of fascism itself, with the effect of relegating its defining characteristic, its politicism, to secondary importance—and, thus, of normalizing fascism.[89] Fascist culture had been effective, however, not only because it fascinated the masses, but also because it transformed the lives of everyday Italians, organizing them through the structures of the National Fascist Party and guiding them via the institutions of the totalitarian state. What's more, in a state that posited the identity of culture and politics, and saw their separation as a legacy of the liberal age, it is impossible to distinguish between these two spheres. In fact, between 1922 and 1943, intellectuals, scholars, artists, and politicians debated how to express a properly fascist culture, which is to say that they ceded the exigencies of their respective disciplines to the higher-order demands of politics.

This interpretation is markedly distinct from those put forth by cultural studies, as one can clearly see in commentary on the religion of politics. In Gentile's opinion, the concept of a political religion is inextricably linked to that of totalitarianism and should not be used to study the relationship between religion and politics in different historical periods. Rather, the sacralization of politics is a key characteristic of totalitarian regimes; it is therefore first and foremost a political phenomenon, quite distinct from the politicization of religion that characterized the relation between religion and politics even in the ancient world.[90]

The American historian David D. Roberts declared his agreement with this position, registering his bemusement at the culturalist approach. Roberts emphasized the importance of the concepts of totalitarianism and ideology for understanding fascist culture and fascism as a whole;[91] as he argued, fascist ideology should not be seen as a stable and codified theoretical system.[92] "Fascism included a common energising insight and aspiration sufficiently coherent to inspire enthusiasm and indicate the general direction for practice" in a political landscape that cannot be reduced to irrationalism, opportunism, or mere activism.[93] Ruth Ben-Ghiat's approach to studying fascist culture also marked a departure from the prevailing narrative in cultural studies. In her view, culture was one of the means by which fascism manifested its efforts to modernize Italy. According to Ben-Ghiat, in fact, fascism developed a project of national regeneration, a new model of modernity that chiefly spread through the instruments of culture.[94]

The third and final trend in scholarship on fascist culture found its most commanding proponent in the English historian Roger Griffin. This trend sought to define the contours of generic fascism—in other words, to define a conceptual model of fascism. Starting in the early '90s, Griffin repeatedly stressed that fascism "has become a less contested concept" than it once had been, such that historians now found themselves agreeing that it was a "truly revolutionary [phenomenon], an interclassist and antiliberal form, and in the final analysis anticonservative nationalism."[95] What's more, in his view, historians had ceased to acknowledge the presence of a fascist ideology that was deeply tied to modernity and modernization, an ideology that assumed a variety of shapes and discourses in order to adapt itself to the historical and national contexts in which it appeared, gathering together diverse cultural and intellectual trends—right and left, modern and antimodern—but also presenting itself as a coherent body of ideas, slogans, and doctrine. It would thus be possible to define fascism as a kind of armed party that tried, for the most part unsuccessfully, to generate a mass populist movement with a religious political style and a radical political program—an armed party that gave rise to a regime furnished with its own ideology and its own political style based on a central myth. According to Griffin, the central myth of fascism, which shaped its ideology, its propaganda, its political style, and its actions, "is its vision of the nation's imminent rebirth from decadence."[96] In 2004 he reiterated the idea that the scholarly debate had recently undergone a period of consolidation and convergence, given that most scholars were now aware of the work that had been emerging on this subject and were disposed to accept that fascism was a politically revolutionary phenomenon.[97]

In point of fact, though, the landscape was a bit less homogeneous than Griffin's description suggested, especially when one considers scholarship in Italy. In 1994 Gabriele Turi recounted the history of the debate about culture between the world wars, identifying a turning point in the early '60s with the publication of Togliatti's lectures on fascism and De Felice's work.[98] This argument posits that De Felice's work expresses an overall positive assessment of fascism, but this is not entirely accurate. According to Turi, Croce's mistaken understanding of fascism as an anticultural phenomenon had been reversed by De Felice and his students, who "tended to reunite the regime's culture and politics under a single positive banner." As such, both intellectuals and culture as a whole, "which had been seen to oppose fascism," were instead depicted as "in peaceful coexistence with a tolerant regime."[99] Thus, while Italian historians following in the wake of Croce and Bobbio thought that the intellectuals of that period had never been fascist, after De Felice's work Italian historiography started down the opposite path, which ended in a description of all Italian intellectuals as fascists. According to Turi, in fact, "to correct or reverse antifascist judgments of the regime, intellectuals—who with the Great War and fascism consolidated their role as mediators between the State and mass society—were seen as one of the keys to understanding a political system erected not only through coercion, but also through consent."[100] As a result, one strain of historiography about culture underwent "the influence of this revisionist work, and landed on an image of a nonconflictual relationship between intellectuals and the regime, reversing the antithetical interpretation born of Croce's work, which had been taken up by Bobbio."[101]

In 2004 Turi reasserted this argument, declaring his agreement with Garin's interpretations in *Intellettuali italiani del XX secolo*, where, as we have seen, Garin denied the very existence of a fascist culture. Turi found it useful to distinguish between "fascist culture" and "the culture of the period," "abstaining from moral judgments about the quality or lack thereof of the period's cultural production, and seeing in the acceptance of fascist culture a collection of values from diverse sources that fascism had succeeded in amalgamating and circulating through its communication channels."[102] Thus, according to Turi, there must have been only a "culture of the fascist period (created by both the fascists and the antifascists) that had not succeeded at permeating the entirety of Italian society, but that, with its efforts at homologizing, elicited in more than one scholar the search for and discovery of intellectual labor's independence, via a process indispensable for making the plant of future antifascist reaction take root."[103]

In the following pages, we shall develop a very different interpretation of fascist culture.

2

Cultural Politics in the 1920s

The Roots of Fascist Ideology

The Italian Combat Leagues (Fasci di combattimento) were formed on March 23, 1919, in Milan's Piazza San Sepolcro, when roughly a hundred young people gathered for a meeting called the month before by Benito Mussolini's newspaper, *Il popolo d'Italia.*[1] The meeting brought together veterans belonging to the socialist left, revolutionary syndicalism, the Republican Party, and Futurism. All these men had been shaped by the experience of the First World War, and by the mythology of an Italian revolution and of war itself as revolutionary.[2] This last notion arose from the belief that the war that had just ended—with its exaltation of sacrifice, its camaraderie, and its cult of heroism—had forever altered human history, along with the face of the nation and the destiny of its individual citizens. Mass warfare had given birth to a new civilization founded on the mystique of the homeland, and therefore, according to the fascists, on an idea of the nation as a sacred entity in whose name the survivors had risked their lives and killed other men. Thus prepared to glorify violence as a means to an end, strengthened by a concept of politics as faith and therefore as an absolute pursuit, and confident that bourgeois society was corrupt and must be purified, the fascists saw themselves reflected in the myth of the Italian revolution. They believed that Italy's participation in the Great War had brought about a revolution in thought, customs, and politics—and had entrusted its veterans with completing the work of nation-building that had begun with the Risorgimento but remained unfinished.

Among the many groups in attendance at that first meeting in Piazza San Sepolcro, the Futurists and the Arditi (a corps of elite soldiers and officers who served in assault divisions during the war) played a particularly important role in early fascism's cultural politics. As an artistic movement, Futurism had begun in 1909. Since then, its proponents had fought to assert new forms of modern life that they believed contained an explosion of energy unprecedented in history.[3] Fierce critics of nineteenth-century bourgeois culture, the Futurists saw themselves as a revolutionary avant-garde. They articulated a model of a new man they believed would change the world: a man moved to power by violent instincts and open to new experiences; a man experimenting with new forms of culture, subduing nature via technological progress, and constantly trying to outdo himself. Between 1914 and 1915 the Futurists had vociferously advocated for entering the war, arguing, as their leader Filippo Tommaso Marinetti put it, that war was "the world's only means of sanitation," the sole event capable of overturning society and giving birth to a new moral, cultural, and political order. In February 1918 they published the manifesto of the Futurist Political Party (Partito politico futurista), presenting themselves to the Italian public as the avant-garde of the nationalist movement of ex-servicemen, *combattentismo*—an elite who, after fighting in the war, were obligated to mobilize the masses against bourgeois society and liberal politics. They were antisocialist, anti-Giolittian, antimonarchical, and anticlerical. As the creators of a modern, revolutionary form of nationalism that demanded bold reforms—from the abolition of the Senate to the confiscation of large sums of capital—they enthusiastically welcomed the rise of the Italian Combat Leagues, sharing their spirit and goals and influencing their ideology.

Unlike the Futurists, the Arditi had been formed during the war, as a special corps of assault troops deployed on the most dangerous missions to enemy outposts.[4] They had not experienced trench life, enjoying instead privileges including better rations and lodging and better pay; they were held up by military leaders as models of bravery and love of country. Certain that bourgeois life was corrupt and nearing its end, the Arditi saw themselves as a kind of military aristocracy, and so, at the end of 1918, they refused to return to the rhythms of civilian life. To the common difficulties faced by veterans upon reintegration, the Arditi added the desire to perpetuate the state of war in Italian politics, convinced as they were that the revolution

sparked by the conflict had to continue in times of peace. With their aggressive, rebellious political style—which would greatly influence fascist political culture—they openly disdained all political parties. Like the Futurists,
they saw themselves as the only ones who could lead the national transformation begun by the Great War. From September 1919 to December 1920,
the Arditi and the Futurists took part in the occupation of the city of Fiume,
led by the poet and war hero Gabriele D'Annunzio, who introduced a new
style of politics during the sixteen months he occupied this small Adriatic
port. As Michael Ledeen has observed, D'Annunzio was fascism's first true
Duce—the first politician to employ secular rituals to create a cult of per-
sonality and a cult of the nation. In Fiume, new ceremonial practices and
new symbols emerged, like dramatic call-and-response with the crowd, the
Roman salute with a raised right arm, and the war cries of *"aia, aia, alalà"*—
all of which would become integral parts of fascist political culture.[5]

As Mussolini saw it, the Italian Combat Leagues were not destined to be
the backbone of a new political party. Rather, they were a republican, anticlerical, antisocialist movement that would defend and justify interventionism, amplify the demands of war veterans, and fight the Socialist Party—all
without troubling themselves to define a clear agenda. Only after their defeat
in the November 1919 elections did the fascists understand that the myth
of the Italian revolution and the exaltation of wartime victory would not
suffice to make their movement a national political force capable of transmitting the demands of a mass society. Thus, beginning with the Combat
Leagues' second national conference in May 1920, they abandoned their
initial premises and decided that they had to develop a political platform
and ideology that could extend beyond the issues that had emerged during
the war.

In the ideology that developed in 1920 we can discern the first signs of
the politics that would motivate the fascists' actions in the years to come.
First of all, the militants in the Italian Combat Leagues declared themselves
antidemocratic and antiliberal because they believed that democracy and
liberalism were made up of individuals engaged in defending their own
interests—the result, in other words, of a narrow, limited notion of political
struggle. The fascists were also profoundly antisocialist: they accused the
Italian Socialist Party of having chosen to stay neutral on the eve of the war,
and thus of having betrayed their country in the name of internationalism.

They condemned egalitarianism and a materialist idea of history in favor of an aristocratic, spiritualist, and antirationalist ideology.

From this point of view, the early fascists' ideas and impulses seem to be well captured in the writings of the philosopher Giuseppe Rensi.[6] In *Lineamenti di filosofia scettica* (The features of skepticism), Rensi argued that in a world of individuals sanctioned to seek their own truths, no true dialogue is possible—thus, politics as a practice of discourse and persuasion is also impossible. To support these skeptical, antirationalist arguments, Rensi marshaled the work of Hume and Hobbes, noting with the former "that debates replicate themselves with the greatest energy, as if everything was certain," and with the latter citing "despotism" as "the only way out."[7] In *La filosofia dell'autorità* (The philosophy of authority), Rensi contrasted the political rationalism that Kant and Rousseau brought to modern philosophy with the irreducibility of conflict among human beings.[8] If different types of justice exist, he wrote, "the only recourse that is left is to a fact outside the field of reason, that is, to the fact of force. It is here that we find the true origin of war and its eternal *raison d'être*."[9] Not unlike the German legal scholar Carl Schmitt, Rensi believed that political power could be based only "on irrationality, assuming clearly irrational forms, like the dominance of some people's wishes over those of others"—that is, the victory of "the irrational, the purely imperial, or simple authority."[10] Thus Rensi offered a means of legitimizing power, presenting his philosophy of authority as one of the theoretical foundations of fascist ideology.[11]

In fact, as Norberto Bobbio has argued, in those early years this ideology was not limited to a critique of political rationalism, or an assemblage of "antidemocratic, antisocialist, anti-Bolshevik, antiparliamentarian, antiliberal— anti-everything" thought.[12] The fascists declared their difference from the bourgeois man who achieved his place in mass society through a series of compromises, from the idea of politics as the site where diverse interests would be reconciled, and thus from all the kinds of reformism that had emerged in the late nineteenth and early twentieth centuries. They presented themselves not as a movement of partisan interests, but rather as a militia at the nation's service, born to create a new antidemocratic state, as both a means of political action and an end to it. This new state would stand beyond any theoretical rationale and would transform Italy by seeking to inject the popular masses into modern politics. In effect, from the very beginning fascist ideology had certain traits that it would maintain in the coming years; it was, in other words, an anti-ideological ideology in the sense that the fascists rejected all categories of political thought, did not accept the primacy of reason in history, viewed politics as life experience and not as the practical application of a theoretical model, and above all presented themselves as a group of war veterans, an armed militia that would create a new civilization in the name of and in defense of a new state. In this sense, fascist ideology was not a reactionary conservative ideology, nor was it a variety of nationalism. While the nationalists were conservative monarchists, the fascists—despite what many historians have argued—shared in the fight to defend the authority of the state but had no wish to return to the past. (We shall discuss this point at greater length below.) They did not present themselves as guardians of the national tradition; above all, they believed that the war had created the conditions for building a new civilization.[13]

To foster this new political situation, the fascists turned to the middle classes. Their movement grew in number and spread geographically, answering the call put forth by the historian of philosophy Emilio Bodrero in his 1921 *Manifesto alla borghesia* (Manifesto for the bourgeoisie).[14] According to Bodrero, after the Great War the Italian bourgeoisie was stuck between the demands of the proletariat and the interests of capital. Indeed, while the great mass parties—the Socialist Party and the Italian People's Party, founded by the Catholics in 1919—were busy defending the proletariat, and while the liberal ruling class worked to conserve its power and direct the capitalists' interests, the Italian bourgeoisie had neither representatives nor defenders. Nonetheless, it comprised the most industrious part of the populace and demonstrated more clearly than any other class the national spirit that had won the war. This was why, in Bodrero's opinion, the bourgeoisie had to abandon the ideologies of the past and mobilize as a revolutionary force to win power and give rise to a new political order that, without questioning market economics, could radically change the status quo. In 1921 fascism came to the same conclusions as Bodrero: it turned to the Italian middle classes as a political force free from class interests and determined to tackle the nation's problems, including education reform. Indeed, from that point on, as a small band mostly made up of young war veterans, the fascists demonstrated their interest in educating the new generations.

The Educational Agenda

When the fascists got involved in education policy, they entered a debate among all contemporary political factions about the crisis in Italian education. In a country with an illiteracy rate of nearly 30 percent—and closer to 50 percent in the south—public schooling reflected the enormous disparity between north and south.[15] While schools in the north were often comparable to those of other European nations, in central and especially southern Italy schools were few and far between, and often housed in dilapidated buildings. For elementary schools the biggest problem was the extremely high dropout rate due to the prevalence of underage workers; for secondary schools, the main issue was crowding, as the number of students had increased enormously starting in the late nineteenth century, rendering the existing buildings insufficient and making an overhaul of the entire educational system urgent. At the end of the 1910s, when the collective mobilization created by the war accelerated the politicization of Italian society via the rise of mass parties, education took on a decisive role in political battles and parliamentary debates. From then on, schooling was a key issue, not only for trade organizations and individual politicians, but also for the parties, which made education part of their platforms, thus pushing the fascists to define their own position.

From 1919 to 1920, fascist education policy represented the culture of *combattentismo*. In the platform they outlined in *Il popolo d'Italia* in early June 1919, the fascists presented an embryonic project in which they declared that the duty of the state was to give the schools the role of "defining national consciousness": "a role of training souls and bodies to defend the Nation," "elevating the moral and cultural conditions of the proletariat," and implementing compulsory education.[16] Though consisting of just a few passages, these notes on education reveal an important aspect of fascism's cultural orientation. In 1919 the fascists were ardent supporters of the public schools, believing that they would shape the moral conscience of the nation. Their platform was quite similar to that put forth by the Futurists in their 1918 political manifesto; like the Futurists, the fascists declared themselves ready to fight against illiteracy to give the proletariat "a patriotic education." And, like the Futurists, they rejected traditional school curricula focused on developing intellectual faculties, instead emphasizing the importance of

"tending to souls and bodies to defend the Nation," and pushing to introduce premilitary instruction into Italian schools.[17] They reiterated this in
the plan published in April 1920 by the Student Vanguard of the Italian Combat Leagues (l'Avanguardia studentesca dei fasci italiani di combattimento),
which in January of that same year became the first student organization to
emerge from within the fascist movement. These young vanguardists, who
not infrequently made up a majority in the Leagues, were republican and
anticlerical. They proposed adapting school curricula to the professional
needs of young people, removing from service those teachers who were ill-
equipped to perform their role, offering support to the poorest students, and
making physical education compulsory in secondary schools.[18]

Starting in the summer of 1920, after the shift to the right established
at the Combat Leagues' second conference, education policy changed. At
the conference, Mussolini declared his agreement with the People's Party,
which for some time had been demanding that civilians be given a greater
role in managing educational institutions. One year later, in June 1921, in
his first speech to the Chamber of Deputies, he would repeat this idea.[19] In
point of fact, this was not a position shared by all fascists. The National
Fascist Party's platform, as formulated in Rome in October 1921, while reasserting support for private institutions' academic freedom, also affirmed
the primacy of the public schools in education, highlighting the "rigorously
national nature of elementary schooling" and its role in "physically and morally" preparing "Italy's future soldiers."[20] With regard to secondary schools
and universities, the fascists declared their support for academic freedom,
while specifying that such freedom would be limited by the state's right to
exercise its sovereignty through rigid control of curricula and teaching staff.
From their point of view, only public schooling could play the role of educating "people capable of safeguarding the economic and historical progress
of the Nation, raising the masses to a higher moral and cultural level, and
developing ... the best students to ensure the continuous renewal of the
ruling classes."[21]

Within the Fascist Party this position gained majority approval. For example, just a few months before the March on Rome, *Gerarchia* (Hierarchy),
the magazine Mussolini founded in January 1922, declared parochial schools
"the opposite of freedom" and came out against academic freedom altogether,
fearing that the principle would benefit Catholic schools.[22] For the same

reasons, during the fascist conference in Naples in October 1922, a majority of the Party declared itself opposed to national high school exams, stressing the need to defend and strengthen public schools in the face of parochial schools.[23]

A minority within the Party, on the other hand, believed that academic freedom would benefit the school system. In this they fundamentally agreed with the philosopher Giovanni Gentile, who had been working on education reform since the turn of the century, arguing that competition among schools would raise the level of instruction throughout the country. Gentile fought to introduce a national exam at the end of each phase of study in both public and private schools—not as a means of favoring private schools, but rather, in the words of a leading Gentilian educator, Giuseppe Lombardo Radice, as a way "of choosing those students who deserve to pursue their studies in the nation's schools."[24]

The conflict between these two positions resulted in a first victory for the National Fascist Party's minority wing in October 1922, when Mussolini called on Gentile to direct the Ministry of Public Education. By doing so, he showed that his government would put an end to the paralysis that had gripped the parliamentary debate over schooling, securing the consent of the People's Party and demonstrating his readiness to welcome an intellectual of Gentile's caliber into his party.[25] When the philosopher began his political activities under fascism, he had long been one of Italy's most influential intellectuals. At the turn of the century, he, along with Benedetto Croce, had written widely on how to transform the nation's culture, taking up the problem of education and, in the 1910s, laying the cornerstones of his philosophy.

The Work of Giovanni Gentile

Scholars who have investigated the motives for and nature of Gentile's participation in the fascist regime have landed in one of three (quite different) camps. According to some, Gentile did not play a decisive role in fascist culture. As we saw in the previous chapter, Eugenio Garin and Luisa Mangoni argued that the most significant proponents of the regime's culture were Catholics, young people, and the many fascist intellectuals who considered Gentile a liberal philosopher extraneous to their movement.[26] This argument was once widespread, and it is still propounded today by those who claim that the philosopher participated in fascism without fully understanding its goals or nature.[27] For other scholars, however, Gentile was the principal theorist of fascism.[28] Augusto Del Noce first asserted as much many years ago, and more recently the American historian David D. Roberts has reasserted it, writing that "a better understanding of [Gentile]'s commitment to Fascism might have much to tell us about why a culture saturated with idealism and historicism also produced the first Fascism, and why it was characterized by an explicitly totalitarian aspiration."[29] Finally, some historians have proposed a third argument, distinct from each of these, which we shall discuss in the following pages.

Gentile published his first philosophical work with significant political implications, *I fondamenti della filosofia del diritto* (Foundations of the philosophy of law), in 1916. In these pages he put forth a spiritualist notion of politics antithetical to any kind of contractualism, and therefore antithetical to the idea that society is produced by the will of rational individuals trying to achieve predetermined goals. Arguing that community develops when an individual's interests are subordinated to their feeling that they are part of a social world, Gentile wrote that "a universal will, or in short, a society," would come into being by overcoming the specific or the individual.[30]

During this same period Gentile began to write for several national daily papers, becoming well known to a broader public and launching a vigorous campaign against nationalism. In March 1917 he argued that "to be really and truly nationalist," it was necessary "to put nationalism aside, if being nationalist" meant "asserting the nation as a positive thing for social man." His critique was built upon a radical refutation of the idea of the nation "as a natural, anthropological, or ethnographic fact," and also "as a historical formation already in existence thanks to a process that is in its turn also taken for granted." In keeping with his earlier claims, Gentile reasserted his general critique of politics understood as action shaped by *a priori* factors, such as premises established once and for all.[31]

Finally, in 1920, with his *Discorsi di religione* (Discourses on religion), Gentile posited the identity of religion and politics: "Our thought cannot but be religious, our action cannot but be imbued with a sense of the divine. And if our action is a political action or an action of the State, our State should also be governed by an unabashedly and deeply religious spirit."[32] Gentile believed that in order to solve its many problems, Italian society needed to foster a national religion. In his view, prior to determining how to manage social forces in the world and balance their various interests; prior to thinking through the state's institutional structure; and prior to addressing the various economic needs present in society, creating a new state must mean rebuilding a community that sees itself as a community and *accordingly* becomes a state. In keeping with this idea, he argued that individual rights amounted to nothing more than an illusion—an illusion that leads us away "from our presumed immediate or natural freedom, and from our sacred inalienable and imprescriptible rights, with which we naturally believe or believed we would show up to take our seat at the feast of life."[33]

On the eve of fascism, therefore, Gentile formulated two major political ideas: a radical critique of the determinism of earlier political ideologies, both nationalism and liberalism; and the necessity of rebuilding Italian politics on the basis of radical self-renewal and moral reform. During the First World War, Gentile, like the fascists, had taken up antidemocratic, antiliberal, and antisocialist positions. Such positions stemmed from his religious notion of politics, which he viewed as a faith that would transform the lives of men because it could speak to their consciences—politics provided a moral tension that could reshape individuals and make them feel like part of a shared experience. It is therefore easy to see why he declared himself a forerunner of the new political movement, and why he joined Mussolini's party, becoming one of its most famous and respected intellectuals.

From 1922 to 1927 Gentile had a veritable monopoly on the development of fascist ideology and the organization of the regime's culture, since he could depend on Mussolini's support, along with that of many key fascist leaders who saw him as a model and were proud to welcome him into their government and their Party. At that time the philosopher had a kind of power that no other Italian intellectual could match, and in 1923 he became a card-carrying member of the Fascist Party. As Gabriele Turi has pointed out, there can be no doubt that the political choice of Gentile as minister of public education, president of the National Fascist Institute of Culture, vice-president of the High Council of Public Education, research director of the *Enciclopedia italiana*, and president of the Commissione dei quindici (Commission of Fifteen, tasked by the Fascist Party with developing a proposal to modify the Italian constitution) was fascist in nature.[34]

From October 1922 until June 1924, Gentile was minister of public education and author of a reform plan that altered every level and type of public schooling. In the elementary schools, which children entered at age six, the most significant change was the introduction of Catholicism. Starting in the early twentieth century, the philosopher had argued that despite their many limitations, parochial schools knew how to "inculcate" their students with the principles of faith and predispose their souls to accept absolutist principles. Gentile, after all, understood religion as a myth that arose "beyond our intelligence"—that is, beyond rational analysis. Accordingly, it could play the role of *philosophia inferior*, preparing children to study philosophy later.[35] Seeing education reform as part of a broader attempt to construct the new state, Gentile believed that Catholicism, the traditional religion of Italy since late antiquity, would help build a national consciousness and conscience. This is why in 1923 he decreed that religion be taught not by clerics, in the form of catechism, but rather by elementary school teachers in cooperation with local religious authorities and the superintendent—and that it not factor into the overall evaluation of a student's progress.[36]

After five years of elementary school, at the age of eleven, children could proceed to secondary school, which was divided into two tiers.[37] The first tier included the *ginnasio* (which prepared students for the *liceo*), introductory courses for the technical and teacher-training institutes, the *scuola complementare* (the subsidiary school, for those who would not be continuing their studies), and lastly the conservatory of music. The second tier included the classical and scientific *licei*, advanced courses for the technical and teacher-training institutes, the girls' *liceo* (for girls who would not go on to university), and the art *liceo*. Only the classical *liceo*, the most selective and prestigious school, prepared students to enroll in all courses of university study; there students were taught history, philosophy, Italian, Latin, and ancient Greek and trained to be the future ruling class. The 1923 reform expanded all Italian students' workloads: entrance to both lower and upper secondary schools was limited to those who could pass the admission exams. Like the exit exams for the *licei*, these tests were administered by the state and became mandatory for both private and public school students. As all this suggests, the decision to add a state exam did not stem from a desire to facilitate parochial school students' course of study; rather, it was a means of exerting control over Italian schooling and allowing private citizens to create their own institutions for students unable to attend state schools.

University reform, too, was guided by the idea that public education should benefit from the contributions of private citizens. The reform envisioned three types of university. The first category comprised institutions entirely financed by the state, which were completely independent and had to offer the four traditional areas of study (medicine, law, humanities, and sciences) plus engineering. The second type included universities that received limited subsidies from the state, being largely financed by private donations and local government contributions. These universities could independently determine how many departments to set up, and they were subject to periodic assessment by state inspectors. Last, there were the free universities, which financed themselves but whose administrative and didactic autonomy were severely restricted. The reform recognized every university's right to broad pedagogical freedom in organizing instruction and developing courses of study; but, at the same time, it specified that chancellors and provosts would be nominated by the king based on advice from the minister of education. Among other changes, the reform transformed the High Council of Public Education into a body appointed by the Ministry, removing any volunteer components and adding the requirement that all instructors swear their loyalty to the state.[38]

In broad strokes, then, such were the contours of Gentile's education reform, which by no means limited itself to altering public education's institutional structure. Though it has been discussed less frequently, another goal of Gentile's education policy was to transform Italy's schools into the cradle of a civic religion. This required a strategy designed by the minister himself, with the help of his undersecretary, Dario Lupi. A Tuscan deputy who was one of the very first fascists and a fervent admirer of Gentile, Lupi has been seen as the most important "creator of rituals" for the new Italy. This is because he instituted the ritual of saluting the Italian flag in schools, mandated that classrooms display the crucifix and the king's portrait, and devised choral competitions featuring patriotic songs. Most significantly, in November 1922 he decided to create memorial avenues and parks and tasked Italian students with decorating every "city, town, and neighborhood" with trees dedicated to those killed during the Great War.[39] As these initiatives unfolded, Gentile himself spoke out in January 1924 to affirm the importance of saluting the flag. "I understand," he wrote to the school superintendents, "that in some schools the ceremony is not performed with solemnity and a religious spirit. This ritual must be performed at least once a month."[40] Similarly, in June 1924, he ordered that all classrooms be furnished with an image of the tomb of the unknown soldier from the monument to Vittorio Emanuele II in Rome.[41]

When this education reform bill was introduced in Parliament, it was greeted with a chorus of criticism, both from members of the opposition and from students, who accused Gentile of having aristocratic notions of education and creating a system that was too challenging.[42] The protests were so widespread that on June 14, 1924, just a few days after the assassination of socialist leader Giacomo Matteotti and in the midst of the resulting political crisis, Gentile resigned, believing that by continuing to serve as minister he would be endangering the reform—but he was in no way distancing himself from the government.[43] Over the subsequent months he strengthened his ties with the National Fascist Party. And indeed, from then until 1927, Gentile proved to be the intellectual to whom fascism would entrust its most significant cultural institutions.

Cultural Institutions

As he set about running fascism's key cultural institutions, Gentile explained that he had joined the regime because he believed that the movement Mussolini had founded would transform Italy into a modern nation.[44] The fascists, he believed, had assumed power to finish the work begun by Giuseppe Mazzini, leader of the Risorgimento battles and prophet of the religious spirit animating the struggle to build a new country in the face of individualism and materialism.[45] Having united those who fought for Italian unification in their youth with the members of the 1919 fascist action squads, fascism, according to Gentile, had "brought back the spirit of the Risorgimento."[46] Recognizing fascism as the result of a process begun long ago was not the same as stripping it of originality, according to the philosopher, nor did it diminish its revolutionary nature. On the contrary, he considered fascism to be a novel, modern political phenomenon that, unlike Italian liberalism, could meet the challenge of admitting the masses into the structures and workings of the state.[47] "The masses who have gathered around the pennants of the fascists," he wrote, gave fascism "the energy missing from the liberalism of a strong State."[48] He reiterated this rationale throughout the period in which he decided to deepen his involvement in fascism. For their part, Mussolini and the fascists granted him more power than any other Italian intellectual. Having chaired the Commissione dei Soloni (Commission of the Solons), instituted by the prime minister to reform the Italian constitution, Gentile helped organize the first convention for fascist cultural institutions in the spring of 1925.

This convention took place in Bologna on March 29–31, 1925, just three months after Mussolini's famous January 3 speech formalizing liberal Italy's transformation into a totalitarian regime. It was organized by Franco Ciarlantini, head of the party's Office of the Press and Propaganda, as a forum for debating the fascist movement's political and philosophical foundations, coordinating among cultural institutions, and showing that fascism could foster culture. Around 250 intellectuals lent their support to the convention, including Luigi Pirandello (who sent a letter of support), Giuseppe Ungaretti, Ernesto Codignola, Gioacchino Volpe, and Ardengo Soffici. To disseminate the spirit that inspired these intellectuals, at the end of the convention the members put together a "Manifesto of Fascist Intellectuals, to Intellectuals of All Nations" and established the National Fascist Institute of Culture (Istituto nazionale fascista di cultura, or INFC).[49] Both were entrusted to Gentile, who wrote the text of the manifesto and assumed the presidency of the institute.

Given the philosopher's statements over the previous months, the manifesto contained no surprises. In it he reiterated his concept of fascism, explaining that the movement founded by Mussolini was religious and radical by nature, as it was born of the spirit of the trenches and expressed in *squadrismo*, the movement of citizen-organized militias violently opposed to revolutionary socialism. After its first three years (1919–1921), fascism had become stronger than ever, proving itself to be a grand idea capable of drawing in every Italian, whether fascist or antifascist. Precisely because it expressed a new way of being political, Gentile believed, fascism could engage the masses in building the state and surpass the usual divisions of political parties. He oriented fascism's cultural politics accordingly, confident that the culture would benefit from the support of both fascists and antifascists, and from contributions from every discipline and branch of knowledge.

In keeping with this belief, when in late 1925 Gentile inaugurated the INFC, the first cultural institution formed to serve the Party, to "create a solid and organic national political conscience,"[50] he remarked that the institute would not shy away from using traditional cultural products, including those belonging to specific disciplines, as means of reflection and knowledge creation.[51] This was why he insisted that the new institute be called the "National Fascist Institute of Culture," rather than the "National Institute of Fascist Culture," as the members of the Party would have liked. Emphasizing the nonpolitical nature of the word *culture*, Gentile thought that fascism would transform Italy by addressing all Italians, over and above their original political loyalties. From this perspective, culture would not serve political interests: just as his reform would foster a national conscience by creating a school system that could ignite students' souls, teaching them to become Italians of the future worshiping at the altar of the nation, so fascist cultural institutions would contribute to the construction of a new Italy.

During the first few years, this belief in no way threatened Gentile's position of leadership in the INFC, which was governed by an administrative committee composed of his colleagues, including Carmelo Licitra, Arnaldo Volpicelli, Ernesto Codignola, Balbino Giuliano, and Carlo Costamagna. The committee included Party men like INFC vice-president Giorgio Masi, who was an admirer of Gentile but was also quite close to Party Secretary Roberto Farinacci, the radical fascist leader; Alberto Calza Bini, national secretary of the Fascist Union of Architects; and figures from the spheres of Italian culture and higher education, like Gioacchino Volpe, the economist Gino Arias, and the historian of law Pier Silverio Leicht.[52] The INFC's work benefited from a network of provincial branches set up in the Party's local chapters nationwide, as well as from works published in its magazine *Educazione politica* (Political education). General directives came from the institute's headquarters in Rome, but the development and implementation of individual programs was left to the ninety-four sections formed in the Italian provinces. The initiative's most conspicuous work consisted in public conferences and conventions, but recreational activities were not lacking, from concerts, excursions, language courses, and museum trips to a wide range of publications distributed in schools, libraries, and Party organizations.[53]

Armed with the same convictions that guided him in managing the institute, and with the same understanding of the relationship between culture and politics, Gentile set about directing the *Enciclopedia italiana*. The *Enciclopedia* was created in 1925 by Giovanni Treccani, with financial support from the fascists and an aspiration to rival the encyclopedias of other European nations. The prospectus expressed the hope that individual entries would benefit from the contributions of the nation's best minds, creating a work of the highest scholarly and cultural caliber. As Turi observed, in fact, Article 4 of the prospectus stated that the Istituto dell'Enciclopedia (Encyclopedic institute) was tied to the consciousness of the Italian people and the glorious destinies that awaited them—but that it was "apolitical" in the absolute sense of that term.[54] This was precisely why, even before the first volume appeared in 1929, various political figures criticized Gentile and expressed their desire to create an authentically fascist work. The most prominent criticism came from the editor of the paper *Il Tevere*, Telesio Interlandi, who sparked a controversy among the *Enciclopedia* contributors with his article "Reflections on a List of Encyclopedians," published in his paper on April 25, 1926. Throwing the first stone in the debate about Gentile, Interlandi wrote:

> What contributions will these ninety "intellectuals" make to an *Enciclopedia* we dreamed would be "fascist"—that is, inspired by the new national spirit that we call Fascism? If the fascists are the bearers of this spirit and the antifascists the bearers of another, the *Enciclopedia* resulting from this horrible collaboration will be a glorious "impartial" mess. O divine impartiality, how willingly we would wring your neck! ... We should, therefore, expel this monumental work from the fascist era, despite its announcement as a faithful reflection of a renewed Italy, that is, a no-longer-liberal Italy. We solemnly swear that when all is said and done, we would prefer the illustrated *Enciclopedia Melzi*.[55]

As we have seen, Gentile considered himself a forerunner of fascism. He said so many times between 1922 and 1925, and reiterated it in the spring of 1926, in responding to his critics and restating his idea of fascism as the occasion for building a new Italy. He believed that the National Fascist Party, by virtue of its very nature as a party—that is, as part of a wider political landscape—embodied the logic of partisanship; and he was convinced that if fascism were to leave the radical transformation of society in the Party's hands, the results would be no different than under previous political regimes. In Gentile's view, the radical renewal that Mussolini and the Blackshirts brought forth in Italian history consisted precisely in imposing a *national* logic on Italian politics, in effectively establishing Italians' identification with the fascist state, and thus in making Italians—all Italians, whether fascist or antifascist—see themselves in the state led by Mussolini. This is why Gentile spoke of the rebirth of a religious spirit in Italian politics, and why he could not imagine a culture in the service of politics. In this sense, Gentile believed that the adjective "fascist" had to become synonymous with the adjective "Italian": to speak of fascism was to speak of Italy, its resources, its best minds and people working to unite the nation, building a new Italian state day by day. This attitude was by no means fearful of the regime. And from this point of view, as Turi has shown, the entries in the *Enciclopedia* fully confirmed the existence of a fascist culture.[56] In the first volume, which appeared in 1929, Gentile noted that what united so many different writers—each with their own temperament, training, and methods—was the spirit of the times, a new unifying sentiment that made the *Enciclopedia italiana* the expression of a people and an epoch. In reality, however, this claim was not met with unconditional approval, as will be clear when we examine the cultural politics of the subsequent ministers of public education.

Making the Schools Fascist

After the brief tenure of the liberal minister of public education Alessandro Casati, which ended with Mussolini's declaration on January 3, 1925, subsequent ministers gave rise to what the French historian Michel Ostenc has deemed a counterreform to Gentile's reform.[57] Pietro Fedele and Giuseppe Belluzzo in the '20s and Balbino Giuliano, Francesco Ercole, Cesare Maria De Vecchi di Val Cismon, and Giuseppe Bottai in the '30s all considered the 1923 reforms unequal to the tasks of making Italian schools truly fascist and inculcating the values and myths of fascist culture in the younger generations.[58]

In January 1925, Pietro Fedele declared in Parliament his wish to alter school curricula, and in particular to make the secondary schools easier.[59] This desire was shared by several powerful members of the government and of the Grand Council of Fascism, not to mention the head of state himself.

In the summer of 1927, chief of staff Pietro Badoglio informed Mussolini that among secondary school graduates drafted into military service, a great number were regularly declared unfit. Accordingly, he asked Il Duce to increase physical education and to continue the work Fedele had begun to reduce secondary school coursework.[60] Mussolini welcomed Badoglio's requests and wrote to Minister Fedele outlining the direction of fascist education policy.[61] Nearly five years after Gentile's reform was passed, therefore, Mussolini too believed that school curricula were too wide-ranging and demanding; he feared that the schools Gentile wanted might be capable of selecting and training a ruling class, but would become a world unto themselves, a place of abstract knowledge where education was in the end nothing more than a cultural grand tour. This is why he authorized Fedele to modify the reformed programs of study and accelerate the process of making the schools fascist. He approved plans to introduce the study of fascism into school curricula and to set aside a day for sports or field trips, believing that political education and extracurricular activities were essential to training a generation of young fascists.[62]

In the months that followed, the Grand Council of Fascism also expressed the need for education reform. At a November 1927 meeting, they addressed the problems attendant upon "fascisizing the schools."[63] On the one hand, the Grand Council expressly declared that Gentile's reform should be considered "one of the regime's best and most fundamental laws,"[64] and concluded by reasserting the untouchable nature of the state exam, which guaranteed the fascist regime's monopoly on conferring academic credentials and its discretion regarding legal recognition of private schools. On the other hand, the regime's governing body distinguished between the results of the 1923 reform in elementary schools and those in secondary schools and universities, deeming the former excellent and the latter merely "satisfactory." In outlining the most urgent measures to adopt, the Grand Council focused on the importance of "physical and sporting education," which in their opinion had not received sufficient attention in the Italian school system, and declared the need to put the schools in more direct contact "with life in all its expressions of force, beauty, and work."[65]

To respond to these needs and move toward truly fascist schools, a March 1928 decree dictated that elementary schoolbooks on history, geography, economics, and civics must conform to the requirements of fascism. Texts already on order would remain in circulation until September 1930, when they would be replaced by a single state textbook for all elementary schools, both public and private.[66] The need to control academic textbooks had been posited as early as 1927, when a Central Commission was established within the Ministry of Public Education to screen all books destined for school use. Chaired by the vice-president of the National Fascist Party, Alessandro Melchiori, the commission examined four hundred texts in October 1928 and declared none of them suited to fascism's purposes. Melchiori accordingly asked the government to move up the publication of the new consolidated state textbook, which appeared in Italian classrooms in 1930, having been shepherded by Minister Giuseppe Belluzzo. Some of Italy's most celebrated cultural figures contributed to the new textbook, including the poet Ada Negri and Nobel laureate Grazia Deledda, the mathematician Gaetano Scorza, and the geographer Luigi De Marchi.[67] The law envisaged a single book covering all the academic subjects for the first two years of elementary school, while several texts would be introduced during the remaining three years; this consolidated textbook was to be revised every three years, published by the state publishing office, and distributed in schools by the various provincial superintendents. Even the book's appearance was carefully curated. In its communications strategy, as Mariella Colin recalled, the regime made ample use of images in children's books, whose covers were to be printed in color and designed by the period's best illustrators. Secondary school texts contained no images but were still subject to strict political control, as programs of study were shaped in accordance with the regime's demands.[68]

During the 1920s, education was not the only arena in which the fascists expressed the desire to inculcate the regime's values in young people.[69] In fact, the domain of the Ministry of Public Education (which was by definition a state body) was nonetheless the sector furthest from the Fascist Party, which throughout the Ventennio invested significant energy into mobilizing upcoming generations.[70] As we shall see, the Party articulated "a concept of politics based on an image of humanity that has been spiritually and physically remade," and for this reason it attributed "primary importance to educating the youth."[71] One might say, furthermore, that the mass politics of the fascist regime was conceived and enacted by the Party "in every aspect ... as a constant enterprise of totalitarian pedagogy, applied to Italians starting at birth," subjecting them to organization, indoctrination, and assimilation.[72]

Balilla: The National Fascist Youth

As we have seen, the history of the first fascist youth organizations coincides with the history of fascism. Students went from leading the movement's earliest fights to being the subjects of a pedagogical experiment upon which the fate of the regime depended.

After the National Fascist Party was founded in November 1921, the Student Vanguard of the Fascist Combat Squads morphed into the Fascist Student Youth organization (Avanguardia giovanile fascista). Open to workers as well as students, this became the Party's youth section, and starting in October 1921 it gradually merged with the Fascist University Groups (Gruppi universitari fascisti, or GUF). The Balilla (or National Fascist Youth) groups were added to this constellation in June 1922. To organize all these different strains of fascist youth activity into a unified structure, and to coordinate their various undertakings, the National Fascist Youth Organization (Opera nazionale balilla, or ONB) was formed on April 3, 1926. A typical example of the osmosis that occurred between the Party's organizations and those of the state under fascism, the ONB was directed by the national Party and was at the same time a charitable organization with its own legal status, subject to control by the head of state. It took its name from Giovan Battista Perasso, known as Balilla, a Genoese boy who in 1746 started a revolt against the Austrians occupying the province of Liguria. The organization provided support and physical education for Italian youths between eight and eighteen years of age. It comprised four groups: besides the Balilla and the Avanguardisti (Fascist Student Youth) mentioned above, there were the Little Italian Girls (le Piccole italiane) and the Young Italian Women (le Giovani italiane). Starting in 1930, it also included the Children of the She-Wolf (i Figli della lupa) for six- to eight-year-olds.

Just a few months after the ONB was created, two decrees in January 1927 banned all nonfascist youth associations, except for Catholic ones, which were reduced in number but not outright prohibited. The Catholic associations were allowed to operate in cities with a population over 20,000, but they had to display the fasces and the initials "ONB." The next year the Boy Scouts, too, were forced to cease all activities. From that point on, as Niccolò

Zapponi has observed, it seemed that nothing could check the ONB's reach, as it expanded its scope and activities until it became one of the regime's most powerful and important institutions, "commensurate with the schools and indeed potentially hostile to them."[73]

For example, in the summer of 1928, the ONB was tasked with managing rural Sicilian schools. These schools had previously been entrusted to the National Association for the Benefit of Southern Italy (Associazione nazionale per gli interessi del Mezzogiorno), one of the delegate bodies charged with improving the southern schools, albeit with scant results. A few months later the ONB assumed control of all "unclassified" (i.e., small and rural) educational institutions in Calabria and Sicily; in 1929 about 700 evening schools for illiterate adults were transferred to the ONB for management, along with similar institutions in the Italian colonies of Eritrea, Somalia, Cyrenaica, and Tripolitania. In March 1930 the ONB secured the management of the municipal aid offices, which supported indigent students by offering medical care, setting up insurance plans, and organizing camps, scholarships, and trips.

Led by Renato Ricci until 1937, the ONB oversaw cultural education, technical and professional instruction, religious assistance, and above all physical education in primary and secondary schools. To this end, in February 1928 the fascist physical education academy was inaugurated in Rome, housed in an enormous gymnasium designed by the architect Enrico Del Debbio. Dubbed the Fascist Upper School for Physical and Sports Education (Scuola superiore fascista di magistero per l'educazione ginnico-sportiva), it aimed to train secondary school PE teachers and sports instructors for the regime's youth organizations.[74] The fascists' goal was to transform physical education into a mass phenomenon, one that could be managed and directed toward the government's ends. Accordingly, in December 1928 the National Fascist Party's press office issued the Carta dello sport (Sports Charter), in which it declared that all sports for children between six and seventeen years of age were now the exclusive purview of the ONB, while the Italian National Olympic Committee would be responsible for sports at every other level. The charter specified that Italian children could participate in private sports associations only if they were also members of the ONB, which organized end-of-year showcases at primary and secondary schools, regional sports tournaments with events determined by local committees, national littorio competitions (i.e., Party-sponsored tournaments), the "Dux" cup, and summer camps for poorer students, which received extensive media coverage.[75]

The enormous amount of energy devoted to sports stemmed from the regime's desire to create a "new man"—strong, modern, able to compete aggressively and thereby demonstrate his superiority. Disciplined athletes were supposed to become valiant soldiers, voluntary servicemen who would greet "the strictest forms of discipline with joy." This description came from a commentator who explained that fascist sports should "be understood like militia, that is as discipline and virile training for the citizen."[76] And in effect, as the years went on, the paramilitary nature of these sporting activities became ever clearer, to the point that, as Ricci wrote in his report on the academic year 1930–1931, the whole of Italy had been transformed into one giant barracks.

Guided by this same logic, the ONB undertook premilitary training for Italian boys: the Balilla were supposed to develop an enthusiasm for military life via frequent contact with the armed forces, which would evoke the glory of military traditions. The Avanguardisti (Fascist Student Youth)— for boys between fourteen and sixteen—would in turn acquire real military knowledge, both practical and theoretical, to facilitate their advancement to the militias and, at eighteen, the call to arms. This is why the 30,000 field trips organized in 1930—in which more than half a million Balilla and fascist students participated—chose military bases, airports, warships, and arsenals as their preferred destinations.

From 1927 onward, all "graduations"—passage from the Children of the She-Wolf to the Balilla and the Little Italian Girls; from the Balilla to the Fascist Student Youth; from the Fascist Student Youth to the Fascist University Groups or the ranks of the young fascists; from the Fascist University Groups or young fascists to the militia or the Party itself—were celebrated yearly along with the military draft. As rites of initiation similar to the Catholic first communion, such ceremonies took place in the provincial capitals and were attended by government and Party officials. Young people advancing to the next level, and in particular those who wanted to join the Party and the militia, were welcomed into the fold by elderly comrades, and, after swearing loyalty until death to Il Duce and the fascist revolution, received their Party card and musket.[77]

In November 1929 supervision of the ONB was transferred to the newly renamed Ministry of National Education. As we shall see, during the 1930s the Fascist Party attempted to regain control of it, as it considered the Fascist Youth Organization one of the regime's most important institutions— indeed, one of the most successful forms of totalitarian pedagogy, *pace* the historians Carmen Betti and Tracy Koon.[78] Both scholars have claimed that the fascist youth organizations, and the ONB in particular, not only failed to achieve their aims but in fact developed into crucibles of antifascism. This argument has been widely accepted and, as we shall see, extended to apply to the entire landscape of fascist youth culture, which many have seen as impervious to the values and symbolism of fascism, and thus able to foster the roots of an antifascist culture.

The National Recreation Club

In an effort to extend their reach into the private lives of adults by organizing their free time, the regime created the National Recreation Club (l'Opera nazionale dopolavoro, or OND)[79] in May 1925. Corporate syndicalist leader Edmondo Rossoni and Party Secretary Augusto Turati fought for control of the OND, and in April 1927 Turati won, officially making it a Fascist Party organization. The National Recreation Club was one of the most important mass organizations of the Ventennio, and the Party's most powerful instrument for reaching the working masses. By the end of the '30s, it controlled 30,000 organizations, associations, and entities involving a total of 4 million Italians.[80] According to its charter, it was responsible for morally and physically elevating the populace through sports, hiking, tourism, arts education, popular culture, professional development, and social, health, and hygiene services.[81] This range of activities made the OND one of the regime's most efficacious instruments for controlling, organizing, and educating Italian workers.

As Victoria De Grazia has observed, foremost among the OND's tasks was the creation of "a mass public." The organization undertook this project in three broad ways between 1925 and 1943. The first was controlling leisure activities that were already woven into daily life in Italy, like bocce, dance, bands, and theater. The second was controlling mass tourism—for example, in August 1931 the OND created "people's trains," which let low-income workers travel at a discounted rate. The trains were a resounding success, carrying half a million travelers in August and September 1931 alone.[82] Third, the OND tried to cultivate the working masses' taste in modern art, which had an intrinsic propagandistic value, as we shall examine in greater detail later. Starting in the late 1920s, the regime also invested a great deal of energy in charitable activities, even as the projects of the OND remained largely focused on sports and tourism.

Such an elaborate undertaking, which had a vast and complex bureaucratic machinery behind it, required an enormous organizing effort. Along with its general management based in Rome, the National Recreation Club created local committees in each provincial capital, which played an essential role in that they brought together representatives from employer and syndicalist associations with public authorities. In fact, these provincial committees supervised all the local leisure organizations—not only the neighborhood or town recreation chapters founded by the OND, but also activities that were popular before the arrival of fascism. The lowest level of this complex hierarchy perfectly mirrored the Recreation Club's general management: it was overseen by the local chapter's secretary, managed by a president nominated by the fascists, and presided over by a committee consisting of the town clerk, the health inspector, the elementary school teacher, the trustee of the women's chapter, and representatives of the fascist unions and employer associations.[83]

In 1928, to incentivize volunteering, the National Recreation Club offered gold, silver, and bronze medals and certificates of merit, conferred in ceremonies honoring those who distinguished themselves by their work for the leisure organizations. Starting in the 1930s, moreover, participation in these clubs became part of the advancement criteria for government positions. And finally, in 1937, a law reforming the OND was ratified, giving the organization greater administrative autonomy. The club had already had a legal dimension, but now it could receive and manage donations, acquire and possess goods, and undertake any legal action necessary to reach its goals. All its revenue was exempt from taxes and fees, since it was considered a public good. Directly reporting to Il Duce, headed by a secretary who by that point had been made a minister, the OND was the equivalent of a government agency.[84]

According to De Grazia, the National Recreation Club failed to reach its goals because "the totalitarian aspiration" to create a mass public faced many obstacles—from communication difficulties to the challenge of reaching parts of the countryside still isolated from the regime's politics. In her view, in fact, the worlds of mass culture and high culture always remained distinct. As we shall see in the next chapter, where we will view things through the lens of fascist culture and cultural politics, this argument is debatable.

3

Intellectuals and Artists
in the 1920s

Intellectuals

Having traced the contours of the cultural politics of the Fascist Party and the government between 1922 and 1929, we now turn to the contributions of intellectuals and artists during that period. As we shall see, there were three main groups engaged in producing fascist culture: the revisionists, the radical fascists, and the Gentilians.

The revisionist wing was led by Giuseppe Bottai, who was one of the regime's most prominent politicians between 1922 and 1943.[1] A volunteer in World War I, a Futurist, and a member of the Arditi, in 1919 Bottai helped found the Italian Combat Leagues and became a proponent of *squadrismo* in his hometown of Rome. After being elected to the Chamber of Deputies in 1921, Bottai took part in the March on Rome. In 1923 he founded the magazine *Critica fascista* (Fascist criticism), convinced that the defeat of the liberal ruling class and the successes of the fascists were only the beginning of the battle. From that point on, he became one of the most authoritative exponents of the revisionist movement, demanding that political strategies and methods be revisited and that a different era succeed the era of *squadrismo*— one that would no longer be animated by violence, but in which a new state could be founded. Bottai thought that to attain this goal, intellectuals should cooperate with the fascist ruling class and put themselves at the service of politics, which in his view had absolute precedence over any other kind of human activity. As Niccolò Zapponi has pointed out, Bottai had a mythological concept of politics and the state. "To be precise, the revisionist ideology encouraged [its followers] to idolize politics as the art of constantly touching up the architecture of the state, with the goal of making timely adjustments for the mutations of history"; theirs was "an idea of politics as creativity, and thus as a gift possessed by only a few elect and carefully chosen souls."[2] Though many historians have argued that Bottai's attention to culture and the intellectual class was a sign of his independence within the ranks of the fascist ruling class, and have accordingly seen him as a moderate if not an outright critic of Mussolini's politics, in reality he was one of the main proponents of fascist totalitarianism.[3]

In a lecture at the Augusteum in Rome in the spring of 1924, the revisionist leader laid out his thoughts about the French Revolution, democracy, and, more generally, the relationship between fascism and modern culture.[4] Though neither a philosopher nor a political theorist by trade, Bottai declared his affinity with modern philosophy and explained how Georges Sorel, the German idealists, and the Romantic intellectuals of the late nineteenth century had critiqued political rationalism, positivistic culture, and the "more decadent" ideas of the Enlightenment, all without denying the importance of modernity. Unlike more reactionary writers, the authors Bottai cited had all demonstrated the limits of individualism and materialism, but without questioning the positive impact of the French Revolution—an event that had definitively changed modern history by inaugurating an era of mass participation in politics.

Through the lens of this notion of modernity, Bottai saw fascism as the most significant expression of the revolutionary impulses that had shaken the Old World over the previous two centuries: a political movement that acknowledged the centrality of the masses in modern politics and, unlike the egalitarian utopias of the nineteenth century, recognized the role of individuals in building the state. Fascism preserved the positive elements of political modernity that emerged with the French Revolution while rejecting those aspects it deemed harmful. It was thus, for Bottai, a modern, revolutionary, and above all *Italian* political phenomenon. In seeking to identify the cultural tradition from which fascism emerged, he argued that Mussolini's movement embodied a politics that had emerged with Machiavelli and Vico, had been promoted by Oriani at the beginning of the century, and had been systematically articulated by Croce and Gentile. He was thus one of the key proponents of Gentile's cultural politics in the 1920s, and he defended Gentile from the radical fascists' attacks.[5]

Among the many young people who wrote for Bottai's magazine *Critica fascista* and shared his views, Camillo Pellizzi deserves special mention. A scholar of literature and sociology, and one of the regime's most prominent intellectuals, he founded the movement's London chapter.[6] Pellizzi, like Bottai, believed that fascism was a revolutionary new political movement; he argued as much in 1924, claiming that the new politics was "a form of religious thought" that expressed myths—that is to say, "faiths and passions that touch and move the vast and varied souls of the populace, as the celestial bodies move the tides."[7] Convinced that only a select few could truly feel the power of political myths, Pellizzi developed a model of an aristocratic society wherein the best of the best would work to carry out the vision embodied in such myths. Like Bottai, he wished to situate fascism within the European history of the previous few centuries, and he did so by borrowing Vincenzo Gioberti's distinction between mimetic and methectic forces (*mimesis* in Greek drama referring to the representation of the real world and *methexis* to the participation of the audience). In Pellizzi's view, liberalism and democracy should be considered mimetic forces because they expressed conservative tendencies aimed at maintaining a pre-existing world order. Fascism, on the other hand, like the Risorgimento and other methectic forces, was the bearer of a revolutionary project that would change history by transforming society and politics through the creation of a new state. In this vein, in a clear reference to Gentile, Pellizzi defined the state as a "dynamo," constantly changing and surpassing itself.[8] Like Bottai, in the early 1920s Pellizzi too saw Gentile as the main theorist of fascism, and he was proud to count the philosopher as a member of the Party and the government.

The second key strain of culture in the 1920s comprised the radical fascists—those who, after the March on Rome, called for no mercy toward their enemies and opposed the ceasefire the government imposed in response to *squadrismo*. In keeping with these positions, they considered cooperating with the liberal ruling class to be an admission of defeat. Instead, they wished to reclaim the Party as a means of gaining power, believing that their movement represented a radical alternative to modernity.[9] The writer

Curzio Suckert—better known by his pseudonym, Malaparte—is a prime example of this school of thought. He developed a notion of modernity as a political, cultural, and philosophical process that sprang from the Protestant Reformation and then began its irreversible decline.[10] Like many intellectuals of his generation, Suckert believed that the Reformation had brought about the triumph of bourgeois individualism and the rise of capitalism, inducing "that paradoxical reversal of values" by which "what the Latinate world had condemned as barbaric" had become "a source of pride."[11] The young writer argued that fascism would achieve its historic mission by saving Europe from ruin, restoring the ancient order, and demonstrating its superiority to liberalism and socialism. Antimodern, anti-European, Latinate, and Catholic, Suckert's fascism was a political movement fighting to valorize its Italian cultural roots and leave behind the foreign ideologies responsible for having corrupted Italy's true spirit as a Catholic, Counter-Reformationist country.[12]

In this regard Suckert's opinions resembled those of his friend, the writer and painter Ardengo Soffici.[13] Soffici too believed that the degradation of Italian politics stemmed from the importation of foreign cultural movements like literary Romanticism and Hegelian idealism. Also prominent among the radical fascists were the ex-Futurists Mario Carli and Emilio Settimelli, who, starting in 1921, articulated a fascist, monarchical, and reactionary form of extremism. From March 1923 on they edited the daily paper *L'Impero*.[14] Fully subscribing to the ideology of violence, they understood politics as a matter of instinct and force; they disdained intellectuals and rejected the idea that it was necessary to culturally legitimate fascism or define its ideological position. Thus, the editors of *L'Impero* were among Gentile and the revisionists' main adversaries. The philosopher had shown no interest in the political battles the fascists fought between March 1919 and October 1922; he had not participated in the squabbles over fascism's political origins, and therefore, in the editors' view, he could not have understood the nature of fascism, which Carli defined as a "phenomenon of temperament, not of theoretical inclination."[15] What's more, their rejection of Gentile was also motivated by a factor unrelated to the politics of fascism and connected, instead, to the anti-idealist and anti-Crocean culture that the Futurists had advocated for in the 1910s.

By the 1920s the ex-Futurists' ideas were shared by the monarchists, a group of radical fascists led by Giuseppe Attilio Fanelli and Giuseppe Brunati, who distinguished themselves in the Italian cultural landscape above all by the violence with which they opposed Gentile.[16] Advocating a return to pre-capitalist society and absolute monarchy, the monarchists made no effort to distance themselves from Malaparte's and Soffici's critiques of Italian neo-idealism and its sympathizers. Like all the radical fascists, they saw idealism as the ultimate embodiment of a culture alien to the Italian tradition. The monarchists hoped that fascism, as a new Counter-Reformation, would restore the principles of the Catholic tradition—which remained uncorrupted by modernity—and bring about a return to a premodern world that rejected individualism and liberalism.[17]

The third main current of fascist culture comprised Gentile and his students, who from 1922 onward campaigned to be the official representatives of fascist culture—to the point that they positioned themselves as "more fascist" than the founders of the Blackshirts. Vito Fazio Allmayer, Guido Calogero, Delio Cantimori, Armando Carlini, Ernesto Codignola, Giuseppe Lombardo Radice, Giuseppe Maggiore, Adolfo Omodeo, Giuseppe Saitta, Leonardo Severi, Ugo Spirito, Arnaldo and Luigi Volpicelli—to name only the most prominent of Gentile's students and those with the closest ties to him—followed their mentor into the Fascist Party and did not leave it until 1943. Among these men only Radice and Calogero chose a different path: the former resigned from his position directing elementary education at the Ministry of Public Education in 1924 and thenceforth refused to hold further political positions; and the latter became an exponent of liberal-socialist antifascism in the late 1930s. All of the others, throughout the 1920s, made up a cohesive group that participated in the Party because the regime offered them the possibility of reforming Italian education and, above all, of authoring a new chapter in Italian history.

The Gentilians believed that unified Italy—the nation born of the Risorgimento—had not yet awakened to self-consciousness as a nation, and that it had to be radically transformed in order to acquire a true political identity. Persuaded that the national character had undergone a growth spurt when Italy participated in the First World War, the Gentilians thought that Mussolini's political movement would finish the process of national identity-building begun by the Risorgimento. On the one hand, they understood themselves as working with the fascists on a large-scale effort of political and cultural renewal; on the other, they thought that Gentile had developed the theoretical premises that gave rise to fascism in the first place.[18] Accordingly, they never saw themselves as wonks merely on loan to politics—in fact, in the early years they were eager to distinguish themselves from liberal "sympathizers" by highlighting their own loyal participation in the fascist cause. This is evident, for example, in the words of the young writer Ugo Spirito, who in June 1924, a few days after the murder of Giacomo Matteotti, declared his readiness to defend fascism, claiming that the parliamentary opposition had no right to protest.[19] Ernesto Codignola was equally clear when he argued that the Matteotti killing was tragic "but salutary" and encouraged all Italians to join the fascist cause "simultaneously and silently."[20] Writing a year later in *L'educazione politica* (Political education), the magazine of the National Fascist Institute of Culture, Spirito elaborated on the idea of fascism's revolutionary character and its relationship with prefascist political authorities, arguing that making "compromises with sympathizers" risked distancing fascism "from its revolutionary goals."[21]

These ideas linked Gentile and his students closely to other key players in the political-cultural debates of the 1920s, including the distinguished historian Gioacchino Volpe, who sought to define fascism's role in the history of Italy. Like Gentile, Volpe—who had been a student at the Scuola Normale in Pisa at the same time as the Sicilian philosopher—had become well known before the war and joined the Fascist Party at the height of his career. Volpe regarded the new movement as a healthy shakeup amid the postwar crisis, and one that could open a new chapter of Italian history. In the late 1920s, having written his most important historical works on the *ancien régime*, Volpe turned his attention to modern and contemporary history, focusing on the relationship between fascism and the liberal era. In his 1927 book *Italia in cammino* (Italy's journey), he traced Italian history from 1861 to 1914, focusing on the processes that brought about the new regime, including both departures from the liberal past and points of continuity with the nation's history. His emphasis on fascism as the best product of a longer national history—of fascism as "continuation, development, [and] elevation of yesterday's Italy"—opened him up to ferocious criticism from the radical fascists, who accused him of being a nationalist who had not fully grasped fascism's revolutionary nature. This did not, however, mean that Volpe was not a true believer: he was the author of the historical portion of the "Fascism" entry in the *Enciclopedia italiana*; he played a key role as an intellectual and eminent historian within the regime, directing the Scuola di storia moderna e contemporanea (School of Modern and Contemporary History) in Rome until 1943 and the section on medieval and modern history in the *Enciclopedia italiana* from 1925 to 1937. He was a member of the Accademia dei Lincei from 1935 to 1947 and general secretary of the Royal Academy of Italy from 1929 to 1934.[22]

For figures like Volpe and Gentile, and for the Gentilians more generally, the desire to distinguish themselves from liberal "sympathizers" and to establish good relations with the Fascist Party did not simply stem from a fear of being labeled as moderates.[23] As we shall see, together with the other key groups we have examined here, in the early years these intellectuals were responsible for developing and diffusing fascist culture in all its many and various forms.

The Debate about Fascist Art

Even before the March on Rome, the fascists had tried to outline the key features of the artistic movements related to fascism, as when the writer and painter Ardengo Soffici wrote in September 1922:

> At the present moment ... there are two key trends: one reactionary and one revolutionary. . . . Which of these shall we understand as best responding to our theory and practice? . . . Fascism . . . is not a movement of reaction, nor of regression . . . and it is not the enemy of modernity. [Nevertheless] Fascism, which is a revolutionary movement, though not a subversive or extremist one, does not tend toward an overthrow of values. . . . So we must reject both of these trends with equal resolve.[24]

Soffici did not explain what fascist art was, and in the years that followed neither he nor other notable intellectuals would identify the style or movement that corresponded to the official art of the regime. Yet from the beginning fascist artists were united in declaring that just as a "conservative, neo-bourgeois, anarchic art" had existed, so fascism would express "its own artistic concept and its own artistic forms."[25]

For example, in his 1923 book *Gli intellettuali creatori e la mentalità fascista* (Creative intellectuals and fascist thought), the Futurist Bruno Corra argued, like Soffici, that fascism had a dual nature, both revolutionary and conservative, and that it would reject individual freedom and reshape daily life by infusing Italians with a mystical revolutionary zeal.[26] Corra did not, however, define the art proper to the regime. In what sense, then, did artists believe that they were contributing to the development of a fascist style of art, if each of them expressed their own style and pursued their own path of inquiry, and if fascist art contained within it various movements, from romanticism to classicism, modernism to traditionalism? In responding to this question, many historians have asserted that fascism was not capable of producing its own style of art, because it got stuck in a sort of "aesthetic pluralism."[27] This claim was first put forth by Philip Cannistraro in 1975 in *La fabbrica del consenso* (Manufacturing consent) and reasserted more recently by Marla Stone. Walter Adamson, on the other hand, has argued that it is not possible to formulate a definitive hypothesis about fascism's lack of cultural coherence because it is not clear whether that lack stemmed from a conscious effort to avoid favoring one artistic trend over another or whether it was a sign of a genuine failure.[28] As we shall see in the pages that follow, however, a different understanding of the so-called aesthetic pluralism of fascist art is possible.

In February 1926 Mussolini participated in an art exhibition organized in Milan by the writer and art critic Margherita Sarfatti. Italy's most prominent artists were there, including Giacomo Balla, Carlo Carrà, Giorgio De Chirico, Fortunato Depero, Giorgio Morandi, and Gino Severini. In this forum, the premier argued that there was a hierarchical relationship between politics and art, such that Italian artists ought to consider themselves civil servants.[29] A few months later, speaking at the Accademia di Belle Arti in Perugia in October 1926, Mussolini declared the need for an art form that would be the glory of fascist Italy. His words provoked a vigorous debate among Italian artists, who weighed in over the following months in *Critica fascista*, explaining their notions of art and its relationship to fascism.[30] Though they had diverse training and distinct aesthetics, artists like Ardengo Soffici, Filippo Tommaso Marinetti, Massimo Bontempelli, Mino Maccari, and Anton Giulio Bragaglia expressed similar sentiments. Each explained his own creative process, illustrated the orientation of his work, and presented himself as a representative of authentic fascist art—indeed, as the one true fascist artist. In this sense, then, all these artists agreed that the new form of art would be at the service of politics.

The position of the writer Antonio Rapisarda (also known by the pseud-onym Antonio Aniante) is exemplary in this regard. He argued that only those writers ready to follow "the fundamental tenets" of fascist thought could be called fascist writers; those tenets were to "passionately love the nation," to respect the principles of discipline and hierarchy, and to "repu-diate forms of literature that glorified class struggle, internationalization, and any type of racial desegregation." The goal, according to Aniante, was "to develop an atmosphere congenial to the ethical principles inspiring fas-cism and Mussolini's government." To do so, Italian writers would have to stop "seeing themselves as superior beings [who exist] above and beyond the state and the nation," and instead strive to "sincerely and passionately" serve "the grand idea inspiring [their] Italian peers."[31] In February 1927, hav-ing collected the opinions of Italy's most prominent artists, *Critica fascista* concluded the discussion by reaffirming that works of art should be moti-vated "by the same tendency" present "in the political arena, toward more solid, more spacious, stronger edifices, in line with the grand tradition of autochthonous Italian art, which would be rediscovered alive and kicking despite the imposition and incrustation of so many foreign artistic tradi-tions." Accordingly artists should not engage with certain topics, such as "psychoanalysis, foreign cultures, Intimism"; they should not formulate "frag-mentary visions" of reality; they should, instead, show themselves "to be mil-itantly faithful to the fascist cause."[32] Everything else would be a matter of "free creation," meaning that choices of style, school, or aesthetics were second-order concerns; the main thing was to declare the subordination of various artistic disciplines to the political contents of fascism. In effect, according to Bottai's influential magazine, defining the art of fascism did not entail identifying an aesthetic responsive to the needs of the regime. The main question concerned artists' ability to make the themes of fascist politics their own. Arguments about style, which obviously had their own importance, ought to remain within the confines of the various disciplines. And, indeed, in the interwar years the debate among proponents of various trends influencing fascist art was lively—but, as Mario Sironi wrote in 1932, "the imagined agreement on a single artistic formula" proved "impossible." The regime demanded of a painter or novelist "the clear, express desire" to "liberate their art from subjective, arbitrary elements and from that specious originality which is wished for and nourished by vanity alone."[33]

The artists of the 1920s were in fact ready and willing to declare their loyalty to fascism, to pledge their contributions to the regime, to compete with one another to be seen as true fascist artists, and to accuse their rivals of heterodoxy. Despite Cannistraro's argument, the existence of different artistic visions does not demonstrate the lack of a fascist form of art. On the contrary, within their various disciplines artists used different methods to declare their membership in the regime, as is evident when we examine the central movements of 1920s fascist literature: the *selvaggi* (primitivists), strident critics of modern culture, and the *Novecento* (twentieth century) school, proud representatives of modernity in all its diverse forms.

Literature

The magazine *Il Selvaggio* (The savage) was founded in July 1924 in Colle Val d'Elsa, Siena, by Angiolo Bencini and Mino Maccari. An early fascist mouthpiece, it counted Curzio Suckert, Ardengo Soffici, Ottone Rosai, Camillo Pellizzi, Leo Longanesi, and Berto Ricci among its contributors. It served as the voice of Tuscan *squadrismo*, both because Rosai, Maccari, and Suckert had participated in the action squads and because they regarded the squads' violence as the revolutionary spirit of fascism (and themselves as its keepers).[34] In the early years, these radical fascists used the pages of *Il Selvaggio* to keep this violent revolutionary spirit alive, fearing as they did that the regime was on a path toward moderation.

The magazine's editorial stance shifted in the spring of 1927, when Maccari took over as editor—a position he held until 1943. Putting an end to the period of *squadrismo* and taking up Mussolini's 1926 call at the Milan fair, the new editor accelerated *Il Selvaggio*'s literary production and gave shape to the *Strapaese* (Ultra-country) movement via a clear strategy. This strategy sought to fight all forms of modern culture, save Europe from ruin, and demonstrate fascism's superiority over liberalism, democracy, and socialism.[35] To achieve this goal the magazine's contributors would valorize Italian cultural roots and give new life to local traditions, especially peasant culture, which they viewed as the source of authenticity in Italian daily life.[36] This was not a form of reactionary regionalism *per se*; *Il Selvaggio* was not trying to be a literary circle of Tuscan intellectuals worshiping the past. Their reverence for Italian peasant life served as "a bulwark against the invasion of fashion, foreign ideas, and modernist cities," part of the widespread conviction among the magazine's contributors that popular culture, faithful to the values of Italian civilization, could triumph in the battles of modernity.[37] Maccari, the magazine's editor, was a case in point. He penned both simple verses and sophisticated essays, explaining popular issues with the biting irony of a satirical poet, attacking careerism, false artistry, and traitors to fascism's pure origins; he strove to demonstrate that the political revolution would require Italians to change their habits, customs, and daily activities.[38]

The other key trend of the 1920s took its name from the magazine *900* (i.e., Novecento), which was founded in 1926 with an editorial stance that seemed directly opposed to that of *Il Selvaggio*.[39] To drive home its intention to renew Italian literature and integrate it into the broader landscape of modern culture, the magazine was published in French for the first two years and leveraged the contributions of artists and intellectuals from around the world. Their group—which included Sironi, Carrà, De Chirico, Severini, and Morandi—was led by Massimo Bontempelli, a fervent fascist and one-time Futurist, along with Curzio Malaparte (who departed after two years to join *Il Selvaggio*).

In the first issue Bontempelli set forth the magazine's poetics by adopting the notion of magical realism, which sought to describe the world not through realism but rather by unveiling the invisible relations woven through it. The intent was to create a form of modern art born of intelligence and imagination, which could surprise and entertain its audience.[40] Thus the contributors worked to create a novel form of literature based on the "creative imagination," on the "inventive ability to create myths, fables, [and] characters"—and to leave the residues of nineteenth-century literature behind.[41] As Bontempelli wrote in one of his more polemical articles, "I would like to meet the wretch who first spread the word that it was necessary to bind oneself to tradition. . . . This was a more fateful move than the introduction of cocaine. The craze for cocaine only affects perfect idiots, whereas the craze for tradition has also affected people who, though not the sharpest tools in the box, nonetheless showed some gleams of intelligence."[42]

Though they criticized those who defended tradition, Bontempelli and the contributors to *900* did not in fact cast themselves as an elite avant-garde. In their view, the battle over modern art was part and parcel of a political battle. Convinced that fascism represented a break with tradition, they declared that the poet was dead, and that the literary man of the new century would be a writer and intellectual destined for a specific job in modern society, and conscious of his role in the service of politics. "We are antistylists," Bontempelli asserted, explaining that Futurism had "been an avant-garde, aristocratic movement," whereas the Novecento school's art must "become 'popular,' winning over the public."[43] As Luisa Mangoni has observed, this was a clear definition of culture work as a job, a technical and specialized profession from which one must make a living—work not only aimed at producing art but also explicitly subject to public opinion.[44]

These two movements were at the heart of a debate that typified the culture of the 1920s: the conflict between defenders of fascism as a modern phenomenon and critics of modernity immersed in the history of Europe over the previous two centuries. From the arts to philosophy, from literature to politics—as we have also seen in the clash between the revisionists, the Gentilians, and the radical fascists—the question of fascism's relationship to modernity galvanized debates among fascist culture's key figures. At the end of the 1930s, Bottai and his collaborators would propose a solution to this conflict in the pages of *Critica fascista*.

Between Politics and Culture

In November 1928, in a long article titled "La filosofia del fascismo" (The philosophy of fascism), Gentile wrote:

> Every political concept deserving of the name is a philosophy, because its object—which is political life in general and therefore the political life of a given populace in a given time—cannot be isolated, whether from other forms of human experience that are usually distinguished from politics or from universal, historical, or natural experience. . . . Despite the attacks on philosophy that many fascist writers seem to enjoy, [fascism] gives philosophical meaning and universal application to its assertions, as assertions of principles whose consequences affect not only politics in the strict sense, but also economics, law, science, art, and even religion—in short, every theoretical or practical human activity.[45]

Gentile believed that the distrust many fascists felt for intellectuals in the early 1920s was rooted in the new regime's culture—that the radical fascists' efforts to declare the independence of politics from culture was a matter of choice. For Gentile, fascism was linked to Marx's socialism, Sorel's revolutionary syndicalism, and Italian idealism, all of which had given rise to a new culture around the turn of the century. He therefore declared himself a forerunner of fascism, citing the role his idealism had played in fighting rationalist and positivist intellectualism many years before. Many fascists, however, took a very different view of the relationship between culture and politics. While Gentile and his followers argued that *every* form of politics *was* a form of culture, the fascists held that the congruence of politics and culture had to be seen as a benefit to politics, and thus that culture, philosophy, and indeed all other aspects of life were in reality forms of politics.

This topic was taken up in the late '20s by *Critica fascista*, which hosted a lively debate between two camps: on one side, those who defended the autonomy of culture; on the other, those who championed the primacy of politics. The former emphasized the importance of defining fascist doctrine. In this vein, Francesco Formigari observed that some fascists claimed to want nothing to do with culture, not realizing—"those billy club mystics"— "that their pugnacious enthusiasm derived from the materialistic notion of culture that had prevailed in the late nineteenth century." Unwilling, therefore, to reject "culture *tout court* by taking refuge in a hypothetical form of pure action," the young contributor to *Critica fascista* wrote, "let there be no confusion, and let us repeat for the umpteenth time that we are against agnostic, Enlightenment culture."[46]

Those who believed Gentile had played a decisive part in defining fascist ideology supported this position.[47] Codignola, one of the philosopher's frequent collaborators, addressed believers in the primacy of politics when he argued that subordinating culture to political praxis would only create a new form of agnosticism—a set of ideas he had developed in his 1933 book *Il rinnovamento spirituale dei giovani* (The spiritual renewal of young people), dedicated to Mussolini.[48] Thus, Codignola argued that intellectuals should not distance themselves from political life and that culture could in no way be subjected to laws outside itself, contrary to what the champions of the sovereignty of politics believed.[49] In reality, this argument was far from clear-cut, since Codignola did not explain how to delineate the borders between culture and politics, as Delio Cantimori, a history student at the Scuola Normale in Pisa, pointed out.[50]

Cantimori—a harsh critic of reactionary, conservative, and nationalist notions of politics, and an advocate of a universalist and revolutionary form of fascism—conceived of the relationship between culture and politics in radical, totalitarian terms. Accordingly, he argued, following Carl Schmitt, that "it is genuine liberal folly to wish to posit a sphere of culture independent from politics."[51] Citing the German political theorist, whose work he had studied extensively, Cantimori noted, "In the meantime we have recognized that politics has totalizing value (*das Politische als das Totale*), and we accordingly also understand that deciding whether something is pertinent to politics or not is always a political question, no matter what sphere it touches, no matter what proof it rests upon. ... If we grant politics the totalitarian nature that even Codignola seems unable to deny, removing cultural life from political decisions becomes unthinkable."[52]

Ultimately closer to Cantimori's than to Codignola's position, in the 1930s *Critica fascista* would publish many pieces arguing that fascism's originality lay in the relationship it instantiated between theory and praxis, and thus in the possibility of defining fascist ideology on the basis of political acts. The problem, for these writers, would not be solved by identifying a single corpus of doctrine that would find its application in the politics of fascism. On the contrary, according to one contributor to *Critica fascista*, it was necessary "to create a totalitarian fascist spirit, in which thought [would] necessarily" be situated and equated "with action."[53] As we shall see, in the 1930s there were many Gentilians who chose a path other than the one laid out by their teacher, drawing closer to Bottai and coming to embody a revolutionary, totalitarian brand of fascism. From the late '20s onward, in fact, the Roman politician recognized that Gentile could not serve as the philosopher of fascism because he held a position on this very question—the relationship between politics and culture—that the fascists wished to move beyond. It was then that Bottai redoubled his efforts to resolve the conflicts among the various strains of fascist culture, becoming the regime's most influential proponent of totalitarian cultural politics.

4

The Ideology of the Totalitarian State

Myth and Ideology

As we observed in chapter 1, for many years most Italian scholars denied the existence of a fascist ideology, reducing fascism to a purely practical phenomenon. As evidence for this claim, many historians pointed to the fact that the regime proved incapable of producing its own doctrine comparable in coherence and solidity to those of the great political traditions, from liberalism to democracy, from socialism to communism. Furthermore, they argued, during the twenty years in which Italy was transformed into a totalitarian state, fascism managed to formulate a series of heterogeneous ideological positions. Reactionary and modernist, Catholic and atheist, nationalist and statist, corporatist and syndicalist, the ideologies of fascism would ultimately give rise to that "political and cultural machine" that Sergio Luzzatto in 1999 called "a bazaar."[1] As we have seen, many American historians concurred with this interpretation. Jeffrey Schnapp, for instance, claimed that the weakness of fascist ideology engendered the regime's massive aesthetic output, as it tried to use propaganda to compensate for the absence of a coherent ideology. Other historians have argued, instead, that the issue had to be addressed by first clarifying what the term *ideology* means. In this vein, David D. Roberts wrote that if ideology is understood as synonymous with political doctrine, with an emphasis on its systematic nature, then one is forced to conclude that fascism did not have an ideology. On the other hand, if we understand ideology as a collection of visions, values, and ideals, then one must conclude not only that fascism expressed its own ideology, but that this ideology was definitely capable of guiding political action.[2]

Ever since the appearance of the term *ideology* in the late eighteenth century, a great many interpretations of it have been put forth. It is not our intent to evaluate the merits of the debate about this keyword in the history of political thought, but merely to highlight the fact that among the diverse interpretations of the concept, the one advanced by the founder of the sociology of knowledge, Karl Mannheim, is of particular importance for the study of fascist ideology. In 1929 Mannheim defined *ideology* as a system of visions, values, and ideals capable of guiding political action and simultaneously expressing a worldview.[3] In keeping with the tradition of Marxist thought from which he emerged, Mannheim believed that ideology expressed a worldview characteristic of a specific social group. Unlike the Marxists, however, he stressed the cognitive aspects of culture, arguing that the various viewpoints expressed in political ideologies are genuine and valid, even when they are partial and contradictory. In fact, he argued, their authenticity derives precisely from the fact that they express a specific aspect of their period's society and history. From this perspective, following Mannheim's position, through ideologies we can discern the dominant classes' way of being, rather than seeing ideologies simply as instruments of domination or means of justifying power; and we can reason about the social determinants that condition each group's worldview. Despite the fact that, broadly speaking, most contributions to the study of fascist ideology have come from historians rather than political theorists,[4] Mannheim was among the first to identify the distinguishing features of fascist ideology, in particular emphasizing that it "has its own conception of the relations of theory and practice."[5]

On this note, Zeev Sternhell has observed that the history of political doctrines is marked by disagreement about the semantic value of terms that ought to refer to corresponding concepts within the history of political thought. For example, the term *democracy* has provoked wide and seemingly interminable debates about its meaning, its scope in the world, and its ability to be concretized as political praxis.[6] And yet no one denies the existence of democratic thought because of a lack of agreement about its contents, or because of the difficulty of reaching its goals. In the case of fascism, on the other hand, commentators have pointed to programmatic and intellectual inconsistency, contradictoriness, and the contrast between declared scope and achieved results as major features of its political culture. In this regard, Emilio Gentile has observed that in every political movement one may encounter a certain degree of dissonance between ideology and action—a mismatch between predetermined goals and actual outcomes—and that ideology is never a philosophical system that respects the principle of non-contradiction: "If fascism appears illogical and unsystematic when subjected to historical inquiry, this does not mean that fascism did not have its own ideology, distinct from its predecessors, contemporaries, and successors. This would be equivalent to saying that if a person doesn't think like a systematic philosopher, then she lacks a worldview."[7] A rigidly conceptual definition of *ideology* cannot explain a political phenomenon like fascism, which critiqued all forms of rationalism and proclaimed the power of myths to organize the masses, thereby introducing a new way of doing politics.

From the beginning, the fascists espoused a notion of politics no longer, or not only, aimed at changing the world, but rather at experiencing life—that is to say, a notion of politics as a religious faith. The German philosopher Ernst Cassirer observed this at the end of World War II, pointing out that in totalitarian regimes, mythical thinking prevailed over rational thinking. In *The Myth of the State*, Cassirer argued that for National Socialism and fascism, myths played a crucial role in building consent because they weakened individuals' intellectual autonomy, making them feel subordinate to political power.[8] In reality, if it is true that myths constitute a powerful instrument of totalitarian power, it is also the case that the creation of political myths does not derive solely from the ruling class's will to dominate. As we have learned from the work of anthropologists, sociologists, and philosophers, in particular Émile Durkheim's work on forms of religious life, myths are not merely instruments by which the powerful subjugate the masses; they are collective beliefs that affect everyone, both the governed and the governing. As methods of control internalized by an individual consciousness, myths are social in nature and thus make up the structure of an individual's identity, not just the context in which she finds herself living.[9] This means that imagining a clear distinction between producers and consumers of myths, or between mythical thought and rational thought, can be misleading in the context of an ideology like fascism. And indeed, observing the rites of fascist ideology, or feeling yourself to be part of a collective

religious experience, does not equate to being subjugated to the blind enthusiasms of irrationalism, or forced to behave in a certain way rather than
another because you have been deprived of your reason. In the following
pages we shall analyze fascist ideology by exploring its myths and attempting to show that it had its own, quite rational, coherence.

The Myth of Mussolini

Among all the myths and legends that nurtured fascist culture, the myth of
Mussolini was by far the most significant because it was, unlike the others,
a living myth.[10] As the absolute apex of political power, the unchallenged
ruler of the regime and the Party's complex organizing machinery, the head
of state was everywhere, as the writer Henri Béraud observed in 1929. Upon
returning from a trip to Rome, the Frenchman noted that Il Duce's image had
become part of everyday life in Italy, presiding over "the circumstances of
life"—not simply over "public acts," but "day-to-day life, street life." Béraud
painted an anxious picture: "Wherever you go, whatever you do, this gaze
follows you.... Mussolini is as omnipresent as a god," he wrote: "you see
him everywhere, in all possible forms, from realistic movie sets and candid
photos to the decorative figuration of stylized portraits."[11]

Thanks to the fascists' monopoly on information, wide-reaching propaganda apparatus, and constant efforts to educate young people, the myth of
Mussolini inundated the popular masses, who attributed extraordinary abil-
ities to the prime minister—from inexhaustible wisdom to immense kind-
ness, absolute genius to physical prowess—and greeted him as the leader
of a historic mission to transform Italy and the world. In effect, after three
years of world war and four of economic and social crisis, members of the
bourgeoisie and proletariat alike proved ready to welcome a strong, authoritarian leader who declared himself capable of solving the grave problems facing Italian society.[12] The myth of Mussolini grew stronger in the immediate
aftermath of the March on Rome, when the new premier toured the city and
the provinces in an effort to establish direct contact with the masses and
demonstrate a style unlike his predecessors'. Mussolini presented himself as
an implacable adversary of the politics and rhetoric of the ruling class he had
defeated and, right from the start, wielded his eloquence as a weapon. As Ugo
Ojetti noted in November 1921, the future Duce typically employed three
rhetorical devices: the periodic sentence, which was never left unresolved;

incisive definitions that impressed themselves on the minds of his listeners; and urgent, imperative statements, the legacy of his militant socialism.[13]

Thus, from October 1922 onward most Italians, though not fascists themselves, were nonetheless fascinated by this young, energetic head of state, who was directly engaged in disseminating his own legend: a self-made man who had emerged from obscurity thanks to the strength of his will, and was thereafter summoned and sustained by the crowd. As Ferruccio Parri has written, from the beginning everyday people placed "the head of state on a pedestal out of blind trust, naïve and almost physical admiration."[14] In the eyes of the bourgeoisie, Mussolini would save the nation from Bolshevism and anarchy, and for the nonsocialist proletariat (or at least those without a political identity), he was a child of the people who had become prime minister without hiding—and, indeed, by vaunting—his humble origins. In this context, in a culture strongly shaped by religious sentiments, the myth of Mussolini brought together various "elements of the popular Christian tradition," in such a way that the premier became the object of a devoted and superstitious cult widely promulgated by fascist propaganda. In effect, during the regime's years in power, writing to the premier, petitioning him directly, and sending him statements of faith or anonymous complaints all became popular practices.[15] "I'm a young Italian girl," wrote one, "a member of the Party since my first year at school (that is, since 1926), where I learned to love Il Duce like a God."[16] In a child's diary entry for March 29, 1938, one reads: "This morning my schoolteacher handed out our membership cards for the Balilla and the Little Italian Girls. Written on the cards is the oath the one [*sic*] that we learned in our first year, that pledges us to follow Il Duce's orders and to serve the cause of the Fascist Revolution with all my powers and if necessary with my blood."[17]

Similar examples abound in the titles of essays written by Italian youths, such as "Why I Love Il Duce," and in letters to the premier. Mussolini was described as a kind of demigod always available to the people, ready to receive their hopes; a man who pondered the fate of the world, watched over the fortunes of Italy, and looked after the destiny of all his children like a father. Pope Pius XI, after signing the Lateran Treaty, called him "a man of Providence."[18]

The reach of this image of Mussolini was not limited to the popular masses indoctrinated by propaganda and fascist culture. The upper echelons of the regime, including government officials and Party leaders like Giovanni Gentile and Giuseppe Bottai, also expressed their devotion to Mussolini. On the eve of the March 1924 elections, while serving as minister of public education, Gentile gave a speech in Palermo in which he exhorted, "Always remember, O young people, the Man in Palazzo Chigi who works day and night, laboring under a flaming passion for the glory of our Fatherland, his large eyes intent, trained on you, on all Italians. Entrust your souls to him—for your future, for the fortunes of this island which for twenty-five centuries has been sacred to every civilized people, for the glory of a victorious new Italy!"[19]

This was not just the usual dramatic peroration of an election speech. In the years that followed, Gentile described Mussolini with unabashed fascination. For instance, at the inauguration of the National Fascist Institute of Culture (INFC) in December 1925, the philosopher cast Mussolini as the personification of the fascist idea, "a hero, a privileged and providential spirit who is thought incarnate, constantly vibrating with the powerful rhythm of a young life in full bloom,"[20] "a will and intelligence beyond every trick and every particular, subjective interest,"[21] a creator and political artist. Betraying no embarrassment about such rhetoric, he concluded: "No one is encompassed more than he is by the religious respect due to a form of thought unfolding without personal interest, through a tireless consciousness permeated by an understanding of a great national and human phenomenon in the divine process of becoming. No one is prouder than he is of his mission; no one more humble than he is in devoting his entire being to the mission that he so deeply feels is his duty."[22]

In May 1927 Gentile's enthusiasm outdid itself. In the opening remarks for a series of lectures organized by the INFC, he explained that the fascist revolution was an unstoppable force "larger than the will and ideas of individual men," a "historical necessity" that had been incarnated "in a Man endowed with a singular gift for achievement, who step by step, as if inspired and moved by a mysterious intuition, is creating this new Italy, amid the world's profound admiration and anxious trepidation."[23] And again in 1936, celebrating the occupation of Ethiopia, he described the prime minister as a man moved by a mysterious instinct, shrouded in a halo of sanctity, a "genius aimed at saving the entire human race,"[24] to which end he brought word of a new civilization.

When it came to showing his admiration for Mussolini, Bottai proved even more impassioned than Gentile. Unlike the philosopher, Bottai had known the premier since fascism's early days and had fought side-by-side with him in their struggles for power. In 1932, leaving his post directing the Ministry for Corporations, Bottai told Il Duce that in private life he would think of him as a guide and a force for improvement. The pages of his diary in 1938 attest to this, as he writes that Mussolini was more capable than anyone else of directing energy and power, of taking action and giving concrete shape to political ideas. And as late as 1941, when his political faith had begun to waver, he confessed in his diary the anguish he felt at the prospect of having to separate himself from Mussolini. "This feeling, which for more than twenty years has quickened my pulse.... Now I am alone, without my leader.... Now I know what fear is: a sudden loss of *raison d'être*."[25]

The myth of Mussolini did not live only in the thoughts and speech of the fascist masses and the Party ranks; from 1926 on, in fact, the Party worked to transform the cult of its leader into out-and-out mysticism.[26] After that point the veneration was boundless, and Mussolini became one of the main engines in the process of converting new generations to fascism. In the 1928 handbook of the Fascist Student Youth (Avanguardia giovanile fascista) one reads, "You exist, Avant-gardist, only because before you, with you, and after you, He and He alone exists."[27] Two years later, in April 1930, the School of Fascist Mysticism (Scuola di mistica fascista) was created in Milan, as part of the Fascist University Groups (Gruppi universitari fascisti, or GUF) and the INFC, of which the GUF represented the youth wing.[28] Niccolò Giani, its founder, explained that fascist mysticism was neither a "mystical religion" nor a theory rooted in irrationality or generic spiritualism, but rather a doctrine based on Mussolini's thought.[29] Il Duce's writings and speeches would make up a corpus of doctrine for fascist orthodoxy. In the first issue of the monthly magazine *Dottrina fascista* (Fascist doctrine), the mystics claimed that the "infallible guidance of Il Duce, who, in addition to being Duce is also *Maestro*" (i.e., "Master" or "Teacher"), would make it possible to unmask heretics.[30] Giani would explain as much in 1940, during the first National Conference on Mysticism, in which many of the regime's notable intellectuals participated. And many of them, in the preceding years, had been theorists of the myth of the state, that true fulcrum of fascist ideology.

The Myth of the State

From the beginning, fascism gained power by presenting itself as a movement to re-establish the authority of the state, first by undermining the authority of the post-Risorgimento ruling class, and then by demolishing the authority of liberals. "Everything in the State, nothing outside the State, nothing against the State," as Mussolini asserted in 1925,[31] summarizing fascist ideology's central thesis, which would be developed in the following years by philosophers, jurists, and historians, along with philologists and literati.

Between 1922 and 1943, the fascists strove to create a new state in which the masses would be hierarchically organized. Every aspect of Italian society and culture, along with the economy, would be stripped of its autonomy; and every institution, whether new or inherited from the liberal Italian state, would become an articulation of the new state, subordinated to its general ends—that is, to the unconstrained expansion of its power. Denying the existence of individual rights and of social groups that could limit the state's power, the fascists saw themselves as the founders of a new civilization based on the myth of the state. Giovanni Gentile and Alfredo Rocco, and to a lesser extent Sergio Panunzio and Carlo Costamagna, lent their energies to developing and diffusing this myth.

As we have seen, Gentile joined the Fascist Party in October 1922 and, having led the Ministry of Public Education, became one of the most influential voices articulating the regime's cultural politics. Starting in 1925 he decided to intensify his political efforts. In addition to leading several cultural institutions, he penned various ideological pieces, the most important of which was an entry on "Dottrina del fascismo" (Fascist doctrine) for volume 14 of the *Enciclopedia italiana*, published in 1932. This entry, a true manifesto of the regime's ideology, consisted of two parts: the first was written by the philosopher and entitled "Idee fondamentali" (Foundational ideas); the second was compiled by Mussolini and entitled "Dottrina politica e sociale" (Political and social doctrine). In the first section Gentile argued that the focal point of fascist ideology was the concept of the state: "The cornerstone of fascist doctrine is the concept of the State, of its essence, its role, its finality. For fascism, the State is an absolute which renders individuals and groups relative. Individuals and groups are only thinkable within the State."[32]

This state would know no limits and would express its power without restricting itself to the simple tasks of maintaining order, as happened in liberal regimes; it would be an "interior form and norm," "disciplining the entire person"—a presence that could reach "the heart of man." As Gentile himself declared, it was the nucleus of an absolute, religious notion of politics: "Fascism is a religious idea, in which man is seen in his immanent relationship to a superior law, with an objective Will that transcends the specific individual and elevates him to conscious member of a spiritual society. Those who, when considering the fascist regime's religious politics, stop at considering the opportunities it presents have failed to understand that fascism, more than just a system of government, is also and first and foremost a system of thought."[33]

For Gentile, fascist politics represented a mission: a constant existential effort and spiritual communion that would transform consciousness and give birth to a new state, lending Italians a sense of identity. A few years later, in 1937, he reiterated these ideas in a text that was a far cry from an ideological manifesto. For the third edition of *I fondamenti della filosofia del diritto* (Foundations of the philosophy of law), Gentile added two new chapters: one about the state and another about politics. In the first, he examined Hegel's political thought, praising it for demonstrating the limits of contractualism and understanding that the state is "a self-consciously ethical entity," that is, a moral phenomenon and not a tool for attaining individual aims. Having gained this ground, which in Gentile's view represented "one of the major achievements of modern political and philosophical consciousness," it was necessary to start moving beyond Hegel—in other words, to view the state as an expression of a collection of individual wills. The state, he argued, is not *inter homines*—that is, it is not the result of an agreement among citizens, or a product of rational choice; rather, it is inside each of them, *in interiore homine*, as the fruit of the individual will and therefore the highest achievement of its freedom.[34]

If Gentile was the regime's most prominent philosopher, Alfredo Rocco holds the title as its most notable jurist and legal scholar.[35] Serving as minister of justice from 1925 on, he publicly propounded the so-called *leggi fascistissime* ("ultrafascist laws") and the transformation of the liberal state into a fascist, totalitarian one, a project achieved between 1925 and 1929. Like Gentile, and even more decisively, Rocco materially influenced the construction of the totalitarian state; and he, too, albeit without the Sicilian philosopher's powers of speculation, linked the theoretical work of fascism to its political work. As early as the First World War, when he was an influential champion of Italian nationalism, Rocco defined the nation as the highest expression of contemporary sociality and argued that making policy meant disciplining social forces in order to attain a society's higher goals.[36] From this point of view, faced with the novelties of a mass society and the rapid transformation of Italian life, the politics Rocco advocated for would have to manage conflict without denying it, govern the people while orienting them toward the nation's ends, and avoid letting their needs undermine the solidity of the nation.[37] In the early years of fascism, unencumbered by his Party colleagues' legalistic reservations, he had become one of the staunchest advocates of the alliance between the fascists and the nationalists.[38] Named undersecretary of military assistance in March 1923, by May 1924 he had become president of the Chamber of Deputies, and one year later minister of justice. From that point on, he was able to carry out the authoritarian project of consolidating and reinforcing state power, which was framed as an alternative to the liberal state created by the Risorgimento.[39]

This was not simply a question of building the new state's legal system. In the summer of 1925, Rocco illustrated the motivating principles behind his work as the legislator of fascism in a speech that reverberated widely, in no small part because it earned Mussolini's stamp of approval. Addressing those who argued that fascism had no doctrine of its own and who viewed fascism merely as "feeling and action," Rocco explained that fascist ideology constituted an intellectual upheaval no less dramatic than the one brought about in the seventeenth and eighteenth centuries by the emergence and spread of natural law.[40] In service of this claim, he highlighted the links between democracy, socialism, and Bolshevism, defining them as "logical derivations" of liberalism: democracy had tried to give substance to the demands raised by liberals; socialism had posed to democracy the question of citizens' fundamental equality in a modern state; and Bolshevism had held that to guarantee equality for all, the proletariat would need to have the means of production at their disposal. Only fascism, Rocco asserted, had put forth an organic concept of society that had refuted liberalism's natural law assumptions, upending the terms of the debate and giving primacy not to individual rights but to the rights of society and the state—that is to say, theorizing the state's right to exist and to subordinate other nations, and the duty of individuals and classes alike to contribute to achieving the state's ends. As he had argued since the 1910s, Rocco believed that in order to give rise to a new politics, it was necessary to overcome the "philosophy of the French Revolution."[41] From this point of view, he was the most consistent advocate of the authoritarian doctrine of consolidating state power.

We can see substantive differences between Rocco's authoritarian and nationalist fascism and Gentile's totalitarian and statist one, differences taken up by scholars interested in the role each man played in the regime and, more generally, in the relationship between fascism and nationalism. Before diving into this issue, however, we must first examine a pair of writers who were less famous than Gentile and Rocco but who nonetheless made significant contributions to the development of a political theory founded on the myth of the state: Sergio Panunzio and Carlo Costamagna.

Unlike Rocco and Gentile, Panunzio was a philosopher of law and a scholar of syndicalism.[42] He had worked for *Il popolo d'Italia* from its earliest days, and after the war he remained in close contact with Mussolini. Having been national syndicalism's most noteworthy advocate, and one of the primary players on the Italian political scene, Panunzio became one of the main theorists of the concept of fascism as a state-party, typified by his notion of the state as "like a trial, like a play, like a fit of will," and of the Party as the engine of revolution.[43]

As he wrote in 1929, the "feeling of the State" summoned an absolute faith in the synthesis of various social and political worlds. Thus, he could speak of "the moral and social unity of the people expressed, living, and personified in the State,"[44] and refer to "the sublime" in politics—its ability to elevate souls.[45] In Panunzio's view, within the structure of the state, the Party would play a decisive role: as a revolutionary party, the PNF made itself into the state; it had "the awareness of being the State, the entire State";[46] and thus it would have to promote and carry out the transformations necessary to perfect the political system.[47] In this vein, Panunzio claimed that "despite being subordinate to the State," the Party had "so much influence over the development of the State itself" that no one could deny "its constitutive nature."[48] In keeping with this position, in his book *Teoria generale dello Stato fascista* (General theory of the fascist state), which was a veritable compendium of fascist doctrine, Panunzio posed a radical problem: "If all fascism ends in the State and directs itself toward the State, is it really possible to distinguish between the two disciplines, the Doctrine of Fascism and the Doctrine of the State? Or do they not, at least in terms of their objectives, duplicate one another?"[49]

In effect, he believed that the "Doctrine of fascism" was broader than the "Doctrine of the State," and that while the latter ought to be taught solely in political science departments, the former should be imparted by all university departments. Based on Mussolini's thought, the "doctrine of fascism" did not simply address the nature and features of the state, but extended to spheres from art to politics, from law to economics. Unlike Gentile and Rocco, Panunzio celebrated the role of the PNF, which he believed should point the state's way to revolution, creating a ruling class, leading the youth, and transforming the structures of the state into a new fascist and totalitarian edifice. This position was quite common among fascists, not only among Party leaders but also distinguished legal scholars.[50]

Among the theorists of fascism, the jurist Carlo Costamagna also deserves special mention. In his youth, Costamagna served as secretary of the Commissione dei Soloni (Commission of the Solons), convened to study constitutional reform and presided over by Gentile; in the 1930s, Costamagna became a harsh critic of the philosopher.[51] In 1930, to "keep pace with Mussolini's revolution" and denounce the slowness of law, economics, and the social sciences to adopt the totalitarian aspects of fascist politics, Costamagna founded the magazine *Lo Stato*. And in 1935, when the Party began offering political training courses for young people, he seized the opportunity to point out that their initiative would have to make up for the deficiencies and delays of a university system incapable of creating a fascist ruling class. Critiques, directed at the National Fascist Institute of Culture, Italian public schools, and the Treccani *Enciclopedia italiana*, appeared in the pages of *Lo Stato*.[52] These reproofs were certainly not new, but Costamagna incorporated them into his reflections on the totalitarian state. In *Fascist History and Doctrine*, he argued that during the period Carl Schmitt defined as "wholesale politicization," the fascist state introduced itself as a "condition of civilization" in which "maximum politicization" was embodied;[53] and in describing the main features of this state, Costamagna asserted that it was a higher power that could transcend and dominate individuals—that is, "an absolute value" with "totalitarian contents."[54] The fascist state was certainly not the result of an agreement among partners; it would create only itself, as the mani-festation of a divine entity that went beyond individuals, with no need for them other than as a means of exercising its power. This is why Costa-magna believed that Gentile's definition of the state *in interiore homine* derived from a wish to legitimate its existence via philosophy, by imagin-ing a state expressed by the individual. By contrast, in Costamagna's view the fascist state did not require any legitimation, being an autonomous and immensely powerful political fact that "transcends and dominates" every-one and everything.[55]

These writers were the primary theorists of fascist ideology. In empha-sizing the most important aspects of their political thought, and therefore the main features of their contributions to the myth of the state, we have aimed to highlight the differences between their views. These distinctions should serve as a reminder that fascism was not a monolith, but rather a system of totalitarianism in which diverse personal and cultural histories were intertwined. The challenge is to understand whether these differences were greater and more significant than the unifying elements; or, vice-versa, if that which bound these writers together was more important and thus decisively united their politics. On the one hand, we could conclude this dis-cussion by arguing that a fascist ideology based on the myth of the state did exist, beyond the distinctions made by any given theorist—an ideology in which all these thinkers would find themselves at home, and yet one which, like all ideologies, did not automatically translate into political praxis but rather directed the political action of its adherents. On the other hand, if the differences between these thinkers were effectively more significant than what united them, we should conclude that each of them expressed a distinc-tive political doctrine, and that therefore no fascist ideology ever existed.

The ideologues of fascism agreed in claiming that the political doctrine they supported was founded on the myth of the state and its primacy within the regime. Between 1922 and 1943, in fact, all of them claimed that the fas-cist state would be impeded by nothing—neither individual nor group nor institution; nothing could compromise its power. For Rocco this power was pre-established, positioned as a ballast that could counterbalance the cen-trifugal forces of society. In Gentile's eyes, it was a new Italian civilization founded on a radical transformation of consciousness, and thus on individu-als' ability to feel like part of the state. For Panunzio, it was a new state order fed by a revolutionary party that would point the way to totalitarian politics. For Costamagna, it was a kind of modern Leviathan, infinitely powerful and independent of its constituent parts. Yet each of them believed that the fascist state, *qua* state, would have to come into being by subordinating all other ends to its will.

Ultimately, as we have seen repeatedly here, all these thinkers expressed a religious notion of politics rooted in the myth of the state. All of them recognized in themselves a shared sentiment that nurtured an idea and experience of politics understood no longer, or not only, in traditional terms, as a project undertaken to transform daily life, but rather as a faith celebrating the state. This explains why, from 1922 to 1943, the writers we have examined here never questioned their faith in fascism, confident that they were participating in building a new civilization: summoned by the regime to lend their talents, proud of being intellectuals in the service of politics, they saw their different theoretical positions as an aspect of fascist politics and culture, and they fought, like other intellectuals, to assert their position as theorists of the fascist state. And it is in this sense that fascist ideology was an ideology based on the myth of the state and not a form or variant of nationalism, as many commentators have argued.

Fascism and Nationalism

The relationship between fascism and nationalism is one of the primary and most exhaustively examined topics taken up by those who study fascist ideology. Some scholars have argued that fascism is a variant of nationalism, while others have emphasized the differences between fascist and nationalist ideologies. Especially after the Lateran Treaty in 1929, according to the first group, the regime shifted toward a reactionary and conservative position with nationalist underpinnings, in line with the Catholic church. For instance, writing in 1974, taking a cue from Togliatti's *Lectures on Fascism*, Luisa Mangoni highlighted the centrality of nationalism and Catholicism in the fascist dictatorship's cultural politics. Citing the communist leader, Mangoni argued: "Not for nothing was Rocco, a nationalist, the legislator of this dictatorship; and not for nothing was Bottai, also a nationalist, one of its most important leaders. Every step of the way there was a battle between the nationalists and the fascists over solutions to the fundamental problems of state and Party. The solutions to these problems were always substantively derived from the nationalist [faction of the] Party—in substance they were always distinctly reactionary and bourgeois."[56]

In a similar vein, in 1981 Franco Gaeta claimed that Rocco was "the true creator of the totalitarian State," while other ideologues, like Gentile, played rather less significant roles, frequently confusing their own theoretical arguments—that is, what they would have liked to achieve via fascism—with the regime's political decisions.[57] In 1994 Gabriele Turi put forth a different argument, remarking that Gentile and Rocco integrated themselves perfectly into a regime to which they made influential contributions, even if they were sharply criticized by the radical fascists. In this sense, according to Turi, Gentile and Rocco were the most significant proponents of a moderate, conservative fascism derived from nationalism, which arose from the ruling class's desire to play a decisive role in building the new state. For Turi, too, therefore, nationalism constituted one of the principal elements of fascist ideology and politics—that is, of a regime giving voice to a conservative vanguard that reacted differently to the crisis of emerging mass society than early twentieth-century liberalism had.

As we have indicated, other scholars have argued that nationalism was merely one of several political movements that converged in fascism, and certainly not more important than the idealism espoused by Gentile. According to Renzo De Felice, in 1925 Rocco enjoyed a position of great prestige within the Party and was close to Il Duce:[58] among nonfascists, he had been among the most successful at integrating himself into fascism, and he was seen as one of the government's "great minds." He had avoided participating in the debate between older fascists and ex-nationalists and had asserted himself as "the most influential representative of true, sane fascism," even if he had "very little of a true fascist about him."[59] Unlike Rocco, Gentile did not perfectly integrate himself into fascism in the '20s and, indeed, had to defend himself against the attacks of many Party supporters who saw him as a liberal. Despite this, in De Felice's view the philosopher had had a decisive influence on fascist culture and above all on Mussolini, who had allowed Gentile to compose "the first part of the 'Doctrine of Fascism' entry" for the *Enciclopedia italiana*, while "substantively endorsing the underlying structure of the second part," which Mussolini "personally edited and signed along with the first."[60] On a closer look, De Felice wrote, the entry "clearly shows what Il Duce had accepted in Gentile's thought: the condemnation—

not only in terms of politics and practice but also in terms of doctrine—of classical liberalism, socialism, and democracy; the concept of the ethical State and, therefore, of the Nation, as the expression, or rather the creation, of the State; the idea that fascism, as a religious and historical concept, was not only law-giver and founder of institutions, but educator and promulgator of spiritual life, capable of remaking man even in his very character."[61] As we can see, for De Felice, while the nationalists were fascist sympathizers among the old ruling class, and Rocco the capable politician who had understood how to assimilate into fascism, Gentile was the theorist of a new, revolutionary culture, welcomed with open arms by Mussolini and the fascists, who were much more influenced by the philosopher than by the nationalists.

In the late '60s, in keeping with De Felice's arguments, some scholars claimed that Gentile and Rocco represented two antagonistic strains of fascism, stressing that nationalism had not constituted the ideological heart of the fascist regime but was simply one of many political trends in Giolittian Italy—one whose influence on early fascism was no greater than that of other movements like Futurism, idealism, and revolutionary syndicalism. And, in effect, in his pioneering study on Rocco, Paolo Ungari warned against understanding nationalism as the "intellectual roots of twentieth-century totalitarian revolutions, or the antecedent of their coercive strategies."[62]

In this regard, Emilio Gentile has written that Gentile and Rocco were flagbearers for the two primary strains of fascism in the years between the March on Rome and the first laws creating the regime.[63] To be sure, these were two opposing strains, even if they had certain commonalities, including a shared aversion toward liberal democracy. Rocco championed an authoritarian and reactionary brand of fascism, devoid of the radical fascists' demands but also quite far removed from the reformist spirit espoused by Bottai. He had a naturalistic view of history and society in which the state was configured as an organic, absolute power that imposed and preserved the nation's internal cohesion.[64] Gentile, on the other hand, had joined the Fascist Party out of the conviction that the Blackshirt movement would finish the process begun by the Risorgimento. Starting from a religious and totalitarian concept of politics that had developed from a specific interpretation of Mazzini's thought, during the war years he had clearly articulated the problem of shaping a national consciousness—a problem that, to his mind, constituted a moral question.[65] This is why, in Emilio Gentile's view, "the statement to the effect that nationalism and fascism were identical and that nationalism had successfully ideologically captured fascism" had created "for the most part groundless" common grounds.[66] In the 1930s, in fact, an authentic "displacement" materialized in the hierarchy of fascist cultural values, a displacement between the concept of the state and that of the nation. If while gaining and consolidating power the Party had presented itself as a nation aspiring to become a new, modern state, in the following years, and even more visibly beginning in the '30s, the "'Fascism-state' proclaimed itself the creator of the nation."[67] For example, while in the statutes of 1921 and 1926 the Fascist Party was described as "a militia serving the nation," in 1929 this reference was removed, and in 1932 it was replaced with "a militia serving the State." From this point of view, the fascists expressed an idea analogous to that of Gentile and his followers. When he was still one of the thinkers closest to Gentile, Camillo Pellizzi wrote that fascism celebrated the myth of the state and not that of the nation.[68] Pursuing this point, he highlighted the differences between fascism and nationalism: while the nationalists, with their naturalistic and materialistic concept of politics, believed that the nation had created the state, Pellizzi observed that, with fascism, "the country made itself into the State" and "in the State attains its ideal form." In his view, nationalism had subordinated the state to the nation and had introduced a political orientation according to which the state would interpret and guarantee "the natural rights and natural demands inherent in the phenomenon of the nation." Thus, he argued, "no concept of an Italian nation exists," and "the fascist State not only rules the nation, but absorbs and eliminates it."[69]

In 1940, in the *Dizionario di politica* (Dictionary of politics) edited by the PNF, Costamagna wrote an entry for "Nation" that portrayed the nation's absolute subordination to the state. Yet again the fascists emphasized the statist (not nationalist) nature of their political ideology, and thus their conviction that the state would create the nation and not vice-versa—an idea aimed at the future, to celebrate the construction of a new imperial civilization glorifying the myth of Rome.[70]

The Myth of Rome

One does not encounter the myth of the Roman empire among the original myths of fascist culture. The very term *fascism* derived not from *fascio littorio,* which was one of the key symbols of republican Rome (the bundle of birch rods gathered with a leather strap, symbolizing the Roman magistrate's power to punish), but rather from *fascio* ("fasces" or "bundle"), a word belonging to the late nineteenth-century political left and indicating the close union of revolutionary groups and movements. And indeed, beneath the masthead of the newspaper *Il Fascio* we see not the emblem of the *fascio littorio* but rather a fist grasping ears of wheat. In the Party's 1919 program, there was no mention of values derived from the Roman empire, just as there was no reference to the myth of Rome in the program assembled during the Second Congress, after the turn to the right in May 1920. Only in 1921 did Roman culture become fascism's primary symbolic tool; from then until the regime's end, fascism constantly referred to Rome to define its political identity, organization, lifestyle, and goals.[71]

In reality, various interpretations of the myth of Rome circulated in fascist culture. Luciano Canfora, for example, has observed four themes tied to Roman history that converged in the regime: antidemocratic sentiment, the concept of the "Third Position," the idea of Rome, and an antagonism toward the modern world.[72] The ancient world's rejection of democracy stemmed from classical culture's pejorative view of the masses. Some European intellectuals based their rejection of modern democracy on this view, as was the case with Friedrich Nietzsche and the German philologist Ulrich von Wilamowitz. For Canfora, this contempt for the popular masses was characteristic of fascism, which venerated the myth of ancient Rome as a means of legitimizing the antidemocratic nature of its politics. It also derived its search for the "Third Position"—an alternative to capitalism and communism—from Roman culture. This is why, being interested in the origins of the guild system, the fascists promoted research on trade associations and participation in civic life. Furthermore, the fascists used a model of imperialism derived from classical history to show how, like the Romans, they had instantiated a positive and peaceful relationship with their colonies. And finally, according to Canfora, the fascist regime had found in the myth of Rome a useful tool for opposing modernity in the name of a past to restore and a set of ancient values to recuperate.

More recently, Andrea Giardina put forth a different interpretation, arguing that at the dawn of fascism the concept most frequently connected to the idea of Rome was expressed in the term *discipline,* which referred to the power and mystical glorification of the nation. This was not a question of defending mythical past glories. *Pace* Canfora, Giardina claimed that fascist ideology feared and rejected the idea that Roman culture should be seen as rehabilitation, "a kind of misoneism or sign of an inability to plan for the future." Accordingly, the fascists rejected anything that could suggest a passive attitude or could "obscure the creative aspect of the fascist cult of Rome."[73]

Emilio Gentile elaborated on why Roman culture was so attractive to Mussolini and the fascists. In his view, Rome represented *continuity in time*, the endurance of a civilization over the centuries; it was a symbol of *universality*, demonstrated by the phenomenon of Christianity, which became a universal religion only after its center was transferred from Palestine to Rome; it had the *imperial destiny* of a civilization that had conquered the known world, managing to reach places never before reached; and finally it represented *modernity*. Unlike Canfora, and rather more in line with Giardina's conclusions, Gentile argued that fascism wished to take on the legacy of Rome not because of reactionary nostalgia, nor a wish to return to a distant past, but rather because the myth of Rome had a political role linked to the future.[74] As we shall see, Giardina's and Gentile's arguments ultimately appear most convincing.

In the spring of 1921, Mussolini made April 21 a national holiday celebrating Rome's founding. The proclamation was a means of corralling the divergent forces of fascism, which were particularly strong in those days and threatened to put him in danger. After the foundation of the National Fascist Party, Mussolini wanted to reassert his authority over the various currents shaping the Party, basing his initiative on a plan adapted from the military structure of republican Rome. The PNF would be armed, its troops comprising the Blackshirts or *principi* (from Latin *principes*, wealthy, seasoned, and heavily armed fighters), and the *triari* (Latin *triarii*, the rearguard) or reserves. PNF symbols also had Roman origins: pennants portraying fasces and eagles, and the Roman salute. In 1922 the fascist militia was created, divided into squadrons on the pattern of the Roman army. Each squadron was led by one commander and two deputies, all called decurions; four squadrons formed a centuria, led by a centurion; four centurias made up a *cohors* ("cohort"), led by a senior centurion; finally, between three and nine cohorts could form a legion, commanded by a consul.[75] It hardly mattered that some of these terms had no exact correlate in the Roman military lexicon. From that point on, the myth of Rome spread unchecked. Indeed, immediately after they conquered real contemporary Rome—a city whose inhabitants had previously disdained the symbols of ancient Italy as corrupt and devoid of values—the fascists fully indulged in glorifying the myth of Roman culture, presenting it as a fascist political myth.

In January 1923 the government issued new one- and two-lira coins, stamped on one side with the king's portrait and on the other with the fasces. Mussolini chose an image of a bundle of rods with an axe laid across it, claiming that this, unlike the fasces represented during the French Revolution and the Risorgimento, accurately reflected the Roman symbol. And this was no isolated occurrence: a few months later, having by then become a symbol of the Fascist Party, the fasces appeared on a postage stamp and on the reverse of a gold 100-lira coin issued to celebrate fascism's rise to power.[76] Efforts to "fascisize" Roman culture would continue, with the endorsement of eminent scholars like the archaeologist Pericle Ducati, who was happy to announce the return of Roman symbols to Italy.[77] In December 1926 the fasces was declared the official symbol of the state, and in April 1929 the government changed the Italian coat of arms by replacing the rampant lions holding the shield of the House of Savoy with two fasces. In the early 1930s, the regime inserted the fasces encircled by oak and laurel branches into the shields of villages, provinces, and other localities.[78]

The cult of Rome was not limited to the riotous diffusion of the fasces but extended to transforming both the calendar and contemporary Rome itself. Starting in 1926, alongside the year dated from the birth of Christ, calendars noted the year of the fascist era, which began in October 1922—a stratagem intended to spread a sense of the epochal, revolutionary nature of a regime destined to far outlast its contemporaries.[79]

To celebrate ancient Rome, the regime also decided to eliminate what it saw as the dregs of the past. Starting in 1923 it began to demolish large parts of the historical center of the capital, framing this undertaking as a liberation of these sacred places of antiquity from the profanation of degrading accretions. Demonstrating a true passion for demolition, construction of the Via dell'Impero, connecting Piazza Venezia with the Colosseum, started in early 1931. All the buildings in Trajan's Forum were destroyed, and the sixteenth-century neighborhood built on the Forum of Augustus and

Nerva was completely erased.[80] The willingness of architects and urban planners to satisfy Mussolini's wishes matched his complete lack of interest in antiquity. For the prime minister, ancient history had no inherent value but was merely a source of stories. Responding to the Roman governor, who had passed along the concerns of the historian and former minister of public education Pietro Fedele about the destruction of everything that remained of popular medieval Roman city life, Mussolini said: "Continue the demolition, and if necessary we will also demolish the melancholy of Senator Fedele, who is so ridiculously moved by a pile of latrines."[81] In reality, the work to destroy the historical center and build a new capital had a specific goal: to demonstrate the fascists' power to the world, to show off their ability to design and build a modern city based on a notion of space fit for metropolitan life and oriented toward the future. This much was clear in October 1932 when the Via dell'Impero was inaugurated and immediately became the primary location for military parades and Party events.

With the occupation of Ethiopia, the myth seemed to have become reality. On May 9, 1936, from the balcony of Palazzo Venezia, Mussolini declared the return of the empire to the fabled hills of Rome. From that point on, fascism tried to show the world that it was heir to ancient Rome, with the blessing of influential scholars ready and willing to confirm that fascist colonial policy was rooted in Roman history.[82] First in line was Ettore Pais, author of a history of Rome, 1936 winner of the Mussolini Prize, and director of the periodical *Historia*, which had been founded by Arnaldo Mussolini and was affiliated with *Il popolo d'Italia*. Next came Pietro Romanelli, who strove to draw distinctions between Greek and Roman colonialism, claiming that only the latter was based on an intimate relationship between mother country and colonies. Giorgio Maria Sangiorgi, a scholar of African ethnology, declared that fascism would succeed at integrating the colonial territories without abandoning them to exploitation.[83] Mario Attilio Levi argued in 1936 that Rome had never been land-hungry, and that its intention was rather to help subjugated peoples achieve their aspirations. In demonstrating the superiority of its expansionist policies, which were based on political leadership, or *imperium*, Rome had managed to understand the will of various communities and meet the people's needs. Every Roman conquest, as a virtuous expression of *imperium*, was thus sought not to "impose but to extend the concept of the public; to unify the civilized world; to spare those who submit."[84]

With the Ethiopian campaign, the myth of Rome came to play an even larger role in fascist culture and politics, as we can see from the plan to build a new Roman city on the outskirts of the capital, which we shall discuss in chapter 6. Meanwhile, the consecration of imperial continuity from ancient Rome to fascist Rome, from the great emperors to the imperial Duce, from the Roman empire to the fascist one, was sealed by an open-air exhibition in September 1937. This was an extravagant celebration of the bimillennium of Augustus's birth. On the opening day, the archeologist Giulio Quirino Giglioli, the exhibition's curator, declared that Mussolini had resurrected imperial Italy's new Augustus as a "genuine blood descendant of the ancient Romans." According to the distinguished archeologist, the proof was in Mussolini's Romagnan heritage, which made him "a worthy emulator of Caesar and Augustus, as the creator of a new age of Roman culture in the modern era."[85]

In effect, the myths of Rome and empire converged in fascist culture because the fascists presented themselves from start to finish as the architects of a new civilization—a modern civilization that could endure over the centuries, develop a universal mission, and achieve its imperial destiny, conquering the world and creating a new man.

The Myth of the New Man

The first version of the new fascist man was the veteran of the First World War, a warrior returned from the front convinced that his role fighting the enemy was not yet complete. As we saw at the beginning of this book, the young men who gathered in Piazza San Sepolcro in March 1919 and created the Italian Combat Leagues saw themselves as a revolutionary vanguard and, like all movements born of the Great War, believed that they represented a new Italy that had arisen from the trenches. These young men changed quickly from soldiers to *squadristi*—that is, to warrior-politicians staunchly opposed to traditional politics based on a dialectic between parties. They applied the violence of trench warfare to postwar politics and believed that they were the only authentic representatives of the nation, which is why they viewed their adversaries as enemies to be physically eliminated.[86] This version of the fascist man lasted for the duration of the fascist period, from its beginnings to the Second World War, because from the moment they took power, Mussolini and the fascists saw themselves as an Italian vanguard ready to create a new civilization and a new man. They would inculcate their values and beliefs into the younger generations, fight the "old" and "corrupt" bourgeois mentality, destroy its legacy, and shape new Italians, raised to follow the regime's orders.

The fascist Italian, as Lorenzo Benadusi has observed, was supposed to have nothing in common with Italians of the past, who were the product of a long period of political, military, and moral decadence. That past Italian was a weakling, a bourgeois, a liberal, or in any case an antifascist—that is to say, a traitor to his homeland, who had to be eliminated to make way for the virile Italians capable of fighting for the Fascist Party and state.[87] The importance of this goal was even indicated in the "Fascism" entry of the *Enciclopedia italiana*—a text that, as we have seen, was meant to serve as an authoritative manifesto of fascist ideology. In that entry Mussolini and Gentile described the new fascist man. He was "active and engaged in action with all his energies," "manfully aware of challenges" and ready to face them, a man who would view life "as a battle" and an object of conquest. A man in the service of the regime, as Gentile and Mussolini declared: "For the fascist everything is in the State, and nothing human or spiritual exists, much less has value, outside the State. In this sense fascism is totalitarian, and the fascist State synthesizes and unifies every value—it interprets, develops, and strengthens the life of the people."[88]

As these statements show, the anthropological revolution the fascists wished for was part of the process of strengthening and developing the totalitarian state. In fact, it was one of its most important aspects. It would therefore become a political issue, one of the goals—perhaps the most important goal—of the regime's actions as it worked to change Italian citizens.

In the latter half of the 1930s, the myth of the new man took on a strong antibourgeois and anticapitalist cast, which according to De Felice "represented the crown jewel of the fascist cultural revolution."[89] In a famous speech delivered in March 1934, Mussolini claimed that, despite the fact that there was no antifascist threat, the future of the regime could be threatened by the "bourgeois spirit," the "spirit, that is, of satisfaction and adaptation, tending toward skepticism [and] compromise, to a comfortable life, to careerism." In this vein, Mussolini asserted, "I do not deny the existence of bourgeois temperaments; I deny the idea that they could be fascist. The fascist's credo is heroism, while that of the bourgeois is egotism."[90]

   With these words the head of state kicked off an antibourgeois campaign
that culminated in 1938 with Mussolini's decision to land several "heavy gut-
punches" to the Italian bourgeoisie: first, the abolition of the formal *lei* form
of address and its replacement with the second-person plural *voi*. This plan
had a modicum of success, since in many regions of Italy the *lei* form was
little used and the change had the approval of a good number of intellectuals, like Filippo Tommaso Marinetti, Salvatore Quasimodo, Elio Vittorini,
Elsa Morante, Armando Carlini, and Gioacchino Volpe. Next, the introduction of the goose step (rechristened the *passo romano* or "Roman step"),
which Mussolini insisted upon both in public and in private, believing it
necessary "to create a military atmosphere among Italians," making them
live as though "ready for battle."[91] And last, the racial question, the third blow
to the bourgeoisie, which had its own complexity and which we shall discuss
at length later on.

   The antibourgeois nature of the revolution hoped for by the fascists provoked a wide-ranging debate about the character of the new fascist man,
which we can examine only briefly here. De Felice considered this crucial
to any understanding of the regime's totalitarian nature during the 1930s.
George Mosse defined fascism as "a bourgeois antibourgeois revolution"
and claimed that the prototype of the new man expressed those values of
honesty, probity, and industry that were the product of nineteenth-century
culture and morality, while Emilio Gentile argued that defining fascism as
a bourgeois antibourgeois revolution amounted to evacuating the term
antibourgeois of all meaning. In effect, the new man of fascism was in no
way the incarnation of traditional respectability or the liberal ideal of the
bourgeois individualist, but rather "a man collectively constituted," trained
by the principles of a bellicose morality, projected into a public dimension
of existence that was the antithesis of bourgeois respectability and individualism.[92] In this sense, the new fascist man was the product of the militarization of politics that characterized Italian culture in the interwar period.
Different in nature from the bellicosity of other political movements, but
founded nonetheless on the distinction between civil and military life, the
militarization of politics imposed by the fascists eliminated the difference
between the soldier and the citizen. This was the sense in which the myth of
the new man was an antibourgeois myth, just like the myth of corporatism,
as we shall see.

Fascism and Corporatism

Corporatism was one of the most significant aspects of fascist ideology because it had the unusual good luck of becoming, in Gianpasquale Santomassimo's words, "one of the fundamental levers of [fascism's] international success."[93] And indeed, the spread of corporatist ideas trained the attention of many international observers on the fascist experiment, especially after 1929, when the fascist "Third Position" began to be considered as a response to the crash. The Third Position was seen as a potential alternative to traditional market dynamics and at the same time a challenge to the Soviet endeavor. And it is in this regard that we shall examine corporatism in the following pages, leaving aside its political construction and limiting our discussion to its importance for the ideology of the fascist state.

Among the various theorists who helped define fascist corporatism, Ugo Spirito most directly influenced the debate within the regime and had the greatest impact on its culture. Spirito, like many of Gentile's students, followed in the philosopher's footsteps in joining the Fascist Party, but in the '30s he distanced himself from his teacher by articulating a more radical political position.[94] In 1927, together with Arnaldo Volpicelli, Spirito founded the magazine *Nuovi studi di diritto, economia e politica* (New studies in law, economics, and politics) to reinvigorate those disciplines and redirect contemporary debates. A few years later he became the primary theorist of corporatism. As he claimed in his 1930 book *Critica all'economia liberale* (Critique of liberal economics), and in the 1932 *Fondamenti dell'economia corporativa* (Foundations of corporatist economics), Spirito believed that it was necessary to create a new political economy based on the self-sameness of the state and the individual, and on the "statism of every economic phenomenon."[95]

The state that he described was a "unique, harmoniously composed organism ... with which the individual, as a social animal," could not but coincide.[96] As Alberto Asor Rosa pointed out in the late 1970s, such a position expressed "the clearest assertion of the superiority of the ethicist (and, if you like, of the politician, too, but only insofar as the politician descends even more directly from the ethicist) over the economist."[97] And indeed, Spirito too, like the other 1930s ideologues we have examined, declared the primacy of the state and saw economics as the chosen sphere for making that state concrete *in interiore homine*—though he invested the phrase with a different meaning than Gentile had. In fact, in the early '30s, for Spirito "the self-sameness of the individual and the state, and the discovery of the state as the ultimate end to achieve in oneself," threatened to remain purely theoretical if no means of actualizing these ideas could be found.[98] Believing thus that it was necessary to accelerate the construction of a new state to actually achieve fascism's goals, in May 1932 Spirito participated in the Second Conference on Corporatist Studies in Ferrara, where he laid out his thesis on proprietary corporations. He proposed transforming individual businesses into corporately owned entities—that is, the property of owner-shareholders—and allowing workers and employers, in varying degrees depending on their position in the hierarchy, to share in the corporation's ownership and management.[99] Obviously the corporation had to be understood as an organ of the state, "an organ that grafts itself onto organizations through the National Council of Corporations," not because the state would resolve internal conflicts within corporations, but rather, Spirito emphasized, because "[the state] is the national system's equivalent of the corporation."[100]

Spirito's contribution to the conference in Ferrara stirred up protests among all those fascists who, despite calling themselves corporatists, did not recognize themselves in his argument about corporate ownership. Such was the case with the group associated with the magazine *Il secolo fascista* (The fascist century), which accused the young corporatist theorist of Bolshevism; with many university students; with Bottai, who (though he later denied it) immediately after the conference asked Spirito to resign from the School of Corporatist Studies in Pisa; and with Sergio Panunzio, who, as we have seen, had syndicalist roots.[101] Panunzio conceived of the corporatist system as a necessary means of easing the admittance of the trade unions into national economic leadership. Hence, like all the former syndicalists (and unlike Spirito), he feared that the corporatist system would constrain and eviscerate the unions' role within the state. This is why he accused Spirito of overvaluing the corporation's economic role while undervaluing the union's political role.[102]

In fact, beyond these differences in orientation, and beyond the various disciplines in which corporatism was an object of study (economics, law, and fascist publications in general), the crux of Spirito's proposal was an effort to absorb various branches of society into the state. Accordingly, as we have observed, corporatism was proposed "as one of the great veins that, along with the Party," would enable "the subsumption of society into the State."[103] In the minds of the corporatist theorists, the relationship between society and the state would be changed through a new model of political representation that would leave electoral politics behind in favor of an "organic representation" that could link various social settings to the state apparatus.

The project of a new juridical order founded on corporatism thus became, in the minds of legal scholars and theorists, a renewed political project that at its core posited the state as the only legitimate creator of society.[104] In this sense corporatism was one of the most important expressions of the totalitarian fascist state's ideology.

The Debate about the French Revolution

At various points in the preceding pages we have alluded to the modern nature of fascist culture: to the mythology, politics, and ideology of a state projected toward the future, which believed it could meet the challenges of its time by imposing another, alternative modernity on Italians—a form of modernity distinct from that which had emerged in the West at the end of the eighteenth century. The views of fascist intellectuals on the French Revolution, with which we shall conclude this long chapter about ideology, demonstrate precisely this point.

For the fascists, the French Revolution was the symbol against which they would define themselves—the symbol, that is, of modern culture. As Sternhell has observed, this resistance was typical of European culture between the end of the nineteenth and the first third of the twentieth century, and thus of the crisis of modernity that the Enlightenment and the French Revolution made visible.[105] At the turn of the century, the Israeli historian wrote, faith in the "Kantian subject," who had exercised his freedom through judgment and founded a secularized society free of traditional values, was the subject of sharp critiques by prominent European intellectuals. Georges Sorel, Gustave Le Bon, Miguel de Unamuno, Robert Musil, Maurice Barrès, and Friedrich Nietzsche all contributed to the spread of irrationalism and of an antidemocratic, antihumanist worldview in which there was no room for faith in the progressive development of consciousness.

Curzio Suckert (also known as Malaparte) was the most famous fascist intellectual who voiced the position Sternhell described. As we have seen,

Malaparte hoisted the flag of an anti-European, Catholic, counterreformist fascism that did not attempt to disguise its ferocious contempt for the
French Revolution and all it represented. There are many examples of this
strain of fascist ideology. Gastone Silvano Spinetti, for instance, was a young,
less well known academic who in January 1933 founded the magazine *La
Sapienza* (Knowledge) in Rome. Determined to oppose any and all aspects
of modern philosophy, in particular Gentile's, Spinetti made *La Sapienza* a
soapbox for young anti-Gentilians, and in July 1933 he organized the first
anti-idealist conference in Rome.[106] That same year he published an argument that was becoming common in fascist publications: namely, that the
French Revolution was the most significant manifestation of the mentality
that resulted in Bolshevism and communism. Proudly declaring that fascism
was the product of the opposite political culture—that is, of collectivism
and totalitarianism—Spinetti claimed for fascism Catholic origins and an
antimodern, antiliberal, antibourgeois, antimaterialist, and obviously antidemocratic culture.[107]

In fact, there was another, no less important, trend in fascist culture
between 1922 and 1943, espoused by distinguished Party and regime leaders
who believed that fascism was the artifact of a different kind of modernity,
an alternative to the form of modernity created by the French Revolution.
These fascist thinkers believed that they could respond to the "wounds of
modernity" by overcoming modernity—eliminating its negative aspects,
appropriating it fully to their own ends, and thereby seeking to settle the
quarrel between modernity and antimodernity.[108] The most significant representative of this effort—though by no means the only one—was Bottai,
as I have tried to show in summarizing his views on the French Revolution
in chapter 3. In the latter half of the 1920s, commentators noted that fascist intellectuals were vying to ridicule the principles that emerged in 1789.
According to the journalist and historian Giacomo Lumbroso, this contest
was ultimately futile because democracy had already been politically defeated
by fascism, which had "served justice" to the Revolutionary idols and thus
to "popular sovereignty"—to "the triumph of numbers" and the "cult of the
majority." Yet, Lumbroso noted, fascism had not rejected the "conquests of
the despicable French Revolution," which formed the basis for "every social,
political, or juridical structure," and for equality among people, which is to
say "the suppression of the privilege of birth—the right granted to all of a

nation's subjects to choose this path or that, this career or that, according to their beliefs and their intelligence."[109]

In 1928 Antonio Pagano, who had nationalist roots and taught the history of fascist legislation in the political science department at the University of Perugia (and whose political past differed sharply from Lumbroso's and Bottai's), argued that equating the French Revolution with the individualistic culture rooted in liberalism was a serious error. In his view, the Revolution had not merely expressed the individualistic, liberal, democratic character of modern politics; it had also created the national military and made the judicial system an arm of the state. Thanks to Rousseau—Pagano viewed him with ambivalence but acknowledged him as capable of profound insights—the state was no longer an object available to individuals but a political subject. As heir to the positive aspects of this tradition, fascism had succeeded in unifying the state's demands, its dominance, and its power, with the young nation of Italy and the spirit of the Risorgimento; thus it had succeeded at transforming the universal state into a national state. "The public became Fasces and the government became State. And the two of them, through this intimate fusion, formed the fascist State."[110] This was the unique nature of the fascist regime: the presence of a dynamic element—the public—"no longer created as a provisional aggregate body," like an electorate, but rather created as "the fasces, which is to say, as a body of volunteers," who, according to Pagano, represented "the Mazzinians and Garibaldians of the new era." Leaving no room for confusion on this point (and reiterating a notion Bottai had put forth), Pagano asserted: "The fascist regime ... having discarded electoral politics ... welcomes and reconciles the two main principles of the French Revolution: the valorization of the citizen and the valorization of the State."[111] As we can see, this was by no means a return to the past; Pagano expressly declared the modern nature of the fascist struggle, which began as a response to the challenges of modernity and over time sought to create modernity anew.

Panunzio, who, as we have seen, came from the syndicalist tradition and whose intellectual and biographical trajectory was quite different from Pagano's, also questioned the relationship between fascism and the French Revolution. Whereas the Jacobins had fought their battle in a period of economic growth, he claimed, the fascists had faced a period of profound recession and crisis in Italy, and managed to overcome it. He, like Bottai, likened

fascism to the great revolutions of modern history, showing that he understood the historical value of a revolutionary political experience that had
seen mass participation.[112] And he too, in the '30s, would return to a comparison of the French and fascist revolutions, in a collection of writings on
the relationship between revolution and constitutional reform.[113]

In fact, in addition to claiming that they had recuperated the positive
aspects of the French Revolution, the fascists went one step further and,
attracted to the experience of Jacobinism, made politics into a secular religion. As Mosse has suggested, fascism saw the French Revolution "through
the eyes of the Jacobin dictatorship" as a coherent whole.[114] In effect, the
desire to create a new man and found a new civilization, the emphasis on
youth and the cult of war, and the role of aesthetics in politics were all central aspects of fascist culture that bore historical comparison to the French
Revolution.[115] As Emilio Gentile argued, the fascists embraced the legacy of
the French Revolution by creating a political religion articulated through
myths, rituals, and symbols, and by accepting the idea that the national state
would institute a secular religion. In this sense, by rendering the nation sacred,
the fascists continued along the path forged by the French revolutionaries,
who had conferred a religious character upon politics and given the state a
pedagogical mission.[116]

5

Cultural Politics in the 1930s

The Ministry of National Education and the PNF

At the end of the 1920s, most fascist intellectuals and politicians believed that educational reform was dangerously behind the goals set out for it. From that point on, a series of ministers of national education undertook to change the 1923 reform, even if they could never develop an alternative to Gentile's plan that matched its coherence.

In September 1929 Mussolini wrote to Balbino Giuliano, the new head of the Ministry—which had just added "National" to its name—to say that the regime would be graduating from the realm of instruction to the broader sphere of education and upbringing, and that therefore the existence of private schools alongside the public ones needed to be discussed. Education would now be the object of a stricter state monopoly.[1]

Several months later a parliamentary discussion of the government's curricular initiatives turned into an out-and-out attack on Gentile, whom many saw as largely responsible for the delay in creating truly fascist schools, since he had authored a reform bill that emerged from a nonfascist social and cultural context. An initial measure, adopted by the Grand Council of Fascism in late March 1930, dictated that all university chancellors, university department heads, and school principals had to have been members of the Party for at least five years. This measure earned the applause of many fascist intellectuals;[2] for example, in the Chamber of Deputies, the historian Francesco Ercole (a future minister of national education) denounced the current state of the universities and explicitly declared them unequal to the task fascism required of them.[3] Voicing a widespread belief, Ercole claimed that the root of the problem lay in the difficulty of creating a ruling class able to impress upon students a sense of rupture with the past. He argued bitterly that there could be no other solution than the one recommended by the Grand Council—namely, "absolute and incontrovertible loyalty to the regime by those called to support or preside over any level or type of school."[4]

Faced with this debate about Gentile's reform and with the Grand Council's declaration, Giuliano continued to waver. When in April 1931 Mussolini termed the 1923 reform "an error owing to the times and the then-minister's beliefs," Giuliano proposed correcting the reform bill where it was found "lacking or contrary to certain principles," but not replacing it outright.[5] He repeated this approach in Parliament, introducing a measure to alter secondary school curricula by removing Rousseau and Humboldt.[6] In the meantime, persuaded, like his colleagues, that they needed to accelerate the process of "fascisizing" Italian culture, he adopted the consolidated textbook, which, as we have seen, had been two years in the making.[7] In 1931 he was among those who supported requiring university professors to swear an oath to the state.

According to Jürgen Charnitzky, up until that point the fascist regime had not been especially strict with university instructors. Starting in January 1927, it had considered the possibility of licensing them or excluding individuals from consideration for university jobs for political reasons, but it had not undertaken any purges. Before 1931 "not even the philosophy professors Francesco De Sarlo and Piero Martinetti, whom Mussolini personally denounced to Fedele in April 1926, could be easily fired."[8] The former retired in 1933, while the latter occupied his chair until 1931, when he refused to swear fealty to the regime. Charnitzky does not explain why an expulsion for political reasons does not count as a purge, nor what it means to be fired "easily." In fact, the decision to force professors to declare their loyalty to the fascist regime was consistent with the cultural politics that we have attempted to sketch here. First proposed by Gentile to Mussolini as a means of responding to those intent on making Italian universities fascist, the measure was taken up again by Giuseppe Belluzzo and finally introduced in October 1931 by Giuliano. Before assuming their posts, university professors would have to recite the following oath:

I swear to be faithful to the king, to his Royal Successors, and to the Fascist
Regime; to loyally obey the Constitution and the other laws of the State; to
exercise the office of teacher and fulfill all my academic duties with the aim of
training hard-working, upright citizens devoted to the Homeland and to the
Fascist Regime.[9]

Only twelve professors out of more than two thousand refused to swear
fealty to the regime, testifying to both their intellectual independence and
their courage in leaving their careers behind. Despite this, according to Charnitzky (and other historians), the regime and Italian universities "established
a *modus vivendi* that usually allowed even antifascist professors, provided
that they were politically passive, to continue to fully exercise their profession." Without clarifying the evidence on which he based such definitive
statements, Charnitzky admitted that the oath "nullified *de jure* the principle of academic freedom," but claimed nonetheless that for the majority of
instructors this was a "purely formal act" that did not overly infringe upon
their work.[10] It is not clear how one might read an oath of loyalty to a totalitarian regime as the result of an implicit compromise, or the manifestation
of a *modus vivendi* established between the regime and the universities. It is
true, as many historians have observed, that many Italian educators took the
oath to keep their jobs, and not because they were actually fascists. That does
not, however, negate the fact that the oath instantiated in 1931 was one of the
strongest and most important manifestations of fascist cultural politics.

Giuliano's successor, Francesco Ercole, who arrived in Piazza della Minerva
in July 1932, was equally focused on pursuing the project of rendering the
Italian schools truly fascist.[11] Ercole adopted the widest-ranging measures
during his first year: transferring the last schools still managed by local governments to his ministry; developing a consolidated textbook for universities in accordance with the legislation; and revising the secondary school
curriculum. In this case, too, the parliamentary debate over these legislative
measures became an occasion for remonstrating with Gentile. The arguments became so heated that Minister Ercole, responding in the Chamber, was moved to defend the reform of 1923.[12] He declared that Gentile's
reform should be seen as a first step in building a fascist school system, and
that the new measures did not alter Gentile's "three principles"—namely,
"administrative freedom, didactic freedom, [and] a state exam."[13]

Such "touch-up politics" and attempts to preserve certain aspects of the 1923 reform were responses to the new demands of fascism, and they came to an end in July 1933, when Mussolini wrote to the minister of national education to ask him to abandon the updates and give more stability to educational policy.[14] In reality, the stability the premier demanded lasted less than two years, since Cesare Maria De Vecchi di Val Cismon's installation as minister in 1935 brought further changes.[15] The new minister's nomination had been greeted with a chorus of approval from those who were finally seeing a "true" fascist in charge of the ministry.[16] De Vecchi—*quadrumvir* of the March on Rome, fervent Catholic, monarchist, and firm anti-Gentilian— had been a radical fascist from the earliest days. In 1935 he did not disappoint, making himself into a champion for "reclaiming culture," a project in which the schools, once entirely purged of their Gentilian influences, would serve as the fascist state's driving force.[17] De Vecchi's reforms centralized all decision-making power in the minister's hands and eliminated every form of freedom left to schools and universities. Among other things, this concentration of power led him to abolish consulting bodies for school administration, with the exception of the High Council of National Education— which, in any case, he wanted to completely reorganize. He decided, in fact, to eliminate all its chapters, remove the obligation to consult it, drastically reduce the number of its members, and guarantee seats for the Party secretary and the secretary of the ONB, the fascist youth organization. As far as didactic freedom was concerned, De Vecchi barred the free choice of curricular materials for schools and university departments, which had been introduced in 1923, and instead added premilitary training to the schools.[18] These were the grounds on which his bitter clash with Gentile unfolded.

In his lecture "The Italian Tradition," delivered at the Lyceum Club in Florence on the eve of the Ethiopian occupation, Gentile accused De Vecchi (without explicitly naming him, but citing passages from one of his speeches) of having introduced the cult of Roman culture into the schools via empty repetitive formulas, which would not allow young fascists to develop consciousness of and respect for the Italian tradition. Making no effort to hide his rancor, he asserted, "A tradition is genuine and thus efficacious if it is alive. And when today we hear on the other hand endless public approbations … of the Italian tradition or of our modern Roman tradition (which amounts to the same thing), of the tradition of *that Rome where Christ is*

Roman, it nonetheless becomes necessary to say to these Romish enthusi-asts perked up by the Lateran Pacts that their Italy is not the authentic Italy, not our Italy—that is to say, not the Italians' Italy. Much less is it the Italy of today's Italians, or of fascism."[19]

On June 11 De Vecchi wrote to him, "You would do well to concern your-self with philosophers and philosophy, and to refrain from concerning yourself with me and my work as a fascist minister. Toward all that, sir, one should advise, if not restraint, respect." The next day he removed Gen-tile from his post as director of the Scuola Normale in Pisa.[20] In the end his absence from the Normale turned out to be brief: less than a year later, when Bottai replaced De Vecchi as minister of national education, Gentile returned to the directorship. Yet it was a symptom of the growing conflict between Gentile and the Party, which came to a head in March 1937 when Party Secretary Achille Starace, having approved a new statute restricting the autonomy of the National Fascist Institute of Culture and establishing its subordination to the Party, pushed the philosopher to resign from his post as president. The biggest change, however, had to do with the name: despite Gentile's continued insistence, the National Fascist Institute of Cul-ture became the National Institute of Fascist Culture, marking an official shift toward a strictly political idea of the cultural body the philosopher had founded in 1925.[21] Thus ended the most important of Gentile's many posts within the regime. Writing to his student Vito Fazio-Allmayer in March 1937, the philosopher explained what had happened over the preceding months, and how he had experienced this most serious conflict yet since joining the fascist movement:

> For some months the Party secretary has waged an all-out war with me, deter-mined [as he was] to make the Institute . . . into a tool of the Party, stripping it of that small amount of independence that I have always defended in order to preserve something of value in its great imaginative contribution to the Party. I am well aware that people are whispering about Gentile's disgrace, etc. So much the better. I would only be sorry if this Institute that I created became an instrument of torture for Italians who read and write. But I hope that won't happen. And for my part I know I've done my duty: I worked with-out pay for twelve and a half years in the face of hostility from friends and enemies alike, and I have the right to retire.[22]

Gentile's comments reflect his awareness that he had lost the battle with the Party: until 1937 he had insisted that the institute should foster the creation of a new culture, not simply spout political propaganda. Many scholars have argued that Gentile fell prey to a misunderstanding, thinking that he could achieve his own version of fascism and not grasping the nature of the forces that transformed Italy into a totalitarian state between 1922 and 1945.[23] This is far from the truth, however. Gentile tried to carry out his cultural and political project because he had Mussolini's support until the late 1930s, and because this project aligned with the Party's and the regime's work in many important ways.

As we have seen, in fact, Gentile helped create a regime that celebrated the mythology of the state and maintained an absolutist idea of politics—a state in which institutions, organizing bodies, groups, and individuals would collaborate on creating a new order, and a kind of politics, understood as a faith, that would transform thought and build a new national life by giving Italians a sense of identity. Like the fascists, Gentile also saw his work as a mission, a constant struggle, since in politics one might lose or win the battle, but never give up on the war. From 1925 to 1937 he fought to impose his ideas, and he lost in the same way that he had won many other times—without ever doubting his choice in the first place. The Party shared this notion of fascism but with one important difference: while Gentile thought that fascism would, day by day, create the Italian people's state because fascism *was* Italy, or, rather, was the best expression of the Italian people, the Party, which safeguarded the mythology of the fascist revolution and saw its role as an artifact of the conquest of power, did not accept the philosopher's "statalist" approach. If the goal of the revolution was supposed to be the creation of a new state, then the Party would choose the methods and the means by imposing its own will, its own obsessive presence, and its control of society, as was evident in their efforts to turn younger generations fascist.

The Italian Youth of the Lictor (la Gioventù italiana del littorio)

In the early 1930s, government supporters and Party men alike believed it was necessary to carry out the political work of "totalitarian pedagogy," doubling down on their efforts with the younger generations.[24] To achieve this goal, fascism wanted to eliminate its most dangerous rival, Catholic

Action (l'Azione cattolica), an organization that sheltered the last remaining nonfascist youth groups. In May 1931, after a series of clashes, Mussolini ordered the provincial prefects to ban and dissolve all youth groups that did not "directly report either to Party organizations or to the Fascist Youth Organization" (i.e., the ONB).[25] Pope Pius XI responded in his July 1931 encyclical *Non abbiamo bisogno* (We need not), denying that the Church posed a threat to the regime—an accusation that, in his view, "betrayed the regime's true intention, [namely] to rip young people—all young people—from Catholic Action and thereby from the Church."[26] In September 1931 a new agreement dictated that Catholic youth organizations must abstain from sports activities, dedicating themselves exclusively to the spiritual and religious upbringing of young people.

As we have seen, in 1929 the ONB came under the auspices of the Ministry of National Education, fueling an already-intense rivalry between the Party and the government and provoking an immediate reaction from the Party, which was determined to regain control of this powerful tool. This was a clash not between two political systems or two ideologies, but rather between two institutions that fought for pride of place in educating young Italians. The first step in this direction was taken by Party Secretary Giovanni Giuriati, who in 1930 created the Fascist Youth Combat Leagues (Fasci giovanili di combattimento), aimed at training youths between eighteen and twenty-one before they entered the Party. In 1935 Minister De Vecchi advised Mussolini to place the university student organization, Gruppi universitari fascisti, or GUF, under his ministry's direction, in an effort to create a unified organization that would coordinate all aspects of youth education and training. Two years later Party Secretary Achille Starace won the battle: the ONB, now transformed into the Italian Youth of the Lictor (Gioventù italiana del littorio, or GIL), returned to the control of the Party, which thereby gained control of the 5,561,000 Italian young people who were card-carrying members.[27]

With the creation of the GIL, all fascist youth groups were consolidated within a single organization. This new body absorbed the ones who already belonged to the ONB, along with the Fascist Youth Combat Leagues for older youths. Thus, all children and young people from six to twenty-one years of age were brought together under the auspices of a single organization, with the exception of those enrolled in the GUF, which maintained its autonomy.

Article 1 of the GIL's constitution stated its motto: "To believe, to obey, and to fight." Every member, down to the smallest child, would have to take an oath and swear to follow Il Duce's orders.[28]

In November 1937, commenting on the law that created the GIL, Starace pronounced the education of young people to be the Party's primary job, adding that no other entity could play the role of positioning "the people within the life of the State."[29] To this end, he wanted to institute a complete educational trajectory from childhood to adulthood and put state-run schools and those run by the Party on equal footing; he argued, accordingly, that the Party ought to replace the minister of national education where that official had proved ineffectual. Starting in 1935 Starace had instituted bi-annual political training courses within every organization, aiming to prepare the future ruling class. The courses, which were the first attempt to create a political class using wholly fascist means, were voluntary and open to young men between twenty-three and twenty-eight.[30] Beyond providing a theoretical education, the courses allowed young fascists to make direct contact with the regime's institutions and with local politics. This means of creating a ruling class was perfected in 1939 with the founding of the National Center for Political Training (Centro nazionale di preparazione politica) in Rome, a two-year course in advanced political culture, which aimed to prepare high-performing young men to assume political duties. The center reported to the Party secretary and was open to Party members under twenty-eight who had completed their military service, had obtained a qualifying diploma after taking provincial political training courses, and were either members or graduates of the GIL. The center's courses, which were conducted by the GUF, focused on fascist doctrine, the history of the fascist revolution, the Party's organization and roles, the structure of the state, racial politics, and military culture.[31]

As we have seen, the GUF emerged in 1920 as one of the first concrete products of early fascism.[32] Through their publishing activities and actions, they kept key debates over fascist culture and politics alive from the early '20s onward, criticizing any normalizing efforts and pointing out any lapses in the regime's work to render Italian culture fascist. As Luca La Rovere has noted, university students, especially in the latter half of the '30s, pressed for more decisive, radical action in building the totalitarian state. Raised within the confines of the regime, enamored of the myth of Mussolini and the seductiveness of revolutionary fascism, empowered by a Party that saw them as the future ruling class, university students had been born into the regime's ideological universe and were the product of its symbols and culture.

Among the many initiatives they took on, the most significant was the creation of the Culture and Art Tournaments (Littoriali della cultura e dell'arte), in particular because many key members of the future political class who were then GUF members participated in them. Created in 1934 after the pattern of the Sport Tournaments (Littoriali dello sport, which began in 1932), these competitions in science, art, and culture lasted several months and became an occasion for debating, under the Party's supervision, key problems in fascist culture and politics. In this sense it seems hard to argue, as many ex-GUF members and scholars alike have claimed, that they were "training grounds for antifascism," since, on the contrary, the tournaments "comprised an integral part of the educational apparatus created by the Party to achieve its plans to train and permanently mobilize the younger generations."[33] For many years, however, most historians viewed Italian universities as bastions of antifascism, or at least places in which nonconformist strains of fascism could emerge. Charnitzky, for instance, notes that in the early 1930s university students chafed at the disciplinary limitations imposed on them, and adds that the tournaments served "the regime as a safety valve for the pressure of student opposition." For him, the competitions "offered the possibility of assimilating the most talented among the new intellectual recruits," but they mutated "from fascist exposition to antifascist crucible."[34] Thus Charnitzky, like the historian Tracy Koon, argued that not only did the fascist youth organizations fail to achieve their goals, but they actually aided the cause of their antifascist adversaries. Ruth Ben-Ghiat, for her part, recognized the importance of the GUF in fascist culture but saw the youth organizations as a site of dissident recruitment during the war.[35]

Many historians of fascist youth life have based their conclusions on memoirs published in the immediate aftermath of World War II. In those years, many young fascists who had by then become antifascist distanced themselves from the regime in recounting their experiences. In their telling, starting in the latter half of the 1930s they began to understand fascism's reactionary nature and therefore felt an increasing need to withdraw from it, until they finally arrived at an antifascist political stance in the late '30s. Among such writers we find Ruggero Zangrandi, author of a successful book called *Lungo viaggio attraverso il fascismo* (Long journey through fascism), and Domenico Carella, editor of the magazine *Il Saggiatore* (The assayer), founded in 1930 to reassert the spirit of fascism in the face of efforts to normalize it. In 1973 Carella published *Fascismo prima, fascismo dopo* (Fascism before, fascism after), in which he claimed that he had always been a revolutionary, a leftist fascist, and a critic of official fascism.[36] Such an argument seems to arise from a widespread impulse among those who spent their youth within the totalitarian regime to absolve themselves—even those who neither dissented nor simply remained silent, but in fact publicly demonstrated their support for the regime by founding newspapers, participating in debates, and even holding political posts. After the war, many such figures, young and not so young, claimed that they had been fascists but that they believed in a different form of fascism than the Party's.

In reality, raised within the mythological universe created by the regime, young people felt that they represented this revolutionary historical period better than other fascists. They portrayed themselves as the stars of the revolution, the ones who correctly interpreted fascist doctrine and could therefore lay claim to a major role in creating the new, authentically fascist ruling class. Such young people were *not* critical of fascism; if anything, they were *more* fascist than others: in the name of fascism, in fact, they attacked any moderate elements they discovered in 1930s politics, pushing to make society and the state fully fascist, and fighting those who, in their opinion, stood in the way of carrying out the original revolutionary plan.

Historians who have given credence to such memoirs in recounting fascist youth life have, therefore, underestimated the degree to which university students and young people embraced fascism. From this point of view, historiographical opinion seems analogous to that of certain influential supporters of mass parties during World War II. Faced with the problem of an entire generation that not only participated in building the regime but in fact played a starring role in the experiments in totalitarian pedagogy that we have examined here, the antifascist parties justified the actions of young ex-fascists and allowed them to re-engage with politics in democratic, antifascist Italy. A huge number of Italians fell into this camp: in 1941 Party members numbered 24,500,000. The number of members strictly defined was only 20 percent of that figure; the remaining 80 percent was made up of members of associations and organizations run by the Party, including the GIL, whose 8,137,000 members accounted for 33 percent of the total.[37] This was an imposing organizational undertaking, which, as we shall see, also transformed the lives of Italian women during this period.

Organizing Women

Within the vast historiography of fascism, studies of fascist women's organizations and, more generally, of women's lives under the totalitarian regime are far from common. In fact, compared with the many important works on women's role in the Resistance, studies of women under the fascist dictatorship have been scarce until recent years.[38] Yet, as some historians have shown, women played a unique role in the mass politics imposed by the fascist state, and therefore a leading role in its culture.

Maria Fraddosio has observed that a stereotype of the fascist woman— as exemplary wife and mother—has long held sway among historians.[39] This stereotype obviously has its antecedents, since the fascists believed that Italian women ought to occupy a role primarily derived from the Catholic cultural tradition: true mistresses of the home, far removed from politics, devoted to their children and family. Yet during the regime a new model of womanhood emerged that stopped short of questioning the traditional model but nonetheless had unique traits. "As the expression of fascism's revolutionary and vitalist culture," as Fraddosio put it, "this model materialized in the *militant female citizen*, actively involved in the life of the regime."[40]

This important insight has, nonetheless, remained a minority view. In most cases, in fact, historians have argued that the regime's attitude toward women reflected a patriarchal, capitalist culture "that added nothing new to long-standing ideas about women, which women unconsciously adopted."[41] Other scholars have argued that the regime's behavior toward women was marked by a profound ambiguity. On the one hand, the fascists condemned all social practices tied to women's emancipation, attempting to limit their freedom as much as possible. On the other hand, "in their efforts to increase the nation's economic power and mobilize every available resource ... the fascists inevitably ended up promoting the very changes they had tried to avoid," as Victoria De Grazia has written. "As in other social spheres, the regime asserted its intention to restore the past while promoting something new in spite of itself."[42] However, fascism never stated an "intention to restore the past," but rather presented itself to Italians as a vanguard that would found a new civilization.

The first female fascists became active in the movement to mobilize women during the liberal era and continued through the war years. For them, as for men, the exaltation of war served as a new reason to commit themselves to the cause. They too embraced the myth of revolutionary war that we discussed in chapter 2.

Nine women who had previously been active in the feminist movement of that period participated in the gathering in Piazza di San Sepolcro in March 1919. Neglected by historians, they were members of the Milan chapter of the Combat Leagues, and they fought for women's suffrage—a demand supported by the entire movement at the time.[43] Many of these women had political backgrounds: some were old comrades from Mussolini's party, like Regina Terruzzi, who left the Socialist Party after it pushed for Italy to remain neutral in the war; others came from the ranks of the D'Annunzians, like Elisa Majer Rizzioli. Rizzioli, who founded the Women's Leagues (Fasci femminili, or FF), was a Red Cross nurse, a strong advocate for intervening in the war, and a volunteer in Fiume, in addition to being an active propagandist. Other women, like Ines Donati, had been members of the nationalist movement and participated in expeditions run by the *squadristi*.[44]

Organically emerging from local fascist scenes, up until the March on Rome the FF comprised about a hundred women. They focused their energies on fighting for the vote and trying to gain their independence within the fascist movement.[45] As it happened, the first Party charter in 1921 defined the Women's Leagues as subsections of the men's, specializing in certain circumscribed tasks, including propaganda, charity, and welfare. The charter also dictated that while women could attend political proceedings during assemblies, they could not undertake any political initiatives.[46] Nonetheless, in 1923 Mussolini declared that the fascist government would grant the vote to women for administrative elections; and in 1924, at the Congress of Female Fascists in Milan, women asserted their desire to be considered full political actors, while pledging to remain subordinate within the Party hierarchy. The Matteotti crisis, the decision (promoted by the ex-nationalists) not to grant women the right to vote on the administration of charitable institutions, and the eventual formal retraction of the promise of such rights by a 1925 law, all contributed to the failure of these plans.[47]

By 1925 the FF was no longer in a position to demand decision-making rights within the Party or the state. From that point on women found themselves marginalized within the Party, which exalted the virility, soldierly virtues, and military prowess of the new man. Yet, as key players in the project to create a new Italian civilization, and therefore to achieve the totalitarian regime's goals, women received a degree of attention unprecedented in previous political contexts. They were accordingly drawn into the processes of totalitarian political mobilization both within and outside the Party, which explicitly tasked women with most aid activities. In this regard, the fascists' first large-scale undertaking was the creation in late 1925 of the National Aid Society for Motherhood and Children (Opera nazionale maternità e infanzia, or ONMI). ONMI was specifically aimed at women who did not have a strong family-support network and who needed assistance for themselves or their children, up to the age of five. The organization worked to prevent abortions and secret births, offered free medical checkups during the last trimester of pregnancy, and cared for orphans under eighteen with the express goal of "acting every time" a "family's actions [were] insufficient or inappropriate."[48] Starting in 1927, ONMI claimed to have prevented the abandonment of thousands of infants each year, persuading mothers to keep their children and pushing parents to legally marry. In any case, in the interest of a new society and a new Italian civilization, they certainly fostered a more tolerant attitude toward unmarried mothers by promising and delivering practical help.[49]

The regime framed raising children as a service to the state and gave political prominence to the experience of procreation. Having approved a bachelor tax in 1926, in January 1927 the government initiated a natalist policy that would have a profound impact on the lives of women, to which we shall return in the next chapter.[50] Starting in 1933, "Mothers' and Children's Day" was celebrated every December 24, an occasion on which "fruitful" mothers were awarded prizes on the basis of the number of children they had produced. The regime was not merely encouraging Italian women to have children and rewarding the biggest families. As we have stressed, this policy, aimed at mobilizing Italian women, effectively transformed their lives because it introduced something new into traditional female roles.[51]

In the early 1930s, many young fascist women who participated in fascist women's youth groups and were raised in the atmosphere created by the regime admired the ideal of the militant female citizen, engaged in building a new fascist civilization and not limited to the domestic sphere to which she had traditionally been relegated. Certain that they could contribute to the grand project to which the regime seemed to call them, some women imagined that they were participating in the ongoing political process. They assumed a new way of thinking and, perhaps without fully realizing it, began to free themselves from traditional female roles—even if neither they nor the Party ever saw the role of militant female citizen as an alternative to that of model wife and mother. By 1942 the ranks of the FF exceeded one million. As it happened, the National Fascist Party was the first Italian political party that could boast a mass female membership, as it asked women to actively demonstrate their loyalty to fascism and contribute to creating a new Italian nation.[52]

Minculpop and the Press

While the Ministry of National Education and the Party vied for control over young people, cultural politics in the '30s was also profoundly marked by another important entity—the Ministry of Popular Culture (Ministero della cultura popolare). Initially created by the Press Office of the President, in 1934 the organization became the Under-secretariat for Press and Propaganda. The next year it was promoted to Ministry, and in 1937 it took the name Ministero della cultura popolare, thereafter known by the acronym Minculpop. It was initially led by Dino Alfieri. In 1939 the baton was passed to Alessandro Pavolini, who directed it until February 1943, when Gaetano Polverelli assumed the position. From the late 1930s onward, it oversaw cinema, theater, music, and radio, though its initial activities were related mostly to print.[53]

As early as 1923, the Press Office exerted strict control over Italian newspapers, keeping them in line with the government's dictates. This goal was much more attainable after 1926, when stringent fascist laws abolished all opposition publications. From that point on, the regime brazenly displayed its desire to marshal journalists for the fascist cause. In September 1927, as a case in point, a heated debate took place in the press over fascist journalists' ability to express dissent from the regime's policies and in this way, however limited, play the role of provocateur. In November of that year, the Grand Council of Fascism reiterated the importance of the journalists' role, reaffirming that the press should be "permeated and shaped by the spirit of fascism" and asking Party Secretary Augusto Turati to press on with the work of "fascisizing" the nation. A few days later, Turati asked the editors of the major Italian papers to remove nonfascists from editorships and give greater prominence and responsibility to men of proven fascist faith.[54]

This process of "fascisizing" the nation was accelerated in October 1928, when Mussolini gathered the editors of the major papers at Palazzo Chigi and declared that the press ought to become "an element of this regime" that had "emerged from a triumphant revolution."[55] For the first time, as the secretary of the Fascist Journalists' Union Ermanno Amicucci noted enthusiastically, a premier wanted to convene leaders of the press.[56] And, in effect, from that point on the Press Office's role shifted, becoming more and more influential with every passing year. In 1933, for instance, an independent branch of the office was established to systematically disseminate propaganda about certain topics.[57] Thus, having started out as an organization reporting to the head of state and intended to enforce censorship, the Press Office began to take a proactive role in identifying topics that journalists should take up, distinguishing acceptable pictures from unacceptable ones, and in general deciding what could be published and what should remain in the shadows. Projecting a mythical image of Mussolini as a demigod entrusted with duties not shared by mere mortals meant, for instance, that journalists could not make the public aware of his birthday or let Italians know how old he was; nor could they publish stories mentioning any illness or "unmanly" behavior.[58]

Pierluigi Allotti observed that to meet these expectations, journalists played "the role of vanguard for fascism's totalitarian project." In fact, in addition to being "public educators," they were seen as actual "soldiers," as Mussolini put it at an October 1933 meeting with the editors-in-chief of the Italian papers, "ordered to guard the foremost and most delicate section of the fascist front, and to operate the most powerful and dangerous weapon in every battle."[59] Entrusted with this role, the press gave their support at critical points in the regime's history. In 1936, sent to cover the African front, they described the Italo-Ethiopian War "as a battle to civilize a country still stuck in a state of savagery, a country that would offer enormous work opportunities to all those Italians who migrated to the Ethiopian Plateau."[60]

A few months later, they depicted the Spanish Civil War as a crusade against communism; and in 1938, they actively participated in the campaign to disseminate news about "the everyday crimes committed by Jews and in particular the anti-Semitic measures taken by other countries."[61] In doing this they were not merely following the orders of the fascist propaganda machine, as they did *en masse* during World War II; with their words, journalists helped create those cultural and ideological myths which we examined in the previous chapter. What's more, their sector benefited from the regime's largest financial investments.

Alongside its official tasks, Minculpop also managed a vast and wide-ranging system of secret subsidies granted to artists and intellectuals who applied for them, tapping into financial reserves that remained shadowy because "they were not intended for the work of cultural aid, but rather were earmarked, within the totalitarian framework, for discretionary projects aimed at generating consent."[62] Among those who secretly applied for and received funding from Minculpop, journalists made up 55 percent of the total, and thus were the professional group that, more than any other, lent themselves to the labor of fascism in exchange for money.[63] They were not the only ones, however: writers, comedians, musicians, and filmmakers were also financed by the regime, which used them to disseminate its culture through the newest tools of modernity.

Film

In 1975 Gian Piero Brunetta observed that, despite what many influential critics have argued, fascism had in fact shown an interest in film as early as the 1920s. The regime intervened in the film industry using the classic instruments of censorship—and some new ones as well.[64] In 1924 the Instituto Luce (Light Institute) was created from a small film company with the aim of educating the Italian public through moving pictures. In 1925 it became a charitable organization under public law, and after 1926 it obtained a monopoly over the film sector: all theaters were required to include its programming in every screening. These programs were typically short newsreels in a reportorial style. From 1927 on, as these newsreels were run in Italian cinemas before each show, Luce became the regime's primary non-print distributor of information.

Newsreels were not the regime's only outlet in the Italian film industry, however. Starting in the late '20s, intellectuals and politicians took an interest in this new art form, which was uniquely suited to achieving fascism's cultural goals. For instance, writing in his newspaper *Il Tevere* in 1927, Telesio Interlandi asked critics and directors how they might "make use of the cinema to broadcast the regime's good works."[65] That same year, Guglielmo Giannini wrote in *Kines* that the entertainment industry should serve fascism as a political weapon; accordingly, he called for greater involvement in the film industry.[66] Indeed, the '30s marked a shift in terms of both the degree of the regime's involvement, as Giannini suggested, and its intention to create a bona fide film policy. Between 1931 and 1933 two laws were passed to authorize financial support for such work. In 1934 the Directorate General of Moving Pictures (Direzione generale della cinematografia) was created within the office of the Under-secretariat for Press and Propaganda, led by an early adopter of fascism, Luigi Freddi; and in 1935 the Experimental Center (Centro sperimentale) was established to "directly create our own pictures capable of responding to the demands of fascist cinema." That same year Interlandi wrote that by now "all [Italian] film" had been transformed into "political film."[67]

The Directorate General opened up a whole new direction for fascist cultural politics pertaining to film when it created the National Association for Film Production (Ente nazionale industrie cinematografiche, or ENIC) and introduced a new way of financing filmmakers.[68] From then on the regime also actively worked to create new film studios, including Cinecittà, and to play the role of editor and censor. In 1934 censorship moved from the purview of the Ministry of the Interior to that of the Directorate General, where Freddi undertook his role with fascist zeal. He believed that it was necessary "to abandon outmoded and negative ideas in order to undertake positive action aimed at influencing film production, to obtain moving pictures that not only do not offend the spirit of fascism, but rather are suited to, and resonate with—if they do not outright propagandize—the fascist regime."[69] To obtain funding, filmmakers were required to submit their projects to the Directorate, which thereby exerted control over every detail of film production in Italy. As for foreign films, the fascist censors exerted their control by simply prohibiting their importation, in the most serious cases, or by cutting certain scenes, as was the case with Fred Niblo's *Ben Hur* among many others.

Beyond films with the express aim of glorifying war, a genre in which the then-fascist Roberto Rossellini distinguished himself in the early 1940s, the most substantive connection between film subjects and fascist ideology can be found in a handful of thematic clusters, like fascist heroism (with its projections onto history stretching back to the powerful warlords of the medieval period), antibourgeois ruralism, and above all the legend of Rome, which inspired many Italian films from the late 1930s onward. As historians have recently observed, after the earliest films, which focused on ruralism, such as Alessandro Blasetti's 1928 *Sole* (Sun) and 1931 *Terra madre* (Motherland), and after those about the Risorgimento period like Blasetti's 1933 film *1860* or Giovacchino Forzano's *Villafranca* of 1934, fascist cinema turned to the mythology of the Roman republic and empire.[70]

To this end in 1937 it funded the production of Carmine Gallone's epic *Scipione l'Africano* (English-language version: *Scipio Africanus: The Defeat of Hannibal*); though not as successful as its producers had hoped, *Scipione* clearly marked the beginning of a new body of work aimed at celebrating fascism's power as heir to Rome and builder of a new civilization that, like its Roman predecessor, would endure over the centuries. In this moving picture, the viewer could watch a veritable transposition of Italy's invasion of Ethiopia, with a Mussolini-Scipio avenging Adwa-Cannae, the Carthaginians in place of the Ethiopian army, and the Italian troops played by valiant Roman legionnaires. It should come as no surprise, then, that Annibale Ninchi played Scipio using postures and speech patterns modeled directly after Mussolini, making the Roman general "a kind of forefather" for Il Duce.[71]

One year later, Goffredo Alessandrini directed *Luciano Serra pilota* (Luciano Serra, pilot), lauded as one of the best films made during the fascist period. The hero of Alessandrini's film dies in Africa, and his sacrifice serves as a testament of courage and commitment for future generations: Luciano saves his son's life and in doing so passes on his love of country and pride in belonging to a modern nation in possession of a powerful air fleet. Number one at the box office in 1938 and 1939, the film starred Amedeo Nazzari, then a young darling of Italian cinema who, like many other actors, put his talents to use for the regime's purposes.

Music and Theater

Like the artists we have encountered in the preceding pages, many musicians showed their sympathies with fascism early on. Pietro Mascagni, Riccardo Zandonai, and Francesco Cilea, for example, regarded the new movement with obvious interest, as their letters and in some cases public statements made clear.[72] Wishing to express the new national spirit that the fascists saw themselves as representing, some musicians, including Franco Alfano, Ildebrando Pizzetti, and Gino Marinuzzi, signed the Manifesto of Fascist Intellectuals in 1925, after the March on Rome and the Matteotti crisis.[73] For his part, Mussolini loved to be portrayed as a passionate music-lover who could play the violin—a cultured man who stayed abreast of trends in Italian art and frequently hosted writers, actors, and musicians at Palazzo Chigi. This was another reason for the regime's greater attention to music compared with earlier years, and it explains why, between 1922 and 1943, it increased musical education for children, transformed Italian theaters and performance spaces, and directly managed the musical world with the creation of the Directorate General of Music and Theater within Minculpop in 1935.[74]

Besides the long-established conservatories of music, the first parts of a general system of musical education were introduced in Italy via an 1885 circular that established singing exercises in elementary schools.[75] These were inspired by the practical idea of using music as a physical diversion for young students, which remained unchanged until the Daneo-Credaro law of 1911. From that point on, music was regarded as part of a student's educational journey, though it was an elective until 1923. With Gentile's reform, thanks to the contributions of Giuseppe Lombardo Radice, the author of the elementary school reform, music was included in the arts curriculum along with freehand drawing and drama.[76]

Although music was required in the elementary schools after 1923, it remained an elective in most secondary schools. Music was offered in the form of chorale singing only at the teacher-training colleges, the women's *licei* (attended by girls from good families who did not intend to continue their studies), and the vocational schools. The 1923 reform bill also changed the way conservatories were funded, ensuring that each year they were supplied with more adequate financing to meet the demands for their services. In

1926 the Ministry created a committee to expand the time and space dedicated to music.[77] The next year it ordered that concerts be performed in the
schools, and in 1930 it reformed the conservatories' curricula. In 1936 history
of music was added to the curricula of the technical and teacher-training
institutes and the classical and scientific *licei*.

Further expanding musical education for young Italians, in 1932 the Chi-
giana Musical Academy was founded in Siena by Count Guido Chigi Sara-
cini, with economic support from the regime.[78] The academy was an elite
training ground for the country's best young instrumentalists. Graduates
were shepherded into the working world, joining the national trade union
and protected by the entertainment guild, which managed job placements
and offered financial assistance. In 1935 the government announced the establishment of a new Fascist Musical Academy in Rome, which would choose
twenty-five students from among the fascist student youth groups (the Balilla
and the ONB) to receive a free musical education at the Santa Cecilia Conservatory, including room, board, and uniforms.[79]

As we have noted, beyond investing in educating young Italians, the
regime also wanted to get involved in the nation's broader musical culture,
and so it also dedicated a great deal of attention to the opera. To move beyond
the traditional managerial system, as part of a gradual governmental process of centralization, fascism abolished agents and middlemen and reformed
Italian theaters by systematically politicizing them and forcing them to rely
on public funding. When the Inspectorate of Theater and Music (later a
Directorate General of Minculpop) was created in 1935, under the supervision of Nicola De Pirro, this cultural policy became even more pervasive,
affecting both modernists and traditionalists alike.

In music as in other arts, a profound conflict developed between the defenders of tradition and the proponents of modernity. The former—including Pietro Mascagni, Ottorino Respighi, Riccardo Zandonai, and Ildebrando
Pizzetti—viewed nineteenth-century *melodramma* and its twentieth-century
offshoots as Italy's true art form: a popular art capable of portraying the
national qualities that fascism embodied and represented. It was on these
grounds that the traditionalists battled the modernist tendencies supported
by the composer Alfredo Casella and Gian Francesco Malipiero, president of
the Italian Society of Modern Music. Casella believed that in the new atmosphere of the regime, it would be possible to develop a kind of syncretism

between tradition and revolution, and he accordingly strove to keep Italian musical culture up-to-date. This included opening Italian music up to encounters with the revolutionary new works of Ravel, Debussy, Strauss, Stravinsky, and the Second Viennese School. In reality, however, there was absolutely no political difference between the two groups: while Mascagni directed *Nero* in 1935 to exalt the legends of ancient Rome, Casella staged *Il deserto tentato* (The untamed desert) in 1937 to celebrate the Ethiopian undertaking, and Malipiero composed hymns to Il Duce and the soundtrack for *Scipione Africanus* that same year.[80]

Minculpop, as we have seen, commissioned works by artists with modernist tendencies and provided support for the Florentine Musical May festival (Maggio musicale fiorentino), which was founded in 1933 and became a hub for disseminating new trends. But Minculpop also provided financial support for more traditional musicians like Zandonai and Alfano.

The work of reaching an ever-wider public schooled in the art of the regime was entrusted to the National Recreation Club (Opera nazionale dopolavoro, or OND), which, as we have seen, was one of the Party's most influential organizations. Among the OND's many programs and initiatives, a few in particular stand out: the amateur theater companies, the Traveling Thespians (Carri di tespi), and Theater Saturdays. The amateur theater companies, which reported to the provincial offices of the OND, performed a repertoire largely consisting of Italian comedies. They were hugely popular, growing from 113 companies in 1926 to 1,053 in 1928 and 2,066 by 1939.[81]

The Traveling Thespians were mobile theaters that operated outside the confines of traditional theater programming. Divided into two main branches, one for theater and another for music, they brought the classics to the most far-flung corners of the nation. With a caravan including a stage and stalls transported by truck, the Thespians did long tours through parts of Italy not normally reached by the theater.[82] The initiative kicked off on July 4, 1929, when director Giovacchino Forzano staged the first shows in Rome, presenting Alfieri's *Oreste* and *Gianni Schicchi* to an audience that included Mussolini.[83] The tour that began that day was so successful that the next year the OND prepared four large traveling structures: three theaters and one operatic caravan, which was inaugurated in Torre del Lago in 1930 with a performance of *La Bohème*. Designed to impress the public, the *Carri* were true sensations, reaching 1 million viewers in 1936. Within a few

hours of arriving at their destination, the troupe could transform a desig-
nated space into a theater with a capacity of 3,000 to 6,000 seats.[84]

Less extravagant but more common were the Theater Saturdays, which
were aimed at low- to middle-income members of the OND and which succeeded admirably in attracting theater- and concert-goers.[85] Via the offices of
the OND, the Party extended its recreational activities to the least-privileged
social spheres, a goal that it also strove for with the aid of a modern tool—
the radio.

Radio

Like film and theater, radio was a medium for both entertainment and
political education.[86] During the years fascism was active, it became a fundamental tool of mass communication for the regime, which brought radio
to the homes of the urban haute bourgeoisie and the most isolated country towns alike, taking advantage of its unique reach as a mechanism of
propaganda.

In 1927 the Italian Radio Broadcasting Agency (Ente italiano per le audi-
zioni radiofoniche, or EIAR) was made into a public body and assumed a
monopoly over programming. From that point on, the regime accelerated
both programming and radio distribution, and in 1933 it created the Rural
Radio Agency (Ente radio rurale).[87] Assigned to Party Secretary Achille Starace, the new agency promoted the sale of radios at a fixed discounted price
to public bodies and schools, with the goal of bringing the radio to common spaces, in particular in the Countryside. The agency was charged with
creating programming specifically targeted at farmers and rural students,
to leverage the radio's ability to teach from a distance and school even the
most far-flung students in the rituals, legends, and symbols of fascist culture.[88] Then, having brought students into the fold of the Party's organizations, rural radio enlisted the support of schoolteachers. School broadcasts
began in April 1934, with new material broadcast every three weeks, with
the intention of getting all students tuned into a simultaneous listening session enforced by their teachers' supervision. The teaching plan envisioned
a preparatory session guided by the teacher, followed by a core section when
the students listened to the radio, and a final period of writing to build
on and consolidate the program's content.[89] Children were, in fact, the tar-
get audience for most of the programming. For instance, in 1925 *Il giornale*

radiofonico del fanciullo (The child's radio news) went on the air: an extremely popular show made up of short segments about the events of the
day, interspersed with music, and rounded out with a story or a chapter of a
novel. Hosted by the Roman teacher Cesare Ferri, who went by the pseud-
onym Nonno Radio (i.e., "Grandpa Radio"), the show focused on the history
of Italy from the Risorgimento to the Great War.[90]

Sports competed with children's shows for pride of place in the regime's
programming, in keeping with the importance of sports for the regime's
culture as a whole. As Franco Monteleone observed in 1975, "fascist ideology
was present, albeit not explicitly, in shows generally devoted to sports and
athletic activities," which, "taken as a whole, and especially when combined
with news broadcasts about soccer matches, betrayed a totalitarian notion
of sports as an essential element of mass education, of discipline and con-
formism, and, after 1938, also a means of improving the race."[91] Soccer and
cycling were the most popular sports: spurred on by the World Cup, which
Italy won in 1934, Nicolò Carosio's soccer broadcasts reached a wide audience, while the stages of the Giro d'Italia cycling race were closely followed
by thousands of radio listeners.[92]

Committed to their work to educate the Italian public, the fascists did not
stop at entertaining them. From 1930 onward, radio news aired six times a
day; the broadcasts ranged from 10 to 30 minutes and included commentary from high-profile figures.[93] In fact, starting in October 1933, Galeazzo
Ciano, who was working to reorganize the Press Office of the President
(which would then become Minculpop), developed a plan to increase the
flow of information and improve the regime's propaganda machinery. Having obtained Mussolini's approval, he envisaged a broadcast in which a fascist true believer would provide commentary on the events of the day. Thus
was born the main political show of the Ventennio: *Cronache del regime*
(Chronicles of the regime), hosted by Roberto Forges Davanzati, a member
of the Fascist Grand Council and editor of *La Tribuna* until his death in 1936.
His commentary included bulletins from the radio news shows and analysis
of cultural and current events—and demonstrated that there was absolutely
no difference between radio news and propaganda.[94]

In 1932 there were a little more than 300,000 radio listeners in Italy. By
1939 this number had reached 1 million, which roughly translated to one
radio for every 50 people. In 1942 the listening public had climbed to nearly

2 million, the highest number reached by a regime that was in many ways built from words.[95]

The Language of Fascism

In 1934, no less prominent a figure than Giuseppe Bottai asserted that politics had "prevailed over every other factor in shaping the renewal or creation of language."[96] That year, the magazine that he edited, *Critica fascista*, published an investigation by politicians and intellectuals ready to declare that contemporary Italians spoke differently from their forebears.[97] This point was driven home by Bruno Migliorini, one of the period's most influential linguists, who declared in 1938 that "the regime's totalitarian politics and its decentralized organization make it such that there are no Italians who remain untouched by its work and its terminology."[98] Such high-flying assertions are consistent with the diffusion of a bona fide linguistic policy to which the fascists paid special attention, regarding it as an essential part of the new Italian civilization they were creating. Between 1922 and 1943, linguistic policy took the form of three major initiatives: attempting to limit the use of dialect; repressing linguistic minorities; and banning foreign words.

In a country where in 1922 a majority of people spoke *only* dialect, the effort to diffuse and impose standard Italian was a constant struggle. This is why, as a strategy for eventually getting all pupils to use Italian, Gentile's 1923 reform introduced the first stages of a gradual shift from dialect to standard Italian in the primary schools, while in 1934 Minister of Education Francesco Ercole removed all dialect from school curricula.[99]

The strictest policies, however, were reserved for linguistic minorities, and in particular for inhabitants of the South Tyrol region. In 1923 the regime decreed that all signage and documents across the entirety of the country had to be written in Italian, that all bilingual schools should be abolished, and that various places should be renamed. As the geographer Ettore Tolomei, director of the Alto Adige Institute and a zealous proponent of assimilation, put it, "Italy, [as] a national, not multinational State," had "absolutely no obligation to subsidize foreign-language primary or secondary schools."[100] In this same spirit, a 1923 decree introduced a fine for the use of foreign words in signs or shop windows.[101] This Italianization of linguistic-minority areas went so far as to include first and last names. Aiming to eradicate any traces of foreign languages and the presence of ethnic-linguistic groups and traditions "alien" to the Italian race, a 1926 law ordered that "families in the province of Trento" with a last name that had originally been Italian or Latin and had been "translated into other languages" should now begin using "their original last name in its original form." Families with foreign last names could request "an Italian adaptation at their discretion."[102]

The battle against foreign usage was particularly heated in the press, which often took up linguistic concerns. In 1932 the newspaper *La Tribuna* held a contest to replace fifty foreign words.[103] This was far from the only event of its kind: in March 1932, in the Turin *Gazzetta del popolo*, the writer and journalist Paolo Monelli started a very successful column. Aiming to "clean up" the language, each day for more than a year Monelli explained to readers which Italian term to use in place of a corresponding foreign word.[104]

From the late '30s on, this interest in lexical matters—we saw in the previous chapter the attempt to eradicate the use of the formal pronoun *lei*—extended into the uppermost echelons of the regime. This included the Accademia d'Italia, which set out to publish an updated dictionary of the Italian language; although the project stalled out after the publication of the first volume in 1941, the Accademia's contributions to fascist linguistic policy continued.[105]

In 1940 a law was passed requiring all lettering on product labels in foreign languages to be accompanied by Italian translations. That same year, the use of foreign words in shop signs or advertisements was banned.[106] The institutional work of identifying Italian substitutes was entrusted to the Accademia, which, advised by a committee of experts, collected nearly fifteen hundred proposed terms between 1941 and 1943. Riccardo Bacchelli, Filippo Tommaso Marinetti, Emilio Cecchi, and Bruno Migliorini, among others, put forth words that would ultimately enter the Italian lexicon and remain there, like *regista* ("director") for *regisseur*, *primato* for record, and *autista* for chauffeur. Less successful alternatives were *teppista* ("hooligan") to replace the French slang word *apache*, *slancio* for swing, and *lista* for menu.[107]

6

Intellectuals and Artists in the 1930s

Cultural Trends

As we saw in chapter 3, the key players in 1920s fascist culture were the radical fascists, the revisionist intellectuals, and Gentile's followers. By the end of the decade, however, new players had come onto the Italian cultural scene, and trends had changed.

The first significant novelty came from the Gentilians, who in the late '20s began to seek a new philosophical orientation, distancing themselves from their teacher and developing a critique of his political choices. Influenced by the many fascists who saw Gentile as a liberal intellectual, these young men redoubled their efforts to shape the culture and in the 1930s allied themselves with Giuseppe Bottai. In time, Bottai became their main point of reference, as he published their work in *Critica fascista* and gathered a group of collaborators who would stay by his side throughout his years in government.

The radical fascists, too, changed after the '20s. Their critique of modernity, their fight to maintain fascism's radical spirit, and their fear of becoming normalized all continued to characterize their thinking. Yet, at the same time, their ideas lost the rebellious quality of the early days of fascism. If we were to summarize a diverse set of personal histories and collective experiences, it would be fair to say that within the culture of the totalitarian regime, the radical fascists took on traits that had once belonged to the revisionists, changing from revolutionaries and warriors into the intellectuals of the regime, and engaged just like the others in building their present and future.

The literary scholar Berto Ricci is a prime example. Ricci was heir to the antimodernist tradition of *Il Selvaggio*, but by 1931 he had founded a new magazine, *L'Universale*, to consistently and repeatedly assert a new "imperialist and universal" form of Italian modernity.

Another branch of 1930s fascist culture consisted of Catholic thinkers. One theory—which still has its supporters among Italian historians—held that the Catholics dominated the regime's culture, especially after 1929, when fascism let its reactionary, conservative colors shine through. Thus, while the Church abandoned the modernist enthusiasms that had emerged at the turn of the century, fascism would benefit from a different kind of theoretical legitimacy than the one Gentile and his students provided. Eugenio Garin, the earliest and most vocal proponent of this theory, believed that fascism's cultural roots could be found in "spiritualism—the philosophy of repentant positivists, existentialists-*cum*-Catholics, and [proponents of] classical metaphysics alike—which accompanied the arc of fascism in official channels from '29 onward."[1] In this same vein, influential scholars from diverse backgrounds and fields have argued that the Church and fascism had a shared foundation, visible, for instance, in the antimodernity of the 1907 encyclical *Pascendi*,[2] and that this shared foundation was the cultural prelude to a political encounter that proved indispensable for the regime. Fascism, in their view, certainly had no wish to become a religious regime, but it would make good use of Catholicism as a tool for building its own ideology.

As we shall see, fascist culture in the 1930s was not the result of traditionalist trends winning out, nor did it stem from Catholic actions, given that the Catholics were unable to dominate a state that essentially viewed their religion as an *instrumentum regni*. Undoubtedly, however, the regime benefited from the contributions of fascist Catholics, and therefore of some Catholic intellectuals who were genuinely fascist, who imagined that they were building a new nation distinct from liberal Italy, and who hoped that fascism would distance itself from Gentile and other representatives of modern philosophy.

Lastly, there were the young fascists. Convinced that it was necessary to distance fascism from "old factions ... disguised with a membership card and a seal of approval,"[3] the young fascists argued that the generation raised during fascism was the only one that had truly absorbed the regime's political and cultural values. Coming of age in the cultural universe created by

the regime, they felt that they were the best representatives of this revolutionary historical period, and they portrayed themselves as the heroes
of the revolution, those who had correctly interpreted fascist doctrine and
should claim their place as the vanguard of a new, truly fascist ruling class.
Many of them, along with some Catholics, ex-radicals, and ex-Gentilians,
would indeed find their place in the pages of Bottai's magazines, as the editor proved capable of bringing together the aims of the radicals and modernists, the demands of the young and old, and the questions of the Catholics
and atheists alike.

Literature

In 1931 Giuseppe Attilio Fanelli and Mario Carli—supporters of radical fascism in the 1920s, as we have seen—published an anthology of fascist writing in which they outlined some criteria for defining fascist literature.[4] The
editors divided the authors into three groups: political writers, artistic writers, and "writers who belong to both categories, but instinctively keep the two
activities separate from one another."[5] Within each group, moreover, Carli
and Fanelli distinguished between revolutionaries and conservatives. The
revolutionaries included former members of the Combat Leagues (*squadristi*) and the first fascists—essentially, all those who "with their writing and
action in the streets had paved the way for the Blackshirts' Revolution,"[6]
who had fought alongside the fascists against the liberal political system,
and who had worked to create a new way of doing politics. The two journalists explained that to be included among the revolutionaries, it was enough
for a fascist writer to have fought "for the triumph of Fascism."[7] Essentially,
the revolutionaries were men born during an earlier historical period, who
accordingly emerged from the ideological legacies that had been overcome
by the advent of the regime. This was an extremely diverse group in which
ex-*squadristi* mingled with ex-nationalists, ex-Futurists, and syndicalists.[8]
In the second group, the conservatives, Carli and Fanelli included writers
who, because of their youth, had not taken part in the political battles of the
immediate postwar period, and who, nine years after the new regime had
taken hold, most fully represented the new face of fascism.[9] Unlike the revolutionaries, the writers who emerged during the fascist period had to show
that they had fully absorbed the principles of the fascist revolution, according to the two editors. As we can see, in this case, too, this was not a question

of specifying a style, but rather of linking individual artists' literary output to the political themes of fascism. From this point of view, the debates over literature had not changed at all since the previous decade.

On the other hand, in the '30s the landscape of fascist literature itself changed, as is clear when we examine a study published in *Critica fascista* in the fall of 1932. In its pages, the assistant editor of Bottai's magazine, Gherardo Casini, defined fascism as "an introduction to modern life, the bearer of a positive, new, and productive Italian way of being," and expressed his hope that Italian literature would have the courage to embrace the spirit of modernity ushered in by the regime.[10] In a later issue of the magazine, the assistant editor declared that fascism, unlike other regimes, was "a Revolution fully engaged in laying the foundations and raising the imposing walls of a new city."[11] Bottai agreed; the editor was engaged during that same period in a fierce debate with Ugo Ojetti, whom he accused of "distinguishing art from politics."[12] Essentially, as Ruth Ben-Ghiat has observed, the primary characteristic of Italian literature in the 1930s was the effort to create a distinctly fascist version of modernity.[13] In the context of this stated faith in a new fascist form of modernity, realism turned out to be the most successful style, as we can see by examining the literary magazines *L'Universale* and *Il Saggiatore*.[14]

L'Universale was founded in Florence in January 1931 by the writers Berto Ricci and Romano Bilenchi,[15] and it frequently published works by Camillo Pellizzi, Roberto Pavese, Diano Brocchi, and Indro Montanelli. It lasted until the summer of 1935, when the regime shut it down. The two editors had previously written for Mino Maccari's *Il Selvaggio*, and in the late '20s they participated in the *Strapaese* debates, fighting on the side of ruralism and attacking bourgeois European culture. And indeed, during that period, Ricci's writings sought "to embody [a] subversive and impassioned Italian tradition completely intertwined with plebeian realism," which was the "enemy of all rhetoric, all wordy and obsequious academese."[16] After his experience with *Il Selvaggio*, Ricci settled his existential crisis and found in literature the sense of purpose he had sought in fascism.

Ricci wrote in his 1931 book *Scrittore italiano* (The Italian writer) that art and politics were indistinguishable from one another, and that it was not possible to imagine "art without a party or a motherland," or "poetry built on the ether of the absolute ... oblivious to the fixed law that is the clash of

civilizations."[17] On the contrary, he thought that writers must play "a political, moral, pedagogical role"—they had to be aware, that is, of their position as fascist writers, subordinating literature to the demands of politics,
but giving voice to a radically totalitarian culture in which art and politics
would play the same "universal function," since both represented the emergence and establishment of a new civilization.[18]

Ricci's thinking was based on a very specific definition of literature. The
editor of *L'Universale* believed that literature was capable of imagining and
describing a new moral and political order without being obliged to theo-
rize it.[19] Indeed, he was convinced that the new fascist civilization was the
fruit of the Italian character—a religious spirit that art managed to capture
and convey. Accordingly, making no effort to disguise his disgust at "philosophy's presumption" that it could explain reality through reason alone,
he noted that "it would be ludicrous to recommend a specific philosophical
outlook to the Italian writer. He can take it or leave it, according to his pref-
erence: if he's a poet, he would do better without it from a pedagogical perspective, because he will always have his own, spiritual philosophy within
himself, consisting more of vibrations than of lines of reasoning."[20]

In Ricci's eyes, "Italianness" should essentially be thought of as a "natural,
not a political fact"—an instinctive, immediate way of being, not the product
of conscious action. To this end he explained that "Italianness . . . is nowhere
and everywhere; it is a temperament, a laugh from [the painter Ottone]
Rosai, a boy's smirk, a market." For Ricci being Italian meant having a certain kind of character, expressing a certain way of being. As he argued, "the
nation precedes the State" and "the best patriotism is a natural occurrence,
not a political one."[21]

This idea of culture was behind the political battle that Ricci ignited
in the pages of *L'Universale*, where he gave voice to a modern, imperialist,
anti-Christian strain of fascism. His imperialism stemmed from his belief
that the regime had a historic global mission to carry out—namely, creating
a new civilization founded on the primacy of Italian culture. Ricci believed
that fascist Italy had a universal message to spread, bringing to fruition
"Dante's Monarchy and Mazzini's Council," imposing its own social and
political model on the entire world, and fighting against nationalist and bourgeois states. As a ferocious enemy of nationalism, which he saw as a political doctrine born of the unholy union of nineteenth-century liberalism and

European powers, Ricci considered his imperialist fascism the best expression of modern politics.

This was not a means of renouncing the attacks on nineteenth-century modernity that he had formulated in *Il Selvaggio* in the late '20s; rather, it was a way of developing them within the ideology of the totalitarian state, and therefore fighting to continuously assert a novel Italian form of modernity "to come, as the very first precondition of national power." For Ricci, "modern" meant "imperialist and global." As Alberto Asor Rosa has observed, the contributors to *L'Universale* were certainly not conservatives.[22] Indeed, Ricci feared that the regime would not have the courage to choose a single path forward and would instead attempt to reconcile dissenting and at times incompatible positions. Accordingly, he placed his hopes in the advent of an anti-Christian, and therefore revolutionary and imperialist, regime. When in 1931 Pope Pius XI issued an encyclical defending Catholic Action after the skirmishes between the government and the Church, Ricci did not miss the chance to launch an attack on the Catholics and explain the nature of his anti-Christian stance.[23]

Il Saggiatore was founded in Rome in April 1930 by three literature and philosophy students at the Sapienza: Giorgio Granata, Luigi De Crecchio, and the above-mentioned Domenico Carella, who were joined by Nicola Perrotti, then a young doctor working to popularize psychoanalytic theories.[24] From the beginning the magazine's contributors wanted to position it as a publication for young fascist intellectuals that would help transform society and the state by articulating a different strain of fascist culture and a different way of doing politics.[25] To outline the culture they believed they represented, the young editors of *Il Saggiatore* published two series that resonated widely. The first, dedicated to the "new generation," appeared in the pages of the magazine from March to June 1932; the second, addressing the "new culture," was the topic of the October 1933 special issue.

In March 1932 *Il Saggiatore* invited several of the regime's well-known intellectuals to respond to three prompts. The first was "Every new generation arises in contrast to the generation that preceded it. Is it possible to speak of this new generation as a clear and decisive break, instead of just the normal contrast?" The second question was related to the characteristics of the generation raised under the regime. *Il Saggiatore*'s young men put the question thus: "Do you recognize in the new generation a clearly defined spiritual attitude that could give new inspiration to culture and life?" The last question was more general in nature: "What do you think are the seeds of a complete spiritual transformation?"[26]

In their essays, *Il Saggiatore*'s contributors argued that Italian society was composed of three generations:[27] the first, the "prewar" generation, were Italians who had participated in World War I and had joined the fascist movement as mature adults; the second had fought in the war and given rise to fascism at a very young age; and the third generation was made up of the young people raised under the fascist regime, who because of their age had not been able to participate in the Great War. According to the *Saggiatore* writers, the "prewar generation" had been brought up in a cultural climate dominated by Croce and Gentile's idealism and, despite the rise of fascism, had not managed to free itself from the ideological abstractions of Italian neo-idealism. This was a generation of "pacifist bourgeois" people who had not understood the spirit of fascism, whether in 1922 or in the years to follow; in the regime they saw "merely a return to order, to the order that the war had hopelessly destroyed."[28] In the second generation, comprising the first fascists, the magazine's contributors recognized the men who had given rise to fascism by voicing their sincere faith in politics. Yet though they had helped create a new phase in the country's history, their efforts too had ultimately been "more rationalist and voluntarist than real" because they had not yet fully absorbed the spirit of fascism, having been born in a different historical era.[29] The only "truly revolutionary" generation was the "very new" one, which was not limited by the past and which, by means of the fascists' new scientific and pragmatic worldview, had defeated idealism: a generation that was the expression of "scientific realism," "collective will," and a "realistic sense of life"; a generation that fought against humanitarian and communist ideologies[30] and rejected individualism; a generation that was truly and definitively anti-Gentilian. In surveying the traits of this new generation in April 1932, Carella explained that Gentile's idealism could not represent the young fascists' political philosophy; like many intellectuals of his generation, he declared himself a realist: "The attempt to try to interpret contemporary political life through the doctrine of idealism is thwarted by reality itself. Today man is desirous of facts, of problems to resolve practically, not of abstract concepts."[31]

In October 1933, as noted above, the magazine published another issue specifying the traits of the new fascist culture for which the *Saggiatore*'s contributors were the spokesmen. In their concluding remarks, the editors wrote: "In modern life politics is the heart of every event: man is a function of it. The freest action, the most intimate thoughts of any individual, do not acquire concrete significance if they are not directly traceable to some political value. Such value is absolutely new: because today it is no longer man with his ideologies and aspirational ideals which politically colors this or that fact, preordains this or that action—but it is LIFE which, through closer economic relationships, faster spiritual exchanges, a greater uniformity of technological tools and, finally, new constellations of interests, determines man politically, barring him from every more or less ideal, more or less utopian, evasion."[32]

For the young fascists behind *Il Saggiatore*, living concretely—that is, thinking about human existence in concrete, productive terms—meant living politically. Indeed, they were confident that politics represented the most important expression of man's life and that gestures, thoughts, feelings, and words had meaning only when they managed to convey political contents. In fascism they saw a modern phenomenon—that is, a regime that, unlike those that preceded it, had known how to transform Italian daily life into a political experience by instantiating a new relationship between politics and ideology. While in all preceding periods the decisions of the ruling classes had been oriented by various political ideologies, in the fascist regime praxis had replaced theory. In this sense, for the magazine's writers, fascism did not have and did not wish to have a defined ideology, because to impose a new order it did not need to apply any political doctrine.

Our survey of this period's magazines would not be complete if we neglected at least a brief discussion of the Catholic monthly *Il Frontespizio* (The frontispiece), which many scholars have seen as uniquely representative of fascist culture in the '30s. *Il Frontespizio* was founded in Florence in 1929 by Enrico Lucatello and Piero Bargellini with the goal of spreading Catholic thought and its distinctive features through Italian literature.[33] Believing that the regime would give Catholics greater pride of place after the Lateran Treaty of 1929, the magazine's contributors declared themselves fierce critics of modern culture and of Gentile's idealism. Another founding contributor,

Giovanni Papini, edited the *Dizionario dell'Omo salvatico* (roughly, Dictionary of the saved wild man) with Domenico Giuliotti—a veritable manifesto
of *Strapaese* Catholicism, in which the two intellectuals inveighed against
modern philosophy and literature, not mincing words in attacking Gentile
and his students.[34] In point of fact, this cultural battle was quite distinct
from the one waged by other Catholics. Renato Moro has emphasized this
point, observing that while an intellectual like Agostino Gemelli, founder
and director of the Catholic University in Milan, "did not posit a pure return
to the past, but imagined a 'new modernity' that was antimodern," seeing
himself as part of the great river of historical development, Papini by contrast championed an "anachronistic" logic "situated beyond civic development" and "was fully conscious of being, on the social and historical level,
au rebours, 'against the current,' 'quixotic and out of sync.'"[35] These same
observations apply to the Catholic intellectual Giuseppe De Luca, who had
joined Bargellini's project in the hope that the new magazine would become
a leader in Catholic culture's fight against idealism.[36]

As critics of modern thought, which they saw as "Enlightenment, positivist, idealist, and historicist,"[37] the staff of *Il Frontespizio* accepted the fascist
regime and imagined that Catholicism would play a decisive role in building the new state. Antonio Miotto claimed as much in 1935, arguing that
Catholics would have to tackle the problem of relating to the modern world
and initiating positive new relationships between politics and religion. This
did not, however, mean that the fascist regime had in fact decided to give
the Catholics a bigger role in cultural production, as is clear when we examine the landscape of Italian philosophy during this period.

The Philosophers of Fascism

After the Second World War, most scholars believed that the school of
thought that best typified Italy's political climate in the 1930s was the Catholic realism that emerged from the crisis of Italian idealism. For instance,
in Garin's opinion the Catholics won the battle between the philosophical
movements fighting to dominate Italian culture because their alliance with
fascism rested on solid political foundations, and because most influential
Italian philosophers sided with them.[38] More recently Franco Restaino has
made a comparable argument, claiming that after the Lateran Treaty, "Gentile felt the blow: despite his many disciples, with his actualism he no longer

served as the sole philosophical point of reference for the regime." According to this way of thinking, the regime, seeking more effective tools for gaining consent among the masses and young people, would find help in the "Italic Catholic realism" that offered itself as the regime's ideology.[39]

In the following pages we propose a different interpretation, arguing that the Catholics' role was decidedly less significant than has been claimed, and delving into the works of thinkers like Francesco Orestano, Julius Evola, and Armando Carlini, who were among the most influential Italian philosophers in the '30s. Does this mean that a philosophy of fascism did exist, after all? We must unquestionably respond in the negative, because fascism never wished to adopt an official philosophy, as Orestano observed: "Despite many vain efforts by individual philosophers to elevate their own thought to the rank of the official or unofficial philosophy of Fascism, Mussolini never left any doubt about this matter: Fascism had its own doctrine, but it neither professed nor adopted any philosophy, whether officially or unofficially. This is not to say that the doctrine of Fascism did not have its philosophical 'components,' but . . . essentially Fascism proved averse to containing itself within any given philosophical system."[40] At the same time, however, the authors we will examine, like the intellectuals we encountered in the previous chapters, concretely engaged with the regime's cultural politics, interrogating the relationship between philosophy and fascism in their research and in some cases taking prominent positions in the regime.

In 1931, when he was both an influential proponent of realism and a fervent fascist, Orestano became president of the Italian Philosophical Society. The honorary president was the Catholic philosopher Bernardino Varisco; the vice-presidents were Emilio Bodrero and the legal philosopher Giorgio Del Vecchio; and the young Catholic scholar (and enthusiastic fascist) Enrico Castelli was general secretary.[41] In 1933, in addition to the aforementioned thinkers, Vittore Marchi, Carmelo Ottaviano, Sergio Panunzio, Giacomo Perticone, Giacomo Tauro, and Erminio Troilo served on the board of directors; all of them dedicated themselves to representing Italian philosophy and collaborating with the regime.[42]

It was in this spirit that Orestano presided over the Eighth National Conference on Philosophy in Rome in October 1933, where he announced to "those who burn with revolutionary passion" that philosophy could finally "provide the weapons needed to free oneself from the false ontologies and false absolutes inherited from the past like so many assets and pieces of property."[43] In fact, in the preceding years Orestano had boldly claimed to have overcome the fundamental problem of modern philosophy—that is, "of reducing everything to subjectivity" and rejecting the principle of objective reality.[44] Positioning himself against this relativistic drift as the main champion of Italian realism, Orestano devoted the first session of the conference to science, providing a platform for young men determined to show how idealism had impeded the development of a positive relationship between science and philosophy. In this forum, Orestano argued that modern science would resolve the problem of the relationship between a subject's lived reality and "ways of being *per se*."[45] To this end he observed that recent developments warranted the establishment of "correspondences, even if symbolic ones," among certain ways of perceiving and thinking "and certain modes intrinsic to a given reality in itself." In other words, Orestano claimed that the symbols used by science had an ontological significance because they translated reality itself—or, as he put it, "the relations that shape reality." [46] As Michele Federico Sciacca has synthesized this position, to go beyond the outcomes of modern philosophy, Orestano proposed a return to classical metaphysics and positivism.[47]

In critiquing modern thought, Orestano asserted the existence of a world independent of philosophy that was materialized in science and politics. He made this claim quite clearly in the late '30s, stating that one of the regime's most revelatory aspects was the fact that, despite having its own doctrine, it had not adopted any one philosophical stance.[48] Analyzing the main features of the doctrine of fascism at length, he located them in a radical refusal of the key political philosophies of the nineteenth century: Enlightenment, liberalism, and historical materialism. Against these, fascism counterposed the "political reconsecration of a religious, Christian, and Catholic ideal" and managed to develop a new ideology whose main trait was the synthesis of opposing ideas. "And above all else: the synthesis of revolution and tradition,"[49] thanks to which, according to Orestano, the regime had signed the treaty with the Catholic church in 1929.

If we wished to find a thinker who expressed a position diametrically opposed to Orestano's, we need look no further than Julius Evola. When he was a young Dadaist painter and proponent of Italian theosophy, Evola proclaimed himself a follower of modern idealism because, in his view, it was the only philosophy that understood that the real world is the world known by mankind—the human world, "the world of which one can speak, even if it's only to say that it's all a mystery."[50] Essentially, in contrast to Orestano, who sought an objective reality and found it in science, Evola located modern philosophy's innovation in the discovery that reality was subjective.

In 1926 Evola began writing for *Critica fascista*, and in December 1927 he summarized his view of politics and philosophy in its pages.[51] His thinking was rooted in a notion of "empire:" a theoretical model proposed by the Roman world, "with that harmonious synthesis of spirituality and politicism, of regality and sacrality, understood by Rome." With the advent of Christianity, the sacrality of politics had been replaced by faith in the equality and liberty of individuals, and in a decidedly worldly, modern notion of politics. In effect, unlike the antimodernist intellectuals among the fascists, Evola believed that modern culture was a product of Christianity itself, not of the Protestant Reformation, which from his point of view had only carried out the work of the early Christians. To "save Italy from the Protestant threat, the Euro-American threat," fascism would have to assert itself as "an anti-Christian revolution" that would reinstate the sacred nature of political power and allow the fascists to rebuild the "empire"—that is, to rebuild a political model based on hierarchy and a sense of the sacred.[52]

Evola was accused of being an atheist by the Catholics and by most fascist intellectuals, who in late 1927 supported the treaty negotiations between the regime and the Church. In the '30s, he redoubled his fight against the traditionalists, and, to this end, in January 1932 noted that many fascists proudly asserted the primacy of politics over culture. In his view, this strong anticulture sentiment, limited to "reclaiming practical life," was certainly not the harbinger of a new "aristocratic and Roman" lifestyle.[53] According to Evola, in fact, a broadly anti-Hegelian stance had spread through Italy, stemming from resentment toward Giovanni Gentile—"hated by many who could not accept that he had so many positions of cultural power, and who think that Hegel and Gentile are the same"; but its adherents were not able to develop a critique of modernity, limiting themselves to superficial traditionalist views, not antimodernist ones.[54] Thus, for Evola, the battle against modernity would take on a very different form from the one described by traditionalists, who were unable to see that the radical fight against modern life would also turn against them.

Such attacks on traditionalism were intertwined with Evola's struggle against modern culture. From the late '30s on, he contributed regularly to Roberto Farinacci's *Regime fascista* and Carlo Costamagna's *Lo Stato*, where he continued to develop these ideas. For Farinacci's paper he worked on the culture section, "Diorama filosofico," where he featured writings by prominent foreign intellectuals and articulated his own ideas about the relationship between philosophy and fascism. Like Orestano, Evola reminded readers that the regime was not aiming to build "an official system of thought." "Fascism," he wrote in January 1935, "is a vision of life," a "way of life" independent of any philosophical orientation. Envisioning history as a progressive decline from a hierarchical world to one ruled by the masses, Evola became the theorist of the myth of empire during those years. He put forth an aristocratic, antimodern notion of politics—a minority position within the Party, where he remained an isolated figure.[55]

From this point of view his position in the regime was quite different from that held by Armando Carlini. Among Gentile's collaborators, Carlini was the one who gained the greatest recognition, even when he decided to abandon his teacher's idealism and seek answers in a different philosophical milieu.[56] In 1921 he was named to the chair of theoretical philosophy at the University of Pisa; in 1922 he became a fascist; and in 1925 he officially joined the Party. In 1927, when he was still one of Gentile's most influential collaborators, he became rector of the university in Pisa. Closely involved in the efforts to make the universities fully fascist, Carlini believed that it was necessary to educate the new generations "from within, not superficially," by creating a "fascist way of experiencing life." Like most fascist intellectuals, he emphasized fascism's religious and antirationalist nature, declaring, "One does not become fascist: one is born that way. Just as one is born a Christian." Accordingly, he argued that young people born and raised "during the war or after the war, or even after the March on Rome," were fortunate in having been born during a revolutionary period.[57]

Unlike Evola and Orestano, Carlini was not a critic of modern philosophy, as he explained in his 1931 *Orientamenti della filosofia contemporanea* (Movements in contemporary philosophy). The book emerged from the need to show which school of thought best expressed "the tone and nature of fascism's mindset and culture."[58] To this end, he asserted that the main proponents of Italian philosophy were the neoscholastic and idealist philosophers,[59] and that he had distanced himself from Gentile not because he himself rejected modern philosophy, but because he had understood that the time had come for a "distillation of idealism in its original precept, so as to explain the question of pure spirituality."[60] This was the beginning of what he would later describe as the most prolific period of his intellectual life, signaled by new thinking about the relationship between religion and philosophy and, we might add (since he omitted it from his autobiography), by his renewed and ever-growing engagement in the cultural world of the fascist regime.[61]

In 1934 Carlini published *Filosofia e religione nel pensiero di Mussolini* (Philosophy and religion in Mussolini's thought), a book in which he demonstrated his distance from Gentile and defined fascist doctrine. In the opening pages he posed a question: "Does Mussolini contain the seed of an idea that, from a philosophical perspective, even in the most rigorous sense, is significant for its originality and capacity for further development?"[62] To this query he responded without hesitation: "Mussolini's temperament is the antithesis of every speculative attitude," and he added that this same consideration could be extended to the "religious question":

> Mussolini is secular, a wholly secular being. He understands and feels the human and historical aspects of religion in general . . . it's true that he is responsible for destroying the Freemasons, and for the Conciliation with the Vatican. But these undertakings were not carried out by him, or in fact justified for reasons other than essentially political or social ones. . . . Not to mention that also in the—shall we say—practical sense, no man seems farther from the ascetic and mystical behavior that characterizes truly, deeply religious souls . . . the morality of the fascism he founded is a wholesale glorification of essentially pagan principles, as many others have pointed out.[63]

Carlini believed that fascism was a modern regime and that its leader was a profoundly secular politician. In this sense he did not construe the regime's fight against the Freemasons or 1929 treaties with the Church as the actions of a conservative or Catholic-leaning government; instead, he traced the motives for such actions back to the regime's political needs. At the same time, he identified the philosophical trends that had influenced Mussolini's cultural and political development. At the turn of the century, according to Carlini, the future fascist leader had been influenced by pragmatism and intuitionism, while during the war years he had subscribed to idealism. This had been a firm conviction, one he publicly declared on multiple occasions, such that idealism, Carlini wrote, was one of the main components of fascist ideology in the 1920s. As a new decade began, however, Mussolini's political thought could no longer be considered an expression of idealist philosophy, since he had profoundly diverged from that school. In this vein, Carlini argued that, in contrast to Mussolini's thought, in idealism man was moved "by the universal spirit," as "depersonalized man" who was missing "a magic word: faith."[64]

Like all the writers we have encountered in the preceding pages, Carlini tried to position himself as the theorist of fascism. In doing so, he ascribed his own intellectual journey to Mussolini—that is, the journey that Carlini himself had taken starting in the 1910s, when he was one of Gentile's closest collaborators, through the late 1920s, when he arrived at spiritualism. This was not a means of proposing a conservative Catholic brand of philosophy, as many scholars have argued, seeing Carlini—like Orestano—as an influential proponent of the union of fascist ideology and Catholic thought. Instead, Carlini had in mind a secular and humanist spiritualism, which is to say a philosophy for fascism that, prior to being Catholic, was decidedly political. He explained as much quite clearly, writing, "Mussolini has spoken many times about a concept of religious fascism and political faith as the defining characteristic of fascism."[65]

In the latter half of the '30s, Carlini wished to assume a position of prestige and power in fascist circles, and like Ugo Spirito, he became one of the fascist intellectuals closest to Bottai. In *Critica fascista*, he examined the problem of fascism's modernity and its relationship to Christianity, arguing that fascism accepted "modernity by stripping it of its antireligious aspect, indeed making this a defining feature." Fascism, therefore, was not merely a "political revolution" but also represented the beginning of a "new civilization" that brought together the best aspects of the past in an original way. So Carlini put it in 1938, at a time when fascism was focused on giving rise to a new civilization in which Jews would have no right to participate.[66]

The Culture of Racism

For many years historians helped to disseminate the reassuring myth that Italians—influenced on the one hand by idealist culture and on the other by

Catholic life—were opposed to the racist policies the regime adopted in 1938. Incapable of atrocities and accustomed over the centuries to cohabitating with Jews, Italians were supposed to have proved themselves "good people," averse to the brutality that characterized National Socialist politics.[67] In reality, the racial laws were not an isolated incident in the regime's history, nor were they a novelty unrelated to its culture, as we shall see. Here we shall limit our discussion to the issues most relevant to the history of fascist culture. We shall attempt to summarize the work of scientists and researchers who tried to develop theoretical support for racist policies; examine the role played by racist intellectuals; and, finally, analyze key cultural figures' reactions to the regime's policies.

As many scholars have noted, between 1922 and 1945 Italian researchers lent their efforts to race-based culture and politics. This included anthropologists, statisticians, demographers, and physicians who were already well known in the scientific community at the turn of the century, when demography and eugenics—the attempt to "perfect" the human race by favoring the procreation of individuals considered "fit" (positive eugenics) or suppressing those individuals considered "unfit" (negative eugenics)—took up the issue of the declining birth rate in many Western countries,[68] a problem exacerbated by the Great War. Tasked by the ruling classes with responding to this crisis (seen at that time as a rampant sign of degeneracy), these scientists were given a much more prominent role in the new regime than they had had in previous governments. In exchange, they offered generous support to totalitarian and racist policies.

As has been widely observed, from the beginning fascism demonstrated its desire to create a new race of rulers and world conquerors. In May 1927, in his famous Ascension Day speech, Mussolini asserted that the fascists would preside over the destiny and health of the race and argued that the strength of a populace was dictated by the number of people in it. In doing so, the premier borrowed an idea from the statistician and demographer Corrado Gini, who propounded an organicist theory of demography and who, in 1926, had been named president of the High Council on Statistics (Istituto nazionale di statistica, or Istat). In keeping with Gini's theories, Mussolini explained that populations, just like living organisms, could be divided into the young, who were capable of proliferating, growing, and conquering territory, and the senescent, who were destined to experience decreasing birth rates and political power, and ultimately to die off. Accordingly, he reminded Italians that the issue of birth rate and procreation was a grave political problem, not a private matter. Thus intensifying the demographic campaign begun two months earlier with the introduction of the bachelor tax, Mussolini mobilized the nation's scientists.[69]

Fascist scientists, understanding that they had a decisive role to play in the regime's racial policies, sprang into action, and between 1928 and 1938 they published an enormous number of tracts and articles about racism and demography. In doing so, they clearly demonstrated the nexus of politics and the development of demographic knowledge.[70] Notable among such thinkers was the anthropologist Nicola Pende, who in 1933 published a book in which he declared that human biotypology had become a political discipline. In *Bonifica umana razionale e biologia politica* (Rational human cleansing and political biology), dedicated to Mussolini and quickly established as one of Italian racism's key points of reference, Pende argued that "the fascist Regime's grand idea was profoundly rooted" in biology—that is, the idea "that individual freedom is determined by collective freedom and interests."[71] Accordingly, he explained, a sick citizen should be seen as a malignant cell, and politics should look to biology to learn operating instructions for human beings. Just as in the human body there is "a principle of vital unity" that regulates "physical and psychic strength," deriving from the "perfect collaboration and interpenetration of the organ system," so too in the constitution of the social organism there were "energetically distinct cellular classes." "And so we have it," Pende wrote, "that the corporative system of the fascist State is precisely copied from the governing system in individual human biology."[72]

Pende's work was not limited to justifying the origins of racism; he also addressed the differences between the theories popular in Germany and those with more currency in fascist Italy. When Mussolini denied the existence of pure races in a 1932 interview with the German journalist Emil Ludwig, Pende took it on himself to comment on the premier's opinion. "Yet again," he asserted, "we fascists, with our approach to the political question of race, have demonstrated our balanced Mediterranean realism in the face of Nordic abstraction and mysticism." Believing that racial policies based on prejudices and errors would lead to "comical and illogical" results, Pende wished to be very clear on this point. He stated that racism had a biological foundation but added that recognizing a biological basis for race did not mean believing in the existence of pure races, because within a single nation one encountered "ethnic polyvalency."[73] He was in no way denying a biological basis for race but rather pointing out the error of those who, like the Germans, thought that pure races existed.

Pende was a firm believer in the existence of different racial types based on physical and psychological traits, which could be masked by environment and upbringing. He argued that politics should intervene in order "to improve the innate qualities of every bloodline with the natural tool of selection, with an anthropocentric state body that aims, as zootechnics does for animals, to select and raise varieties of the plant 'man' without pollutants, thanks to the physical and mental education of the population."[74] As we can see, despite his harsh criticism of the German racists, Pende nonetheless stressed the importance of using the tools of politics to select a new line of Italians and to improve it physically and psychologically; as a scientist, he believed that human biology should form the basis for political decisions.

In reality, setting aside the question of the origins of racism, such arguments testify to the willingness of fascist scientists (like many other Italian intellectuals) to offer significant support to the totalitarian regime, and to bend their disciplines to political ends. In this sense it is true that scientific culture offered its theoretical support to the fascist project of creating a new Italian race. This does not mean, however, that racial policy was the product of Italian science in the interwar period. It was not that the fascists became racists because they decided to enact the scientists' proposals; in fact, they did not codify any single scientific theory of race. On the contrary, they were racist because they believed they were part of a dominant race that would subjugate other men, modifying them in their image. For their part, the scientists enthusiastically welcomed fascism because it created a new alliance between the social sciences and politics. Like the philosophers, writers, and architects—indeed, like all fascist intellectuals—these scientists seized the opportunity to use the power the regime granted them as consultants to totalitarianism.

In 1937 the first racist laws were inflicted on the African colonies, forbidding Italian citizens to have "conjugal relations with any subject of Italian East Africa or any foreigner,"[75] specifying a punishment of up to a year in prison. In February 1938 Mussolini charged the anthropologist Guido

Landra with putting together a research department within Minculpop to support the ministry's racist agenda. After a series of clashes among scientists over whether race was a biological or a cultural trait, Landra, who was a supporter of the minority, biological theory, set to work preparing a manifesto for racist scientists. First published in *Il giornale d'Italia* in July 1938, it also appeared on August 5 in the first volume of the magazine *La difesa della razza* (The defense of the race), founded by Telesio Interlandi and subsidized by the regime to accelerate its racist agenda.[76] The manifesto's ten propositions asserted the existence of race on the basis of biological principles. The signers declared that Italians were living under a regime waging a constant battle over racism; they emphasized the importance of preserving Italians' physical and psychological traits and argued that Jews were not a part of the Italian race. Though the racist scientists who believed in the biological origins of race would find no further platforms for expressing their views, the battles over race and anti-Semitism intensified.[77]

To oversee the enforcement of racial laws, the Directorate General for Demography and Race, the so-called Demorazza, was created under the Ministry of Internal Affairs in August 1938. It immediately mandated a census of Italian Jews and foreign residents in Italy. The main goal of the 1938 survey was to draw a clear dividing line between Jews, who shortly thereafter would be subjected to persecutory laws, and all other citizens. And indeed, on September 7, 1938, the first anti-Jewish regulation was enacted, requiring that non-Italian Jews—who were less well integrated into their communities and thus more easily isolated and persecuted—be deported. In the months that followed, additional laws would forever change the fabric of Italian Jewish communities, "Aryanizing" Italian schools and universities, banning "mixed" marriages, setting limits on owning property, running businesses, and practicing professions, firing Jews from public offices, and barring them from the armed forces.

Italian intellectuals did not raise a single protest over the racial laws that enacted discrimination right under their noses in the education sector.[78] In fact, they actually contributed to creating a cultural landscape in which the state's anti-Semitism could flourish—and then they reaped the benefits by rushing to take up the vacant posts of their Jewish former colleagues. For this reason, Giorgio Israel has urged us to reject both arguments that attempt to diminish fascist anti-Semitism and those that attempt to frame it as a defining characteristic of fascist ideology.[79] In reality, anti-Semitism was not a defining characteristic of fascist ideology—but racism certainly was, as we can clearly see from the many influential political and cultural figures who eagerly declared their racism in the late '30s. In 1937 Julius Evola wrote *Il mito del sangue* (The legend of blood); Giulio Cogni published *Il razzismo* (Racism); and Paolo Orano wrote *Gli ebrei in Italia* (Jews in Italy).[80] In 1939 Leone Franzì, another, less well known theorist of fascist anti-Semitism, wrote a book invested with the trappings of authority because it was published by the National Institute of Fascist Culture—in other words, by the main cultural arm of the regime. In its pages, Franzì argued that for fascists race was understood as a political community and not as a biologically determined group. Rejecting any biological basis as deterministic, Franzì denied that a community could be founded on a fact instead of a choice but asserted that such a choice could be experienced as naturally occurring. Comparing Italian racism with the National Socialist variety, Franzì asked how one might reconcile the idea of empire—an idea tied to the desire to conquer and thus to a political plan—with the idea of a biological race. Science had lost, Franzì claimed, "and now politics speaks."[81] In this vein he cited an exchange he had had with certain German intellectuals who admired the Italian laws targeting foreign Jews: "We are especially gratified, Professor Gross said to me, by your laws pertaining to foreign Israelites, insofar as, despite our strong desire to do so, we have not dared to attack such elements, given the consequences that would likely result due to their possession of foreign passports."[82]

The book's thesis was quite clear: Italian racism had proven itself superior to the German variety because "the former had shaped the spirit and the desire of a populace according to the spirit and desire of a Man capable of violently changing the course of his country's history. The latter [i.e., the German variety], on the contrary, [had been shaped] by means of a man who had brought forth the repressed ideals of a populace that could not find within itself the strength for the rapid rebirth that events required."[83]

The key point, Franzì continued, was that "ours is a type of racism that can be universal because it is political. Theirs is at bottom a type of 'biological nationalism.'"[84] Essentially, after the anti-Semitic laws were introduced, fascist ideologues wished to banish any suspicion that their decision to adopt the new laws could be tied to their relationship with their German allies. And, indeed, in the *Dizionario di politica* published by the Party in 1940, the fascists claimed that anti-Semitism had been present in their movement from the beginning.[85]

It has often been written that fascist intellectuals did not protest against racial policies because they could not express any criticism of the totalitarian regime, and that, in any case, Italian culture was not really racist. It merely acquiesced to anti-Semitic laws that it not only did not approve of but did not actually recognize as its own. This is also how Giovanni Gentile's behavior has been interpreted, when, for instance, scholars have recalled his support for Paul Oskar Kristeller, a lecturer in German at the Scuola Normale in Pisa, whom the philosopher helped to flee Italy and find a position in the United States in 1939. Scholars have pointed out that Gentile's philosophy could in no way be linked to anti-Semitism,[86] reiterating that there was no room in his philosophical and political thought for materialistic conclusions, much less for the idea of race.[87] One could retort that in the National Institute of Fascist Culture's 1939 definition of racism there are no naturalistic criteria, and that, on the contrary, as we have seen, for the fascists racism meant identifying a political community, not a biological reality. We might also note that Gentile helped Kristeller on a purely personal level—that his intercession was on behalf of a young man whose studies he had closely followed and whom he loved, and that the episode does not therefore constitute an example of his distance from fascist anti-Semitism.

In the preceding pages we have seen how Gentile saw himself as a forerunner of fascism. This, along with his closeness with Mussolini, is precisely why he intervened again and again in the regime's policies, and why he did not hesitate to express his dissent at other crucial moments, as happened between 1927 and 1929, when he felt it necessary to repeatedly state his opposition to the regime's treaty negotiations with the Catholic church. Are we therefore to imagine that Gentile thought it more important to voice his opposition to the Lateran Treaty than to the racial laws? The truth is that in the pages of his *Giornale critico della filosofia italiana* (Critical journal of Italian philosophy), not only was there no condemnation or protest; there was not even the slightest indication of one. Gentile's behavior was consistent with that of most Italian intellectuals and university professors, who, as noted above, hurried to assume the chairs and positions vacated by Jewish colleagues who were forced by the 1938 fascist legislation to leave their posts.[88]

The Fascist City

The totalitarian nature of fascist culture, which we have attempted to sketch in the previous pages, also typified Italian architecture between 1922 and 1943, perhaps even more than it did other cultural spheres.[89] The regime's desire to design, build, and change the day-to-day life of Italians, all the while demonstrating its ability to create a new civilization, was unprecedented. It began with transforming public spaces—and the results are still visible today in many Italian cities. Yet instead of analyzing the relationship between this new kind of public space and politics, most historians of architecture have focused instead on two distinct and opposing trends in interwar architecture, rationalism and neoclassicism, as a means of arguing that fascist architecture lacked its own characteristic style. According to some scholars, what is more, these different styles correspond to two different ways of interpreting fascism: the proponents of rationalism are supposed to represent a revolutionary, modern form of fascism, while those more closely tied to tradition and therefore to neoclassicism represent a moderate, conservative strain.[90] According to Bruno Zevi, for instance, only the neoclassicists, and in particular Marcello Piacentini, can be seen as true fascists, while Giuseppe Terragni, Giuseppe Pagano, and Edoardo Persico, all influential rationalist architects between the two wars, should be seen as antifascist. In reality, as we shall argue here, the differences between these two schools of thought were rather less prominent than the relationship that the regime instantiated with architects, and less significant overall than the contributions these architects made to fascism.[91]

Within the rationalist movement there were various styles that repurposed the vocabulary of recent European tradition. At the heart of this movement were the young architects of the so-called Gruppo 7, which was created in Milan in 1926 by a group including Giuseppe Terragni. In the late '20s, Terragni founded the Italian Movement for Rationalist Architecture (Movimento italiano per l'architettura razionalista, or MIAR), to bring together various regional expressions of this trend. The rationalists believed that with fascism the moment for "new architects" had arrived, "as the narrow mindset of [their] forebears from the Umbertine period [i.e., the late nineteenth century] had matured and Mussolini's conquests had exuberantly flowered."[92] In this way they clearly articulated their desire to be identified with the architecture of the fascist state. In his 1931 article "Architettura, arte di Stato" (Architecture, State art), Pier Maria Bardi explained that rationalist architecture was the only architectural style capable of interpreting fascism and representing the "mission" that Mussolini wished to carry out and bring to the world.[93] With this goal in mind, from the early 1930s on the rationalists made themselves into a bona fide political and academic establishment, entering competitions that the regime created and involving architects in a new way of doing city planning.[94] Thus, contrary to what historians like Zevi have claimed, the rationalists were not outsiders in the regime but, rather, saw themselves as representing the only real expression of fascist architecture.

On the other side were the critics of the avant-garde, who were closely linked to the Novecento group that emerged in Milan in the early '20s, aiming to popularize a new artistic style as an alternative to turn-of-the-century avant-garde experiments. As we have seen, in the literary sphere Novecento's most influential member was Massimo Bontempelli; among architects the best-known "anti-rationalists" were Gio Ponti, Emilio Lancia, Ottavio Cabiati, Giovanni Muzio, and Marcello Piacentini, who was especially influential in the realm of city planning. Considered by many to be the regime's architect, Piacentini theorized and built an urban landscape of neoclassical and theatrical monuments, directly opposed to the rigor of the rationalists. This was a kind of simplified neoclassicism that featured symmetrical plans and classical architectural details like marble surfaces, colonnades, columns, and arches.

As Richard Etlin has noted, despite the debates between these different schools and the disagreement among rationalist architects and those fascists who did not always recognize as their own an art form that was also successful abroad, fascism "favored the appropriation of the rationalist aesthetic in service of the fascist cause." Such a dynamic was at play, for instance, in the Exhibition of the Fascist Revolution (Mostra della rivoluzione fascista), organized in Rome in 1932 to mark the ten-year anniversary of the regime's ascension to power.[95]

Opening ten years after the March on Rome, the exhibition welcomed such huge throngs of visitors that it remained on view for two years, only to be repeated in 1937, 1939, and again in 1942.[96] Mussolini was personally engaged in the planning and demanded that the exhibit "be a thing of today, therefore extremely modern and daring, with no sentimental attachments to the decorative styles of the past," discarding solemn, "Roman-ticizing" elements. The period's most famous painters participated, led by Mario Sironi, as did the most influential rationalist architects, like Terragni, Adalberto Libera, and Mario De Renzi, united by their ideological fervor and their desire to build monuments that could respond to Mussolini's dictates. As Margherita Sarfatti wrote, the exhibit, which recounted the history of fascism from 1914 to 1922, aspired to be history in action, history lived and presented in a tangible way, not from a contemplative distance.[97] Drawing near, a visitor would be struck by the aerodynamic black, red, and silver façade of the Exhibition Hall, whose geometric purity was meant to symbolize the order created by the regime's totalitarianism. Four enormous fasces eighty feet high stood in front of it, resembling smokestacks, along with two twenty-foot-tall Xs representing the regime's ten-year anniversary.[98]

While the rationalist architects worked on the public-facing walls and the arrangement of interior spaces, Sironi created one of the most important galleries. A Futurist, early fascist, and radical artist, Sironi had begun to paint deserted, silent urban landscapes in the '20s. He deployed techniques borrowed from Giorgio De Chirico, removing the energy and movement of Futurist landscapes from the cities he painted. To lend an epic quality to the urban landscape, where the only animated objects were streetcars and trucks, in 1926 he began painting allegorical scenes, with figures appearing in barren, incomplete, or altered spaces. In the early '30s he began work on a series of fishermen, farmers, and workers, whose dimensions seemed limited only by the size of the canvas: enormous men painted in an exaggerated, aggressive, anguished chiaroscuro. The most influential fascist painter, the one most committed to sharing his talents with the regime, was an artist who fought against the bourgeois values of naturalism inherited from the nineteenth century and instead painted workers. He wanted to evoke in his viewers a kind of catharsis prompted by the epic events depicted by his canvases and murals. The work of art would be a catalyst and the artist a maker of myths.[99] Sironi achieved this aim through mural paintings, which he described as "social painting *par excellence*" because they could work on the popular imagination more directly than any other form of painting. "The current renaissance in mural painting, in particular in frescos," he wrote in a 1933 manifesto, "facilitates an approach to the question of fascist art. In fact: the practical destination for mural paintings (public buildings, everyday places with a civic function), the governing laws, and the artist's intimate knowledge of architecture, all prevent him from falling prey to improvisation and glib virtuosity."[100] According to Sironi, therefore, the goal of fascist art was to transform the city via a shared effort in which painters, architects, and urban planners collaborated to achieve the regime's plans.

In effect, planning cities, whether by revolutionizing the shape of existing cities or designing those founded *ex novo*, was one of fascism's decisive challenges: a task that could concretely measure the intensity of its revolutionary force.[101] There were various factors behind the enthusiasm for meeting this challenge, from demographic to economic ones, that are outside the scope of our discussion here; but there was also an intuition that planning cities would give rise to an important means of imagining the new Italy.[102] In fact, urban planning—which was much discussed starting in the '30s, as we can see from the establishment in 1930 of a National Institute dedicated to it—was a key point of contact between modernization and fascism, as it "rationalized" historic city centers, rethought the relationship between the country and the city, and founded new cities that, in their entirety, gave shape to the myth of the new fascist community. Old cities were accordingly subjected to radical "renewal" projects that continued and extended work begun in the Umbertine era, modifying it by further simplifying space and inserting into ancient landscapes unmistakably modern features. The new ones, meanwhile, arose under different stars in many regions, in particular in Lazio, where the Pontine Marshes were being reclaimed.[103] This movement to found new cities spanned the entire decade and culminated in the early '40s with the construction in Rome of the EUR (Esposizione universale di Roma) district, then called the "Esposizione del '42" or "E42."

The idea of building a new city on the edge of the capital arose from Rome's bid to host the 1942 World's Fair, directly after the Ethiopian occupation. Clearly the idea was closely linked to empire building. The Italian section of the Fair, with its temporary and permanent buildings celebrating the history of Roman and Italian civilization, was intended to serve as the nucleus of a new fascist imperial Rome. E42 was meant to be the most grandiose urban expression of this new fascist Roman culture: a monumental complex that architecturally, symbolically, and functionally represented a new idea of man, politics, and the state.[104] And through E42, detached from the historic city center but an effluence of it, Rome would become "the capital of a country in which past, present, and future" were "finally connected."[105]

It may seem paradoxical that the fascists decided to use a fair as the impetus for building a city, constructing something permanent on the basis of something so temporary. But in fact there is nothing strange about this if one considers the fact that from the mid-1920s on, exhibitions were one of the regime's primary tools for disseminating propaganda and concretizing their worldview. As we have seen, exhibitions were the site of the fascists' most successful efforts to concretize the totalitarian notion that politics and culture were one and the same, amalgamating eclectic styles via a unified goal: to make the myths of fascism visible through a sacred experience of politics.[106]

On December 26, 1936, a law was passed designating Rome as the site of the World's Fair in 1942, the twentieth year of the fascist era. The fair would feature various nations' contributions to the development of civilization. The same law established an autonomous body with legislative capacity, directly reporting to the premier, and financed by state contributions and proceeds from the fair itself. The executive portion of the project began on April 26, 1937, when Mussolini visited the site of the future complex and planted a Roman pine tree. Two months later, the general commissioner of the fair, Vittorio Cini, publicized the goals of E42: to affirm the power and prestige of fascist Italy in all sectors and to realize Mussolini's plans for a new city—a version of Rome oriented toward the sea. As for the style in which the pavilions would be built, Cini confirmed that the fair would meet the demand to be both modern and historic: "an understanding of Rome as eternal and universal will reign in the inspiration and execution of buildings destined to last, such that in fifty or a hundred years their style will neither age nor, God forbid, appear stale."[107]

The new site was traversed by the Via dell'Impero, a large roadway that on one side linked E42 to the center of Rome, proceeding north until it reached the Mussolini Forum, and on the other side stretched to Ostia and the Tyrrhenian Sea. The road added to the urban transformations that had already been made to the Fori quarter, the Colosseum, and Piazza Venezia, and served as the major artery for the new Rome, a city that was modern and monumental at the same time.

It is beyond the scope of our analysis here to delve into the debates that accompanied the planning and building of E42, which also touched on

Rome's future urban development. We can, however, note that architects from diverse schools of thought were called upon to help design and develop the new district, under Marcello Piacentini's leadership. There was no shortage of debate during the competitions the regime sponsored for the design of permanent structures, from the Palazzo dei Congressi (Convention Center) to the Palazzo della Civiltà Italiana (Palace of Italian Civilization), which remains one of the most celebrated buildings of the Ventennio. Nonetheless, Italy's most influential architects worked to create E42's most important monuments and buildings in accordance with a "maximalist design"—that is, in a style that strove to reconcile an aesthetic of grandiosity and monumentality with the principles of rationalism.[108] And indeed, the EUR district was conceived of as a representation of an eternal Rome that had returned in the modern era.[109] As Etlin has observed, the rationalists who worked on the early designs for EUR had high hopes that they would prevail, especially considering that a few years before they had won competitions to design and build Florence's central train station along with the town of Sabaudia in the province of Lazio. In reality, however, as Piacentini put it, the new architecture for the World's Fair in Rome needed to define the "great era of Mussolini" in a style that could not be pigeon-holed as either rationalist or classical because it was instead "*littorio*" (i.e., fascist).[110] This was a new type of architecture that would synthesize imperial grandeur with the architects' plans, as we can see in the influential structures the young rationalists built: the Palazzo dei Congressi and the Palazzo della Civiltà Italiana. "Modernity and monumentality, rationalism and classicism were to be fused together in the service of an imperial vision of the Fascist state"[111]—a vison perfectly embodied during those same years by Giuseppe Bottai.

7

Cultural Politics and Intellectuals in the 1940s

The School Charter and *Primato*

In the preceding chapters we have encountered Giuseppe Bottai many times, since he was a key player in fascist culture from the early 1920s on. In those years Bottai was the leader of the revisionist branch of fascism and the main supporter of a modern totalitarian notion of fascism. He believed that fascism had not gained power simply to restore a premodern political order but, rather, that it belonged to the tradition of great European revolutions, and that the regime would show the world an alternative modernity quite distinct from that produced by the nineteenth century. This is why Bottai was one of Gentile and his followers' primary allies in the early years. He believed that the philosopher had contributed to developing and diffusing a fascist school of thought, and that defining the movement ideologically would strengthen the identity of the entire regime.

His certainty about that contribution had already begun to waver by the late 1920s, when he stopped seeing Gentile as the regime's ideological guide and lost faith in the importance of developing fascist political theory. From that point on, he was the politician most attentive to the regime's cultural politics, the main proponent of an idea of fascism that could unite modernists and traditionalists, Catholics and secularists, early fascists and university students, Gentilians and anti-Gentilians alike.

In February 1939, when he had been Minister of National Education for a little over two years, Bottai introduced the School Charter (Carta della scuola) to the Grand Council of Fascism:[1] a policy document containing twenty-nine declarations that laid the foundations for the new fascist school system. The motivating principle was articulated in the first declaration, which went like this: "Within the moral, political, and economic unity that is the Italian Nation, and which is entirely fulfilled by the Fascist State, the Schools, that first bedrock of solidarity for all social forces, from the family to the Corporation and the Party, shape the human, political consciousness of the new generations."[2]

The primary objective of Bottai's reform was thus "the complete education of the new fascist man." For this reason the charter defined the schools as essentially political and rejected the idea of culture as a matter of personal growth for an individual. Its second declaration asserted that the schools, the Italian Youth of the Lictor (Gioventù italiana del littorio, or GIL), and the Fascist University Groups (Gruppi universitari fascisti, or GUF) would all become "a single tool for fascist education," and that young Italians would be required to participate in these groups from a very early age up until they turned twenty-one. "This service," the charter explained, "consists in attending school and the GIL from four to fourteen years of age, and for those who do not continue their studies beyond that age, to continue attending [the GIL] until the age of twenty-one." University students would have to participate in the GUF, which, like the other youth organizations, had now become obligatory. In addition to defining goals for the schools, Bottai introduced two other novelties into Italian student life: the *libretto personale* ("personal booklet"—a service log) and the incorporation of work experience into the scholastic curriculum. Both changes aimed to strengthen the ties between schooling and politics.[3]

Personal service logs recorded students' performance in the classroom and in the military training undertaken by GIL members. Grades for behavior took notes from the GIL into account, meaning that academic evaluations were clearly linked to political activities.[4] Because of the other new element introduced by the charter—work as a school subject— manual labor was for the first time framed within an educational system as a pedagogical tool and a means of fostering young people's integration into society. Contrary to the traditional educational divide between humanities and vocational subjects, which had been firmly ensconced in the 1923 reform, the charter's fifth declaration stated that work should be "taught by the State as a social duty," and that it would play a role in the curricula "from elementary school on up through all other grades and types." Accordingly, "special work shifts, regulated and managed by the scholastic authorities, in workshops, factories, fields, and at sea," would help cultivate the productive social conscience proper to the corporative system.[5]

In May 1939 Bottai presented the charter in the Senate, to unite "the work of the schools with the GIL, the discipline of culture with that of physical and military education, the meditative cult of tradition with that of action that forges ahead and turns to the future."[6] He made the same argument in *Critica fascista*, where in March 1939 he wrote at length about Gentile's reform and his opinion of the effect the philosopher had had on fascism. The minister clearly stated that the School Charter was not intended to be a "counterreform" to Gentile's reform. And he added that, having acquired the values set forth in 1923, it was necessary to move forward— that is, to "create . . . a School that does not simply and generically strive for the cultural values Fascism recognizes as valid and for a generic fascist mentality, but [rather] a School that is naturally incorporated into the system through which national life articulates itself and unfolds; [a School] that lives and participates in that fascist mentality we feel today—which after 17 years laden with spiritual and historical events has clarified and enriched the fundamental intuition of Mussolini's Revolution."[7] These same ideas were set forth in a book edited by the Ministry of National Education, which traced the history of fascist educational policy from Gentile's reform through Bottai's, the "starting and ending points" of the road to "fascisizing" the schools.[8]

Bottai did not need to recognize the value of the 1923 reform, or to acknowledge any of the philosopher's virtues, since by 1939 their relationship was far from what it had been in the early years. He truly believed that Gentile had laid the foundations for a "fascist worldview," but by the late '30s his reform could no longer meet the regime's needs. Framing things thus, Bottai gave the philosopher more credit than he did anyone else, including Fedele, De Vecchi, and especially Belluzzo, Giuliano, and Ercole. When considering fascist educational policy, Gentile remained his primary point of reference; and when comparing the School Charter with the 1923 reform, which had arisen as part of a broad cultural program, Bottai compared himself to Gentile, presenting himself as the star of a new fascist policy, the creator of the regime's new culture and education.

In the press, too, most commentators compared the two reforms. For instance, the young pedagogue Luigi Volpicelli credited Gentile with having introduced the idea that "education is autodidacticism, the free and unfettered development of our spirituality."[9] Yet he stressed that only with Bottai's reform had the regime eliminated the traditional division between classical and vocational education and begun the process of integrating man into society. Accordingly, he was proud to announce, with the advent of fascism, "the first and most exemplary popular revolution of modern times: the masses have entered the bourgeois schools, multiplying institutions and classrooms and throwing the traditional hierarchies into confusion."[10]

Like Volpicelli, everyone who participated in this conversation pointed out the need to move beyond the 1923 reform.[11] Paolo Orano, professor of fascist history and doctrine at the University of Perugia, claimed that Italian schools had finally become one of the totalitarian state's greatest achievements, with the help of its institutions, methods, and spirit, "such that there is perfect continuity from the schools to private life and from there to public life."[12] Armando Carlini, a frequent contributor to *Critica fascista* in the late 1930s, made the same claim. He too wished to tease out the differences between the School Charter and Gentile's reform, and in this vein he argued that the new reform "fundamentally" overturned "the prevailing notion of education" up until that point. Like Orano, Carlini saw the charter as revolutionary in that it framed education not as a matter of individual development but, rather, as something that "first and foremost" affected "the Nation, that is to say society and the State."[13]

In effect, as we have suggested, Bottai's project represented totalitarian fascism's response to the conflict between various currents in culture and politics—the triumph of those who had been able to politically synthesize fascism's various animating spirits in a way that satisfied both anti-Gentilians, like Costamagna, and intellectuals who had collaborated with Gentile for years, like Carlini, Spirito, and Pellizzi. We encounter another important instance of this approach in the magazine *Primato* (Primacy), which Bottai began editing in 1940 and which in the postwar period became famous as an opposition publication. In reality, the magazine brought together young fascist intellectuals, modernists and antimodernists, anti-Gentilians and ex-Gentilians, all united in believing that they had solved the problem of making the Italian schools fascist, all celebrating the achieved fusion of culture and politics, and all in agreement that fascism was a revolutionary, modern, total-itarian regime.[14] *Primato* was, in short, a magazine for young fascist intel-lectuals, as their writings up until 1943 unequivocally demonstrate.

In February 1941 the historian Carlo Morandi responded to a question *Primato* posed about the relationship between university life and students' extracurricular lives, describing students in the early '40s thus: "There's a profound difference between this generation of students and that of ten or twenty years ago: fewer purely literary interests, more advanced political ones."[15] The literary critic Luigi Rosso expressed a similar view: "Our politi-cal life was 'a little modern world,' in which everyone, though active in dif-ferent parties, was united and recognized one another as brothers.... Today the mood has shifted among young people; to speak of the 'fatherland' would seem milquetoast to them, [and] memories of our little modern world in '14 have, alas, come to seem ancient. Above and beyond the fatherland, a new political religion has been taking shape."[16]

Luigi Volpicelli even claimed that by then, in 1940s fascist Italy, the dom-inant political culture was indistinguishable from academic political culture. In fact, he believed that "the time when universities disdained the third page [i.e., the cultural page of the newspaper], and preferred tomes to articles, or academic publications to immediate, essential observations," was long gone.[17] Pellizzi made similar arguments. Named director of the National Institute of Fascist Culture in April 1940—thanks to Bottai, who made a case for him to Mussolini[18]—Pellizzi declared in March 1941 that there was absolutely no distinction between university life and students' extracurricular lives. The challenge facing fascist education, in his view, had more to do with the regime's organizing efforts. Pellizzi believed that in a totalitarian regime like the fascist one, it was necessary to maximize contact between universities and political bodies in order to continuously involve academics "in the admin-istrative and political-educational work of the Regime."[19] For this reason he did not dwell at length on the relationship between politics and culture, which, like most contributors to *Primato*, he saw as a problem that had already been solved.[20]

Dizionario di politica

We find another clear declaration of the new totalitarian culture in the pages of the Fascist Party's *Dizionario di politica* (Dictionary of politics), which was published in four volumes in 1940 with the help of various intellectuals willing to collaborate on the project.[21] Its director was the philologist Antonino Pagliaro, who was professor of comparative literature and classical languages from 1934 on and one of the best-known figures in Rome's School of Linguistics, as well as a teacher of fascist doctrine for the politics courses organized by Rome's fascist organizations. In 1933 he published a study of Mussolini's thought: a slim volume in which each chapter consisted simply of his commentary on one of Il Duce's most famous sayings.[22] Good fascist that he was, Pagliaro devoted himself to developing the *Dizionario* project together with Guido Mancini, who directed the Party's Ufficio studi e legislazione (Office of Research and Legislation).[23] When Pagliaro announced its publication in the pages of *Civiltà fascista* (Fascist civilization) in January 1940, he stressed the political character of the work. Unlike the *Enciclopedia italiana*, the *Dizionario* was to be an expression of "politics in action, which included everything that could benefit the rigorous fascist spiritual training of the new generations, freeing them from the superstructures through which demo-liberalism believed itself to be stabilizing people's lives."[24]

Alongside the young men enrolled in the PNF's political education courses, the regime's most influential intellectuals—whom we have encountered in the preceding pages—contributed to the dictionary.[25] Carlo Costamagna was entrusted with several entries that were important in defining fascist doctrine, including "Law," "Nation," "Nationality," and "State"; Sergio Panunzio wrote the entry for "Union"; Luigi Volpicelli took on "Idealism" and "Intellectualism," among others; while Delio Cantimori wrote "National Socialism" and entries on German history. Among the many contributors we should note two historians with very different backgrounds who nonetheless shared an interest in the history of political thought: Felice Battaglia and Carlo Curcio. Battaglia and Curcio played big parts in developing the dictionary, and their work shows how two radically different orientations could meet on the ground of the Party's initiatives. One stemmed from Gentile's school and represented modern philosophy; the other originated in critiques of modernity starting in the '30s.

Battaglia had earned a law degree in Rome in 1925, attending Gentile's Roman lectures, and in 1927 became a lecturer in philosophy of law.[26] In the *Enciclopedia italiana*, where he wrote the entries for "Democracy," "Party," and "State," Battaglia argued that Gentile's political philosophy was the cornerstone of fascist thought.[27] He observed:

> The fascist concept of the State, the advanced concept of the State that characterizes Fascism, certainly also derives from the speculative re-evaluation of the State enacted by idealism; but even more so it originates in the need for an integration of and with the State, which, even if it had been barely visible in the theoretical system, practically speaking had not come to fruition as expected. Of this Fascism was acutely aware, whence the pragmatic nature of its doctrine of the State, which should not, however, make us forget its idealization in Fascism, which was ever-present, in contrast to any other political movement.[28]

According to Battaglia, Gentile had given fascism a philosophical definition of the state, but in the political sphere fascism had independently developed the re-evaluation the idealist philosopher had called for. In the preface to his *Scritti di teoria dello Stato* (Writings on the theory of the state), Battaglia asserted that these essays were conceived in the spirit of idealism and of a theory of the state "to cooperate in studying the political edifice that is rising up before our eyes."[29] With this goal in mind, Battaglia wrote 133 entries for the 1940 dictionary, with a careful eye to the political and ideological character the Party wished to give the entire project. In fact, in the many entries he edited, he never missed an opportunity to compare the topics and figures treated therein with contemporary political topics and figures. Such was the case, for instance, with the entry on "Declaration of Rights," where he argued that the Work Charter (Carta di lavoro), ratified by the fascists in 1927, was superior to British labor laws, to the 1789 Declaration of the Rights of Man and the Citizen, and to the French Constitution of 1795.[30] In his entry for "Enlightenment," on the other hand, after a lengthy reflection on the merits of the Enlightenment and on its modernity, Battaglia observed: "The concessions we have made should not lead us to forget the points at which our own concept firmly opposes enlightenment thought, nor the obvious limits of the latter. The man whom enlightenment celebrates for being [enlightened] too often loses contact with the state and is ignorant of all political bodies."[31]

This argument was quite similar to the one Bottai proposed in 1925, which we examined in chapter 4—an idea that was common among the fascists closest to Gentile in the early '20s, who highlighted fascism's modernity. To such an interpretation, as we have seen, the radical fascists responded by claiming that fascism offered a response to modernity's failings, and that its defining trait was the affirmation of traditional values. Twenty years later, in the early '40s, the Party welcomed Battaglia's musings in the *Dizionario* in praise of the virtues of the Enlightenment, the French Revolution, and Rousseau. In his entry on the Genevan writer, in fact, Battaglia traced his thought starting from the *Discourse on Inequality*, recalling that Rousseau had initiated "those profound perspectives on the state that, through German idealism," had arrived in Italy. He was, therefore, the harbinger of the state as freedom and authority, "of a rational value that expresses itself in each individual, soul of their soul, to use Mussolini's energetic term."[32] In the entry on Sorel, Battaglia wrote that the French theorist's vitality and urgency stemmed from that strain of ethics which distanced him from socialism, and which "even with all its limits, [brought] him close to antisocialist movements, and in particular to Fascism."[33] In a brief entry for the early Italian socialist thinker Carlo Pisacane, Battaglia argued that the absence of mass revolutionary action—an absence that Pisacane protested and decried—explained "the lack of a unified educational system and related crises up until [the arrival of] Fascism," which took up those very problems of the public, its education, and its needs.[34]

If Battaglia's contributions were those of a philosopher of law who subscribed to Gentile's school of thought, Curcio, who wrote more than thirty entries for the *Dizionario*, had a very different philosophical and political trajectory. Curcio taught history of political doctrine at the fascist-dominated University of Perugia and was a regular contributor to Giorgio Del Vecchio's *Rivista internazionale di filosofia del diritto* (International magazine of philosophy of law), to *Critica fascista*, and to Costamagna's *Lo Stato*. In early 1930, Curcio had spoken out against the slow progress toward "fascisizing" Italian culture and finding "a genuinely totalitarian solution" to the problem of educating young people—a problem that would be hard to solve as long as there were still liberal-socialist instructors who were fascist only on paper and antifascist in their hearts.[35] That same year he outlined the political thought of Carl Schmitt for the readers of *Lo Stato*. Hoping that the German jurist's influence would reach Italy, he emphasized the political, nonphilosophical nature of Schmitt's work, which stripped his doctrine of the state of any "cloaking or complicated mechanisms by which to return to its true grounds," which was politics.[36] In 1934 he decided to contribute to the debate about the nature of the Fascist Party and its relationship to the state. On this occasion he declared his agreement with Panunzio and argued that the PNF represented "the soul of the fascist state," the "active and dynamic element of the State," whose essential task would be to provide the state with the best men and "to guard the flame of revolution."[37] Such an idea seemed analogous to Sorel's notion of myth, a concrete phenomenon, "perhaps illogical, but sublime," which represented "the Party's *idée-force*," a "tight-knit, united, powerful *congregatio fidelium*."[38]

Curcio reiterated these beliefs in several of the dictionary's most important entries.[39] One of these was "Party," which he edited alongside the philosopher of law Giacomo Perticone, who was also a frequent contributor to *Lo Stato*. They stressed that the rise of single-party regimes in the postwar period was the most salient novelty in legal and political systems, citing Spain, Turkey, China, Germany, and of course Italy, where, in their view, "a revolutionary party with a broad popular base" and "helmed by a leader of extraordinary prestige" had given rise to a new type of state. Though they highlighted the structural and organizational differences between the Fascist Party and other totalitarian parties, the two scholars emphasized that in Italy, Spain, and Germany the presence of parties with similar features had created new national landscapes. "The new State," they wrote in this vein, "is typified by the active presence of a totalitarian party—to which, though historically it derived its pre-eminent position from a bitter struggle and conquest of power, one must naturally add that it was legitimized by a much more profound revolution that took place in political ideas."[40]

This position was widely shared in the *Dizionario*, to which, as we have noted, intellectuals of diverse backgrounds contributed, all united in affirming the totalitarian nature of the fascist regime, its politics, and, obviously, its culture.

Conclusion

In concluding this book, I would like to return to the distinction between cultural politics, schools of thought, and ideology that I deployed in the preceding pages, in order to synthesize the most salient aspects and moments of fascist culture.

From 1922 to 1943, one of the primary goals of fascist political culture was educating young people. This is why the fascists welcomed Giovanni Gentile into their ranks in October 1922—because Gentile had been engaged in a campaign to overhaul Italian schools since the turn of the century. They granted him powers unmatched by any other Italian intellectual: he was minister of public education in Mussolini's first government, author of the 1923 education reform, and director of various institutes founded to show the nation that the new regime was prepared to benefit from the work of prominent intellectuals and to disseminate a new kind of culture. As early as the late 1920s, however, the philosopher's role changed along with the regime's cultural politics. Many intellectuals and politicians who had defended Gentile against the most radical fascists' attacks began to criticize his reform, arguing that it was incapable of finishing the work of "fascizing" the schools that the government and the Party demanded. From then until 1939, the subsequent ministers of education altered the 1923 reform and stripped the schools and universities of their autonomy, as happened in 1931 when university professors were compelled to swear fealty to fascism, and in 1939 when Giuseppe Bottai, as minister of national education and author of the School Charter, mandated the closest relationship yet between public education and the Fascist Party's youth organizations.

As we have seen, the school system was not the only domain in which fascism enacted its plans to educate young people. As the purview of the minister of education, and thus a branch of the government, this was actually the sector furthest from the reach of the Party, which for its part made every effort to mobilize up-and-coming generations throughout the Ventennio. This task was undertaken diligently and consistently by Party men, who imagined themselves to be giving rise to a genuine anthropological revolution, and who thus had to begin with the young people who represented both the future of fascism and the testing grounds for the totalitarian experiment. From the Opera nazionale balilla, the fascist youth group founded in 1926, to the Gioventù italiana del littorio, which took its place in 1937, the Party dedicated itself to cultural education, instruction, aid, and physical education, as PNF Secretary Achille Starace promised in 1937.

For a regime whose ambition was to create a new kind of humanity, novel in body and spirit, every aspect of Italian society was crucial. And indeed, from the early years the fascists demonstrated their wish to educate women and workers alike, organizing their leisure time to deprive them of their freedom. They used two main strategies to attain this goal: on the one hand, fascism assumed control of old ways of life already embedded in the nation's cultural fabric; on the other hand, they invented new forms of recreation to manage private spaces and transform Italians into a mass public. From the theater to rural radio, from musical performances to the cinema, workers became familiar with new forms of sociality imposed by the totalitarian state, which left not a single sector of Italian society free. We can see this clearly in the case of women, whom they considered veritable reproductive machines.

Queen of the home, far removed from the world of men, dedicated to her children and family, the fascist woman was supposed to be a model wife and mother, observing traditional forms of submission that were, of course, not introduced by fascism. In other respects, however, she was supposed to be a militant, engaged in building the new fascist civilization, not limited to the domestic activities to which she was traditionally relegated, but also committed to carrying out the tasks entrusted to her by the Party and the regime. Believing that they could contribute to the grand project to which the regime seemed to call them, some women imagined that they were participating in the political process then underway. And perhaps without being fully aware of it, they began to emancipate themselves from traditional models, even if the role of militant female citizen was never seen as an alternative to that of wife and mother by Italian women, much less by the Fascist Party.

Though these were the main lines of fascist cultural politics, and therefore can be seen as summarizing the Party and government's most significant cultural initiatives between 1922 and 1943, fascist culture was also the product of artists and intellectuals who, hailing from the most diverse circumstances of life and training, collectively contributed to building the totalitarian regime. That is, they were ready to dedicate their knowledge, their talent, and their energy to the political cause and to declare that their disciplines had no need to defend their autonomy—indeed, they were available to host the "contents" of the totalitarian regime.

It will be clearer now why the absence of shared aesthetic criteria within individual disciplines and the obvious continuity of a certain stylistic and programmatic pluralism within individual fields not only did not indicate a void—that is, an absence of a shared fascist culture—but in fact indicated the exact opposite. If we consider the debates that preoccupied individual intellectual and artistic communities, we can come to see that these different figures and opinions were united by the impetus to mobilize and work at fascism's disposal. Thus, to imagine that there was no fascist architecture because rationalists battled neoclassicists in the '20s and '30s is to risk making stylistic controversies more significant than the works themselves—more relevant, that is, than individual buildings and complex urban developments, from the exhibition marking the tenth anniversary of the March on Rome to the creation of E42 and the many other Italian cities begun from scratch. The case of Italian architecture is emblematic not only because most architects were fascist, but also because they fought hard, each believing himself to be fascism's true representative and therefore deserving of a broader platform than the others. We could cite many examples to show that the debates over style were not more significant than the presence of political themes in the works of individual artists. Are we to think that the differences between Mino Maccari and Massimo Bontempelli's literary works diminish the importance of their shared conviction that literary men should pursue the regime's ends? Or should we forget that both were financed by fascism, to which they devoted their talents? And how should we consider the work of Mario Sironi, who declared that he wanted to contribute via mural painting to a collective effort by which architects, urban planners, and painters would design and build the new fascist city? We must stress that there was no single fascist art form, no single fascist philosophy, no single fascist literature, because the fascists refused to establish fixed aesthetic criteria once and for all. None of this means, however, that these disciplines were not profoundly "fascisized," as should be clear from the materials we have attempted to analyze in the preceding pages.

And, finally, there is ideology. From the beginning, fascism gained power by presenting itself as a movement that would re-establish the state's authority. "Everything in the State, nothing outside the State, nothing against the State," Mussolini declared, distilling the central idea of fascist ideology, which was developed in the following years by Giovanni Gentile and Alfredo Rocco, by Sergio Panunzio and Carlo Costamagna. These were very different writers and thinkers, united by the conviction that the state should not be impeded by anything: not individuals, nor groups, nor institutions—nothing could hinder its power. In this sense, fascist ideology was the most complete rationalization of the totalitarian state.

This infinitely powerful state would give rise to a new kind of Italian: a virile, athletic man, fit in mind and body, aware of challenges and ready to face them; a man who had nothing in common with liberal bourgeois Italians of the past, who would conceive of life as a struggle and a matter of conquest, who would conform to the group and be trained to accept the regime's orders. "For the fascist," wrote Gentile and Mussolini in this vein, "everything is in the State, and nothing human or spiritual exists, much less has value, outside the State. In this sense fascism is totalitarian, and the fascist State synthesizes and unifies every value—it interprets, develops, and strengthens the life of the people."[1]

The new fascist man was to be created in Mussolini's image—a living myth, unlike the other myths that sustained fascist ideology. As the absolute apex of political power, the uncontested ruler of the Party and the regime's organizing machine, the head of state was everywhere. As such his legend spread among the popular masses, who believed he had superhuman qualities and saw him as leading an epic mission to transform Italy and the world. This image of Mussolini was widespread, and not only among the popular masses indoctrinated by propaganda; high-ranking officials in the regime expressed their dedication to him as well, convinced, as Giuseppe Bottai declared, that the head of state was a man endowed with special powers who would create a new imperial civilization based on the mythology and example of Rome.

For the fascists, Rome represented continuity in history. It was the symbol of universality, as demonstrated by the phenomenon of Christianity, which became a universal religion after it transferred its seat to Rome. Rome had ruled the world, reaching previously unreachable corners of it, and ultimately it represented the future. Contrary to what many historians have claimed, fascism declared its intention to take up the legacy of Rome not out of a nostalgic or reactionary impulse, but rather, as we have seen, because the legend of Rome served a political purpose in the project of building a modern, totalitarian imperial civilization.

Can it be said, then, that fascist culture was a homogeneous phenomenon, devoid of conflicts and discord? A cohesive, unified style? A site in which everyone agreed with everyone else in declaring the successful merger of politics and culture and celebrating the primacy of politics—which, as I emphasized in the Introduction, constituted the primary feature of the totalitarian fascist regime?

As I have attempted to illuminate in the pages of this book, within the regime's culture there were divergent strains: in the '20s the main trends were represented by the Gentilians, the revisionists, and the radical fascists, who played the role of fascism's intellectuals and explored the relationship between politics and culture, the position of the new regime in European history, and the regime's relationship to modernity. The revisionists and Gentilians believed that intellectuals should cooperate with the ruling class; they believed that defining fascist culture would strengthen the regime's identity; and they saw fascism as a modern state that would take its place in the arc of history begun by the French Revolution. The radical fascists, on the other hand, believed that fascism did not need any theoretical justification, and that its politics expressed an alternative to the form of modernity that emerged after 1789.

By the late '20s, however, this contrast had diminished, in the sense that trends in fascist culture changed. The criticism of modernity, the fight to protect fascism's revolutionary spirit from being corrupted by opportunists, and the fear of normalization remained among the defining characteristics of radical fascism. At the same time, the radical fascists' proposals lost some of the rebelliousness of the early days. In a sense, we can say that in bringing together a diverse set of personal backgrounds and collective experiences, the radical fascists moved closer to the revisionists on the regime's cultural spectrum, and that to vindicate their role as revolutionaries and warriors, they became the regime's intellectuals, engaged like the others in building a present and a future. For their part, Gentilians like Ugo Spirito began to distance themselves from their teacher, seeking a different philosophical orientation and developing a critique of his political choices. Influenced by the fascists who viewed Gentile as a liberal intellectual, such young people engaged in cultural politics more pointedly and, in the '30s, allied themselves with Bottai, who from that point onward served as their standard-bearer, publishing them in *Critica fascista* and giving shape to a group that would follow him throughout his political career.

In this sense Bottai was the most important figure in fascist culture in the '30s and '40s because he succeeded in creating a totalitarian fascist response to the conflicts between various strains of the regime's culture and politics, as we can see from the fate of his magazine *Primato*. Bottai founded the magazine in 1940 with support from intellectuals of various backgrounds who were united in believing that they had overcome the problem of making Italian culture fully fascist, in celebrating the achieved union of culture and politics, and in defining fascism as a revolutionary, modern, totalitarian regime. If in the 1920s the radicals took on characteristics belonging to the revisionists, the opposite is also true—that is to say, Bottai and his collaborators, in distancing themselves from Gentile in the latter half of the '20s, became less and less concerned with developing a body of doctrine and more and more engaged in ensuring an ever-tighter link between politics and culture.

For all these reasons, I believe that fascist culture in the 1930s was a product neither of the victory of traditionalist elements nor the work of the Catholics, since the Catholics were quite far from dominant in a state that considered Catholicism an *instrumentum regni*. Certainly the regime benefited from contributions from intellectuals who saw in fascism the potential to build a new nation, distinct from liberal Italy, in which Catholicism would play a fundamental role. This does not, however, mean that the Catholics represented fascist culture, or that this culture derived from Catholic thought. This is clear if we look at the young people who grew up in the imaginative universe created by the regime, who felt themselves to be the best representatives of a revolutionary historical era, and who wished to claim their place in creating a new, truly fascist ruling class.

Thus, these young people were not secretly antifascist, as has been argued; on the contrary, they provide the most compelling testimonies regarding the totalitarian experiment that was fascism. Yet there are commentators who see the contests organized by the university students in the Gruppi universitari fascisti as a training ground for antifascism; or who argue that fascist intellectuals were naïfs who sought to transform the regime from the inside, unaware of their own impotence.

In the pages of this brief history of fascist culture, I have made quite different claims, arguing that politicians, intellectuals, and artists, young and old, were fascists in spite of their different backgrounds, intellectual training, and disciplines. What united the people, institutions, and ideas of fascist Italy was therefore more significant than what divided them and thus dictated their political and cultural identities. This does not mean that within the regime there were no conflicts between opposing trends and groups, nor does it mean that the culture expressed by fascism was a monolith.

On the contrary, it means that we must take seriously the choices of those who from 1922 to 1943 dedicated themselves to creating a new culture, who either would not or could not live differently. It means reading the works and recounting the actions of those fascists who offered their labor and their talents to the totalitarian regime, believing that they were participating in a grand project to build history. And, finally, studying fascist culture means tirelessly reflecting on a topic that may seem obsolete to some—that is, continuing to ask ourselves why the Italians became fascist.

NOTES

Introduction

1. National Fascist Party, *La cultura fascista* (Rome: Istituto poligrafico dello Stato, 1936), 4.

2. "Contributo per una nuova cultura," *Il Saggiatore* 4, nos. 6–8 (October 1933): 243–381.

3. Benedetto Croce, *La storia come pensiero e come azione* (Bari: Laterza, 1938), 5.

Chapter 1. The Historiographical Debate from 1945 to Today

1. See Renzo De Felice, *Interpretations of Fascism* (Cambridge, MA: Harvard University Press, 1977), 14–55.

2. Norberto Bobbio, *Politica e cultura* (Turin: Einaudi, 1955), 198.

3. Norberto Bobbio, "La cultura e il fascismo," in *Fascismo e società italiana*, ed. Guido Quazza (Turin: Einaudi, 1973), 231.

4. Norberto Bobbio and Lydia G. Cochrane, *Ideological Profile of Twentieth-Century Italy* (Princeton: Princeton University Press, 2014), 122.

5. Benedetto Croce, *Scritti e discorsi politici (1943–1947)*, vol. 1 (Bari: Laterza, 1963), 7–16, 43–44. On these Crocean ideas, see De Felice, *Interpretations of Fascism*, 14–15, 160–61, 164–65.

6. Piero Gobetti, *La rivoluzione liberale: Saggio sulla lotta politica in Italia* (Turin: Einaudi, 1948), 66. There is an English-language compilation of Gobetti's essays: Piero Gobetti, *On Liberal Revolution* (New Haven: Yale University Press, 2008). See also Pier-Giorgio Zunino, *Interpretazione e memoria del fascismo: Gli anni del regime* (Rome: Laterza, 2000), 5–12; Pier-Giorgio Zunino, *L'ideologia del fascismo: Miti, credenze, e valori nella stabilizzazione del regime* (Bologna: Il Mulino, 1995).

7. Zunino, *L'ideologia del fascismo*, 17.

8. Emilio Gentile, *Fascismo: Storia e interpretazione* (Rome: Laterza, 2002), vi–viii. See also Alberto De Bernardi, *Una dittatura moderna: Il fascismo come problema storico* (Milan: Bruno Mondadori, 2006), 1–20.

9. Eugenio Garin, *Cronache di filosofia italiana: 1900–1943* (Bari: Laterza, 1966).

10. Eugenio Garin, *La filosofia come sapere storico* (Bari: Laterza, 1990), 109.

11. Antonio Gramsci, *L'Ordine nuovo*, September 1, 1924.

12. Zunino, *Interpretazione e memoria del fascismo*; Simona Colarizi, "Gramsci e il fascismo," in *Gramsci nel suo tempo*, ed. Francesco Giasi (Rome: Carocci, 2008), 343. For an alternative line of reasoning, see Benedetta Garzarelli, "Il fascismo e la crisi italiana negli scritti del 1924–26," in the same volume, 530.

13. See Gianpasquale Santomassimo, "L'impegno civile," in *Garin e il Novecento*, special edition of *Giornale critico della filosofia italiana* (Florence: Le Lettere, 2009), 444; Alessandra Tarquini, "Eugenio Garin studioso della cultura fascista"; Giorgio Vacca, "Eugenio Garin interprete di Gramsci"; and Fabio Frosini, "La presenza di Gramsci nella storiografia del Novecento," all in *Il Novecento di Eugenio Garin: Atti del convegno di studi*, ed. Giuseppe Vacca and Saverio Ricci (Rome: Istituto della Enciclopedia italiana, 2011).

14. Carlo Bo, "L'ideologia del regime," in *Fascismo e antifascismo: Lezioni e testimonianze (1918–1948)* (Milan: Feltrinelli, 1962), 1:305–22.

15. For example, E. Faccioli, "La cultura durante il periodo fascista," in *Dall'età giolittiana alla costituzione*, ed. Antonino Répaci and Renato Giusti (Mantua: Unione goliardica mantovana, 1964), 104.

16. See Augusto Del Noce, "Senso del fascismo," *Il popolo nuovo* 12 (May 1945), reprinted in *Centrismo: Vocazione o condanna?* ed. Norberto Bobbio, Augusto Del Noce, and Lorella Cedroni (Milan: Reset, 1995), 34.

17. Bobbio, Del Noce, and Cedroni, *Centrismo*, 35. See also De Felice, *Interpretations of Fascism*, 71–75.

18. Augusto Del Noce, "Idee per l'interpretazione del fascismo," *L'ordine civile* 2, no. 8 (1960): 17.

19. Augusto Del Noce, "Giacomo Noventa e 'l'errore della cultura,'" in *Il suicidio della rivoluzione: Scritti vari* (Milan: Rusconi, 1978), 32–56. This essay first appeared as the introduction to Giacomo Noventa, *Tre parole sulla Resistenza e altri scritti* (Florence: Vallecchi, 1973).

20. György Lukács, *The Destruction of Reason* (Atlantic Highlands, NJ: Humanities Press, 1981). For an analogous interpretation see Marco Rosci, "Il fascismo degli intellettuali," in *Arte e fascismo in Italia e in Germania* (Milan: Feltrinelli, 1974), 154–62. On Lukács's influence on the artistic avant-garde, see Giovanni Cianci, ed., *Modernismo, modernismi: Dall'avanguardia storica agli anni Trenta e oltre* (Milan: Principato, 1991), 32–34.

21. Norberto Bobbio, *L'ideologia del fascismo* (Ferrara: Quaderni della FIAP, 1976), 4. This was also Niccolò Zapponi's argument, as he demonstrated the similarity of Croce's, Mann's, Lukács's, and Nolte's interpretations of fascism in "G. L. Mosse e il problema delle origini culturali del fascismo: Significato di una svolta," *Storia contemporanea* 7, no. 3 (1976): 461–80.

22. Mario Isnenghi, *Intellettuali militanti e intellettuali funzionari* (Turin: Einaudi, 1979), 232.

23. Alberto Asor Rosa, *Scrittori e popolo* (Rome: Samonà e Savelli, 1965), 279.

24. Asor Rosa, *Scrittori e popolo*, 95.

25. Alberto Asor Rosa, "Il fascismo: Il regime (1926–1943)," in *Storia d'Italia*, vol. 4: *Dall'unità a oggi* (Turin: Einaudi, 1975), part 2, 1386.

26. Asor Rosa, "Il fascismo," 1358.

27. Asor Rosa, "Il fascismo," 1415.

28. Palmiro Togliatti, *Lectures on Fascism* (New York: International Publishers, 1976), 7, 10. On the importance of these lectures for the debates about fascism, see Michele Ciliberto, "Sulla filosofia italiana fra le due guerre," *Dimensioni* 3, no. 7 (1973): 28; and Giuseppe Vacca's lengthy introduction to Togliatti in the Italian edition, Palmiro Togliatti, *Sul fascismo* (Rome: GLF Ed. Laterza, 2004). See also Antonio Pellicani, "Ideologie e culture nel periodo fascista," *Rassegna di politica e di storia* 14, no. 161 (1968): 72–80.

29. Togliatti, *Lectures on Fascism*, 10.

30. Zunino, *Interpretazione e memoria del fascismo*, 30.

31. Roberto Racinaro, "Intellettuali e fascismo," *Critica marxista* 13, no. 1 (1975): 177–214.

32. Giuseppe Vacca, "Gli intellettuali nel regime reazionario di massa," in *Matrici culturali del fascismo: Seminari promossi dal Consiglio regionale pugliese e dall'Ateneo barese nel trentennale della liberazione* (Bari: Università di Bari, 1977), 51.

33. Vacca, "Gli intellettuali," 53.

34. Luisa Mangoni, *L'interventismo della cultura: Intellettuali e riviste del fascismo* (Rome/Bari: Laterza, 1974), 74.

35. Mangoni, *L'interventismo della cultura*, 48.

36. Mangoni, *L'interventismo della cultura*, 350.

37. Mangoni had posited a similar argument in the early 1960s in her work on Catholic culture, which she reasserted in the following years. See Luisa Mangoni, "Il fascismo," in *Letteratura italiana: Il letterato e le istituzioni* (Turin: G. Einaudi, 1982), 540, and the new edition of her monograph, *L'interventismo della cultura: intellettuali e riviste del fascismo* (Turin: Aragno, 2002).

38. Eugenio Garin, *Intellettuali italiani del XX secolo* (Rome: Editori Riuniti, 1974). On the links between Marxist interpretations and those indebted to Piero Gobetti's thought, see Zunino, *Interpretazione e memoria del fascismo*, 58.

39. Gabriele Turi, *Il fascismo e il consenso degli intellettuali* (Bologna: Il Mulino, 1980), 82.

40. Turi, *Il fascismo e il consenso*, 7.

41. Turi, *Il fascismo e il consenso*, 64.

42. Ernst Nolte, *Der Faschismus in seiner Epoche: Die Action française, der italianische Faschismus, der Nationalsozialismus* (Munich: Piper, 1963), published in English as *Three Faces of Fascism: Action Française, Italian Fascism, National Socialism*, trans. Leila Vennewitz (New York: Holt, Rinehart, and Winston, 1966).

43. Nolte, *Three Faces of Fascism*. The following year, the historian of modern France Eugen Weber argued in his pioneering *Varieties of Fascism* that to understand

fascism it was necessary to fill a gap in the literature and study the culture that it expressed. Among the first to reflect on the relation between processes of secularization and modern politics, Weber demonstrated the link between the nationalism that emerged from the French Revolution and fascism. Eugen Weber, *Varieties of Fascism: Doctrines of Revolution in the Twentieth Century* (Princeton, NJ: Van Nostrand Reinhold, 1964).

44. Zeev Sternhell, "Fascist Ideology," in *Fascism: A Reader's Guide: Analyses, Interpretations, Bibliography*, ed. Walter Laqueur (Berkeley: University of California Press, 1976). Two years later, he developed this argument in one of his most influential works, *La droite revolutionnaire, 1885–1914: Les origines françaises du fascisme* (Paris: Éditions du Seuil, 1978).

45. Zeev Sternhell, review of *The Fascist Revolution: Toward a General Theory of Fascism* by George L. Mosse, *American Historical Review* 105, no. 3 (2000): 882–83.

46. A. James Gregor, *The Ideology of Fascism: The Rationale of Totalitarianism* (New York: Free Press, 1969).

47. Gregor, *Ideology of Fascism*, 231.

48. Edward R. Tannenbaum, *Fascism in Italy: Society and Culture, 1922–1945* (London: Allen Lane, 1974), 251.

49. Philip Cannistraro, *La fabbrica del consenso: Fascismo e mass media* (Rome: Laterza, 1975), 5.

50. Cannistraro, *La fabbrica del consenso*, 9.

51. See Zapponi, "G. L. Mosse e il problema delle origini culturali del fascismo," 461–80; Stanley G. Payne, David Jan Sorkin, and John S. Tortorice, *What History Tells: George L. Mosse and the Culture of Modern Europe* (Madison: University of Wisconsin Press, 2004), especially 118–22 of Roger Griffin's chapter, "Withstanding the Rush of Time: The Prescience of Mosse's Anthropological View of Fascism," on the reception of Mosse's work in the English-speaking world; Emilio Gentile, *Fascination with the Persecutor: George L. Mosse and the Catastrophe of Modern Man*, tr. John and Anne Tedeschi (Madison: University of Wisconsin Press, 2022), 27–34; and Donatello Aramini, *George L. Mosse, l'Italia e gli storici* (Milan: FrancoAngeli, 2010).

52. George L. Mosse, *The Culture of Western Europe: The Nineteenth and Twentieth Centuries* (Chicago: Rand McNally, 1961).

53. Mosse, *Culture of Western Europe*, 340.

54. Compare the definition put forth by one of the pioneers of modern anthropology, Edward Burnett Tylor, *Primitive Culture: Researches into the Development of Mythology, Philosophy, Religion, Language, Art, and Custom* (London: John Murray, 1871).

55. George L. Mosse, *The Nationalization of the Masses* (New York: Howard Fertig, 1975), 9. On this topic see also Gentile, *Fascination with the Persecutor*, chapter 7.

56. George L. Mosse, *Masses and Man: Nationalist and Fascist Perceptions of Reality* (New York: Howard Fertig, 1980), 161.

57. Sternhell, review of *The Fascist Revolution*, 883.

58. Gentile, *Fascination with the Persecutor*, 115.

59. Paolo Simoncelli, *Renzo De Felice: La formazione intellettuale* (Florence: Le Lettere, 2001); Renato Moro, Luigi Goglia, and Fiorenza Fiorentino, *Renzo De Felice: Studi e testimonianze* (Rome: Edizioni di storia e letteratura, 2002); Emilio Gentile, *Renzo De Felice: Lo storico e il personaggio* (Rome: Laterza, 2003); Giovanni Mario Ceci, *Renzo De Felice: Storico della politica* (Soveria Mannelli (CZ): Rubbettino, 2008).

60. De Felice's decision to highlight consent to the fascist regime elicited the strong censure of some historians, who accused him of wanting to rehabilitate fascism. For a survey of reviews of his Mussolini biography, see Borden W. Painter, "Renzo De Felice and the Historiography of Italian Fascism," *American Historical Review* 95, no. 2 (1990): 391–405. Since then, many have referred to De Felice and his students as "revisionists." As is well known, "revisionist" was the term Lenin used to condemn the German social democrat Eduard Bernstein for attempting to "correct" Marxist doctrine and promote the reformist path over the Bolshevik revolution. In everyday discourse, revisionists are those who intend to challenge the "myths" of traditional historiography, from the heroes of the Risorgimento to those of the Resistance. This label is now part of the historian's lexicon, as we can see in Sergio Luzzatto, "The Political Culture of Fascist Italy," *Contemporary European History* 8, no. 2 (July 1999): 317–34.

61. Renzo De Felice, *Mussolini il duce*, part 1: *Gli anni del consenso, 1929–1936* (Turin: Einaudi, 1974), 102. The words in italics quote the terminology of Gabriel A. Almond and G. Bingham Powell, *Comparative Politics: A Developmental Approach* (Boston: Little, Brown, 1966).

62. De Felice, *Mussolini il duce*, part 1: *Gli anni del consenso, 1929–1936*, 105.

63. De Felice, *Mussolini il duce*, part 1: *Gli anni del consenso, 1929–1936*, 106.

64. De Felice, *Mussolini il duce*, part 1: *Gli anni del consenso, 1929–1936*, 35. De Felice had already expressed this opinion in *Le interpretazioni del fascismo* (Bari: Laterza, 1969), where he had identified Mussolini and Gentile's entry for "Fascismo" in the *Enciclopedia italiana* and Gentile's 1927 "Origini e dottrina del fascismo" as the two most important documents of fascist ideology.

65. De Felice, *Mussolini il duce*, part 1: *Gli anni del consenso, 1929–1936*, 111.

66. Renzo De Felice, *Intellettuali di fronte al fascismo: Saggi e note documentarie* (Rome: Bonacci, 1985), 192.

67. Renzo De Felice and Luigi Goglia, *Storia fotografica del fascismo* (Rome: Laterza, 1981), xix–xx; also Renzo De Felice, *Mussolini il duce*, part 2: *Lo stato totalitario, 1936–1940* (Turin: Einaudi, 1981), 8. On De Felice's thinking about totalitarianism, see also Gentile, *Renzo De Felice*, 99–111.

68. Emilio Gentile, *The Origins of Fascist Ideology, 1918–1925* (New York: Enigma Books, 2012), 382.

69. Gentile, *Fascismo: Storia e interpretazione*, 83.

70. Emilio Gentile, *The Italian Road to Totalitarianism* (London: Frank Cass, 2004).

71. Emilio Gentile, *The Sacralization of Politics in Fascist Italy* (Cambridge, MA: Harvard University Press, 1996).

72. Gentile, *Sacralization of Politics in Fascist Italy*, ix.

73. Isnenghi, *Intellettuali militanti e intellettuali funzionari*, jacket. For an example of the pattern Isnenghi referred to, consider Guido Quazza, president of the National Institute for the History of the Liberation Movement: "Futile, too, were recent efforts to identify a subjective autonomy for the movement on the grounds of ideology.... If we want to speak of the ideology of fascism, then we must attend solely to its foundational characteristic as an attitude toward life ... and look for its features not positively but—as Norberto Bobbio writes—negatively, as being against something.... And we could go on at great length if we wanted to adequately examine the results of a form of historiography that, though it engaged philology and objectivist empiricism, ended in essentially rehabilitating fascism." Guido Quazza, "Antifascismo e fascismo nel nodo delle origini," in *Fascismo e capitalismo*, ed. Nicola Tranfaglia and Paolo Alatri (Milan: Feltrinelli, 1976), 65. In this same volume Enzo Collotti argued that fascist ideology had a merely "instrumental" nature because it was made from a "mystification of reality" (146–50).

74. Zunino, *L'ideologia del fascismo*, 18.

75. Zunino, *L'ideologia del fascismo*, 62.

76. Zunino, *L'ideologia del fascismo*, 371.

77. Zunino, *L'ideologia del fascismo*, 374.

78. Zunino, *L'ideologia del fascismo*, 380.

79. Guido Quazza, *Storiografia e fascismo* (Milan: Angeli, 1985).

80. Marino Biondi, Enrico Ghidetti, and Alessandro Borsotti, *Cultura e fascismo: Letteratura, arti e spettacolo di un ventennio* (Florence: Ponte alle Grazie, 1996), 15.

81. Lawrence Stone, "The Revival of Narrative: Reflections on a New Old History," *Past & Present* 85 (1979): 4.

82. For a discussion of studies of fascist culture in the early 2000s, see David D. Roberts, "Myth, Style, Substance and the Totalitarian Dynamic in Fascist Italy," *Contemporary European History* 16, no. 1 (2007): 1–36.

83. Jeffrey T. Schnapp, *Staging Fascism: 18 BL and the Theater of Masses for Masses* (Stanford, CA: Stanford University Press, 1996).

84. Jeffrey T. Schnapp, "Fascinating Fascism," *Journal of Contemporary History* 31, no. 2 (1996): 238.

85. Mabel Berezin, *Making the Fascist Self: The Political Culture of Interwar Italy* (Ithaca, NY: Cornell University Press, 1997), 29.

86. Simonetta Falasca-Zamponi, *Fascist Spectacle: The Aesthetics of Power in Mussolini's Italy* (Berkeley: University of California Press, 1997).

87. See the observations of Charles Burdett, *Journeys through Fascism: Italian Travel Writing between the Wars* (New York: Berghahn Books, 2007), 5, and those of Luzzatto, "The Political Culture of Fascist Italy," 325.

88. Luzzatto, "The Political Culture of Fascist Italy," 322.

89. Gentile, *The Origins of Fascist Ideology*, 385–86.

90. Walter Adamson also argued that the sacralization of politics constituted the most significant aspect of fascist culture; see Walter L. Adamson, "The Culture of Italian Fascism and the Fascist Crisis of Modernity: The Case of II Selvaggio," *Journal of Contemporary History* 30, no. 4 (1995): 556.

91. See David D. Roberts, *The Totalitarian Experiment in Twentieth Century Europe: Understanding the Poverty of Great Politics* (London: Routledge, 2006), 282–83. See also David D. Roberts, "How Not to Think about Fascism and Ideology, Intellectual Antecedents and Historical Meaning," *Journal of Contemporary History* 35, no. 2 (2000): 185–211. On the arguments discussed here, see especially David D. Roberts, "Myth, Style, Substance and the Totalitarian Dynamic in Fascist Italy," *Contemporary European History* 16, no. 1 (2007): 1–36.

92. Roberts, "Myth, Style, Substance and the Totalitarian Dynamic in Fascist Italy," 11.

93. Roberts, "Myth, Style, Substance and the Totalitarian Dynamic in Fascist Italy," 12.

94. Ruth Ben-Ghiat, *Fascist Modernities: Italy, 1922–1945* (Berkeley: University of California Press, 2009).

95. Roger Griffin, *The Nature of Fascism* (New York: St. Martin's Press, 1991).

96. Roger Griffin, "Il nucleo palingenetico dell'ideologia del 'fascismo genetico,'" in *Che cos'è il fascismo? Interpretazioni e prospettive di ricerca*, ed. Roger Eatwell and Alessandro Campi (Rome: Ideazione, 2003), 100.

97. Roger Griffin and Matthew Feldman, eds., *Fascism: Critical Concepts in Political Science*, vol. 5: *Post-War Fascisms* (London: Routledge, 2004).

98. Gabriele Turi, "Fascismo e cultura ieri e oggi," *Belfagor* 49, no. 5 (1994): 553.

99. Turi, "Fascismo e cultura ieri e oggi," 554.

100. Turi, "Fascismo e cultura ieri e oggi," 552.

101. Turi, "Fascismo e cultura ieri e oggi," 552.

102. Alessia Pedio, ed., *I volti del consenso: Mass media e cultura nell'Italia fascista, 1922–1943* (Rome: Nuova Iniziativa Editoriale, 2004), 119.

103. Pedio, *I volti del consenso*, 121.

Chapter 2. Cultural Politics in the 1920s

1. See Renzo De Felice, *Mussolini il rivoluzionario, 1883–1920* (Turin: Einaudi, 1965), 501–44; Adrian Lyttelton, *The Seizure of Power: Fascism in Italy, 1919–1929* (London: Weidenfeld & Nicolson, 1973); Emilio Gentile, *Storia del Partito fascista, 1919–1922: Movimento e milizia* (Rome: Laterza, 1989), 3–53.

2. Emilio Gentile, *Il culto del littorio: La sacralizzazione della politica nell'Italia fascista* (Rome: Laterza, 1993), 41–46.

3. On the relationship between Futurism and fascism, see Renzo De Felice, *Futurismo, cultura e politica* (Turin: Fondazione Giovanni Agnelli, 1988); George L. Mosse, "The Political Culture of Italian Futurism: A General Perspective," *Journal of Contemporary History* 25, nos. 2–3 (1990): 253–68; Emilio Gentile, *The Origins of Fascist Ideology, 1918–1925* (New York: Enigma Books, 2012), 76–113; Filippo Tommaso

Marinetti and Luciano De Maria, *Teoria e invenzione futurista* (Milan: A. Mondadori, 2001); Emilio Gentile, *"La nostra sfida alle stelle": Futuristi in politica* (Rome: Laterza, 2009).

4. On the Arditi, see Ferdinando Cordova, *Arditi e legionari dannunziani* (Padua: Marsilio, 1969); Giorgio Rochat, *Gli arditi della grande guerra: Origini, battaglie e miti* (Milan: Feltrinelli, 1981); Gentile, *The Origins of Fascist Ideology*.

5. Michael Arthur Ledeen, *D'Annunzio: The First Duce* (New Brunswick, NJ: Transaction, 2002). See also George L. Mosse, *Masses and Man: Nationalist and Fascist Perceptions of Reality* (New York: Howard Fertig, 1980), 87–103.

6. On Rensi, among others, see Augusto Del Noce, "Giuseppe Rensi fra Leopardi e Pascal: Ovvero l'autocritica dell'ateismo negativo in Giuseppe Rensi," in *Filosofi dell'esistenza e della libertà*, ed. Francesco Mercadante and Bernardino Casadei (Milan: Giuffré, 1992), 469–540; Renato Chiarenza, ed., *L'inquieto esistere: Atti del Convegno su Giuseppe Rensi nel cinquantenario della morte (1941–1991)* (Genova: Effe Emme Enne, 1993); Mirella Pasini and Daniele Rolando, "La filosofia a Genova," in *Le città filosofiche: Per una geografia della cultura filosofica del Novecento*, ed. Pietro Rossi and Carlo Augusto Viano (Bologna: Il Mulino, 2004), 163–72; Alessandra Tarquini, *Il Gentile dei fascisti: Gentiliani e antigentiliani nel regime fascista* (Bologna: Il Mulino, 2009), 86–105.

7. Giuseppe Rensi, *Lineamenti di filosofia scettica* (Bologna: Zanichelli, 1919), xxxiii.

8. Giuseppe Rensi, *La filosofia dell'autorità* (Palermo: R. Sandron, 1920), 5.

9. Rensi, *La filosofia dell'autorità*, 163.

10. Rensi, *La filosofia dell'autorità*, 14.

11. Rensi, *La filosofia dell'autorità*, 242.

12. Norberto Bobbio and Lydia G. Cochrane, *Ideological Profile of Twentieth-Century Italy* (Princeton: Princeton University Press, 2014), 122.

13. See Gentile, *The Origins of Fascist Ideology*.

14. Gentile, *The Origins of Fascist Ideology*, 163–66. Emilio Bodrero, *Manifesto alla borghesia* (Rome: La Fionda, 1921).

15. See Jürgen Charnitzky, *Fascismo e scuola: La politica scolastica del regime (1922–1943)* (Florence: La Nuova Italia, 1994), 499; see also Teresa Maria Mazzatosta, *Il regime fascista tra educazione e propaganda (1935–1943)* (Bologna: Cappelli, 1978); Rino Gentili, *Giuseppe Bottai e la riforma fascista della scuola* (Florence: La Nuova Italia, 1979); Michel Ostenc, *La scuola italiana durante il fascismo* (Bari: Laterza, 1983).

16. See De Felice, *Mussolini il Rivoluzionario, 1883–1920*, 743.

17. De Felice, *Mussolini il Rivoluzionario 1883–1920*, 743.

18. Paolo Nello, *L'avanguardismo giovanile alle origini del fascismo* (Bari: Laterza, 1978), 67; Luca La Rovere and Bruno Bongiovanni, *Storia dei Guf: Organizzazione, politica e miti della gioventù universitaria fascista 1919–1943* (Turin: Bollati Boringhieri, 2003), 38–67.

19. See Benito Mussolini, *Opera omnia*, vol. 14, ed. Edoardo Susmel (Florence: La Fenice, 1954), 468. Benito Mussolini, *Opera omnia*, vol. 16, ed. Edoardo Susmel (Florence: La Fenice, 1955), 443.

20. Benito Mussolini, *Opera omnia*, vol. 17, ed. Edoardo Susmel (Florence: La Fenice, 1955), 351-52; Benito Mussolini, "Prefazione al programma," *Il Popolo d'Italia* 8, no. 309 (December 28, 1921), 1.

21. Mussolini, *Opera omnia*, vol. 17, 338.

22. Francesco Meriano, "Il problema della scuola media," *Gerarchia* 1, no. 4 (1922): 230.

23. "Le discussioni dell'ultima giornata," *Il popolo d'Italia* 9, no. 257 (October 27, 1922): 2; but see also "Gli importanti lavori del Convegno Fascista a Napoli," *Il popolo d'Italia* 9, no. 256 (October 26, 1922): 1. See Tarquini, *Il Gentile dei fascisti*, 23–44, for a discussion of school reform inside the PNF.

24. Giuseppe Lombardo Radice and Gino Ferretti, *L'esame di Stato* (Rome: La voce societa anonima editrice, 1920).

25. Renzo De Felice, "Presentazione," in Teresa Maria Mazzatosta, *Il regime fascista tra educazione e propaganda (1935–1943)* (Bologna: Cappelli, 1978), 15ff.

26. Aside from the works already cited by Luisa Mangoni and Eugenio Garin, see Henry Silton Harris, *The Social Philosophy of Giovanni Gentile* (Urbana: University of Illinois Press, 1960); and Maria Luisa Cicalese, *Nei labirinti di Giovanni Gentile: Bagliori e faville* (Milan: FrancoAngeli, 2004).

27. See Guido Verucci, *Idealisti all'indice: Croce, Gentile e la condanna del Sant'Uffizio* (Rome/Bari: Laterza, 2006).

28. Beyond Del Noce's contributions, including Augusto Del Noce, *Giovanni Gentile: Per una interpretazione filosofica della storia contemporanea* (Bologna: Il Mulino, 1990), see also Aldo Lo Schiavo and Giovanni Gentile, *La filosofia politica di Giovanni Gentile* (Rome: Armando, 1971); and Aldo Lo Schiavo, *Introduzione a Gentile* (Rome/Bari: Laterza, 2001). Francesco Perfetti makes reference to Del Noce's interpretation in his introduction to Giovanni Gentile and Francesco Perfetti, *Discorsi parlamentari* (Bologna: Il Mulino, 2004). The most radical criticism of this interpretation, argued from a philosophical standpoint, may be found in Gennaro Sasso, *Le due Italie di Giovanni Gentile* (Bologna: Il Mulino, 1998).

29. David D. Roberts, "Maggi's Croce, Sasso's Gentile and the Riddles of Twentieth-Century Italian Intellectual History," *Journal of Modern Italian Studies* 7, no. 1 (January 1, 2002): 126; Claudio Fogu, "Actualism and the Fascist Historic Imaginary," *History and Theory* 42, no. 2 (2003): 196–221. Roberts has devoted a number of works to the topic: David D. Roberts, *Giovanni Gentile e la politica italiana* (Pisa: Edizioni ETS, 1999); "How Not to Think about Fascism and Ideology, Intellectual Antecedents and Historical Meaning," *Journal of Contemporary History* 35, no. 2 (2000): 185–211; and, more recently, *The Totalitarian Experiment in Twentieth Century Europe: Understanding the Poverty of Great Politics* (London: Routledge, 2006), 299–306, 309–10, 322–23.

30. See Sasso, *Le due Italie di Giovanni Gentile*, 263–316, for a reflection on the structure of Gentilian philosophy; also see Lo Schiavo and Gentile, *La filosofia politica di*

Giovanni Gentile, 182–93; Dario Faucci, *La filosofia politica di Croce e di Gentile* (Florence: La Nuova Italia, 1974), 113–25; Salvatore Valitutti, *Il diritto secondo Gentile. Il pensiero di Giovanni Gentile*, Enciclopedia 76–77 (Rome: Istituto della Enciclopedia italiana, 1977), 873–83; Giuliano Marini, "Aspetti sistematici della 'Filosofia del diritto' di Gentile," *Giornale critico della filosofia italiana* 14, no. 2–3 (1994): 462–83; Luigi Punzo, "I fondamenti della filosofia del diritto di Giovanni Gentile," in *Giovanni Gentile: La filosofia italiana tra idealismo e anti-idealismo*, ed. Piero Di Giovanni (Milan: FrancoAngeli, 2003), 375; Alessandro Amato, *L'etica oltre lo Stato: Filosofia e politica in Giovanni Gentile* (Milan: Mimesis, 2011); Andrea Pinazzi, *Attualismo e problema giuridico: la filosofia del diritto alla scuola di Giovanni Gentile* (Rome: Aracne, 2015).

31. Giovanni Gentile, *Opere complete di Giovanni Gentile*, vol. 43: *Guerra e fede*, ed. Hervé A. Cavallera (Florence: Le Lettere, 1989), 36–37.

32. Giovanni Gentile, *Opere complete di Giovanni Gentile*, vol. 37: *Discorsi di religione* (Florence: Sansoni, 1957), 29.

33. Gentile, *Discorsi di religione*, 29.

34. Gabriele Turi, *Giovanni Gentile: Una biografia* (Florence: Giunti, 1995), 304–67.

35. Giovanni Gentile, *Opere complete di Giovanni Gentile*, vol. 39: *Educazione e scuola laica*, ed. Hervé A. Cavallera (Florence: Le Lettere, 1988), 124.

36. On Catholicism in Gentile's reforms, see Luigi Ambrosoli, *Libertà e religione nella riforma Gentile* (Florence: Vallecchi, 1980). On the relationship between religion and philosophy in Gentile's actualism, see Sasso, *Le due Italie di Giovanni Gentile*, 147–78.

37. Monica Galfré, *Una riforma alla prova: La scuola media di Gentile e il fascismo* (Milan: FrancoAngeli, 2000).

38. Charnitzky, *Fascismo e scuola*, 110–14; Ostenc, *La scuola italiana durante il fascismo*, 205–10.

39. Gentile, *Il culto del littorio*, 69. Cf. Tarquini, *Il Gentile dei fascisti*, 39–43.

40. Ministero della pubblica istruzione and Ministero dell'educazione nazionale, "Saluto alla bandiera," *Bollettino ufficiale del Ministero della pubblica istruzione* 51, vol. 2, no. 3 (January 15, 1924), 65.

41. Ministero della pubblica istruzione and Ministero dell'educazione nazionale, "Raffigurazione simbolica del Milite ignoto nelle aule scolastiche," *Bollettino ufficiale del Ministero della pubblica istruzione* 51, vol. 2, no. 26 (June 24, 1924): 1438.

42. For the criticism from the opposition, see Charnitzky, *Fascismo e scuola*, 217. For the criticism from fascists, see Tarquini, *Il Gentile dei fascisti*, 54–58.

43. See Ernesto Codignola, "Il nuovo ministro dell'istruzione," *La nuova scuola italiana* 1, no. 41 (July 15, 1924): 553.

44. Giovanni Gentile, "Che cos'è il fascismo?" in *Opere complete di Giovanni Gentile*, vol. 45: *Politica e cultura I*, ed. Hervé A. Cavallera (Florence: Le Lettere, 1990), 21.

45. Gentile, "Che cos'è il fascismo?" 22. Cf. Roberto Pertici, "Il Mazzini di Giovanni Gentile," in *Storici italiani del Novecento* (Pisa/Rome: Istituti editoriali e poligrafici internazionali, 2000), 105–58.

46. Gentile, "Che cos'è il fascismo?" 27.

47. Giovanni Gentile, "Riforme costituzionali e fascismo," in *Opere complete*, 45:183.

48. Giovanni Gentile, "Il fascismo e la Sicilia," in *Opere complete*, 45:57.

49. Emilio R. Papa, *Storia di due manifesti, il Fascismo e la cultura italiana* (Milan: Feltrinelli, 1958); Emilio R. Papa, *Fascismo e cultura* (Venice: Marsilio, 1974), 159–86; Philip Cannistraro, *La fabbrica del consenso: Fascismo e mass media* (Rome: Laterza, 1975), 18–21; Gisella Longo and Francesco Perfetti, *L'Istituto nazionale fascista di cultura: Gli intellettuali tra partito e regime* (Rome: Pellicani, 2000), 28–38.

50. Longo and Perfetti, *L'Istituto nazionale fascista di cultura*, 39.

51. Giovanni Gentile, "Discorso inaugurale dell'Istituto nazionale fascista di cultura," in *Opere complete*, 45:256–72.

52. Longo and Perfetti, *L'Istituto nazionale fascista di cultura*, 58.

53. Cannistraro, *La fabbrica del consenso*, 23.

54. Gabriele Turi, *Il fascismo e il consenso degli intellettuali* (Bologna: Il Mulino, 1980), 41.

55. "Considerazioni sopra un elenco di Enciclopedici," *Il Tevere* 3, no. 97 (April 25, 1926): 1. For fascist polemics against Gentile, see Tarquini, *Il Gentile dei fascisti*, 64–67.

56. Turi, *Il fascismo e il consenso degli intellettuali*, 82–100.

57. Ostenc, *La scuola italiana durante il fascismo*, 127–81.

58. See Charnitzky, *Fascismo e scuola*, 211–63, 419–69; Ostenc, *La scuola italiana durante il fascismo*, 127–83.

59. Charnitzky, *Fascismo e scuola*, 223; cf. also "Il programma scolastico del ministro Fedele in un discorso al Consiglio Superiore," *Il giornale d'Italia*, January 10, 1925.

60. Tarquini, *Il Gentile dei fascisti*, 123–27.

61. Benito Mussolini, *Opera omnia*, vol. 40, ed. Edoardo Susmel (Florence: La Fenice, 1979), 405–6.

62. Tarquini, *Il Gentile dei fascisti*, 123–27.

63. Partito nazionale fascista, *Il gran consiglio nei primi dieci anni dell'era Fascista* (Rome: Editrice Nuova Europa, 1932), 282. The term *fascistizzazione* appears frequently in publications from the Ventennio and here has been rendered variously as "making fascist," "making truly fascist," or, as in this case, "fascisizing."

64. Quoted in Benito Mussolini, *Opera omnia*, vol. 23, ed. Edoardo Susmel (Florence: La Fenice, 1963), 61.

65. Mussolini, *Opera omnia*, vol. 23, 61. See also Charnitzky, *Fascismo e scuola*, 247–48.

66. Charnitzky, *Fascismo e scuola*, 393–418; cf. Adolfo Scotto Di Luzio, *L'appropriazione imperfetta: Editori, biblioteche e libri per ragazzi durante il fascismo* (Bologna: Il Mulino, 1996); Anna Ascenzi and Roberto Sani, *Il libro per la scuola tra idealismo e fascismo: L'opera della Commissione centrale per l'esame dei libri di testo da Giuseppe Lombardo Radice ad Alessandro Melchiori (1923–1928)* (Milan: Vita e Pensiero, 2005); Mariella Colin, *"Les enfants de Mussolini": Littérature, livres, lectures d'enfance et de*

jeunesse; De la grande guerre à la chute du régime (Caen: Presses universitaires de Caen, 2010).

67. Charnitzky, *Fascismo e scuola*, 401.

68. Colin, *Les enfants de Mussolini*, 188.

69. See Charnitzky, *Fascismo e scuola*, 249–63; Ostenc, *La scuola italiana durante il fascismo*, 170–81.

70. Nello, *L'avanguardismo giovanile alle origini del fascismo*; Renzo De Felice, *Mussolini il duce*, part 2: *Lo stato totalitario, 1936–1940* (Turin: Einaudi, 1981), 123–29; Niccolò Zapponi, "Il partito della gioventù: Le organizzazioni giovanili del fascismo, 1926–1943," *Storia contemporanea* 13, nos. 4–5 (1982): 569–633; Carmen Betti, *L'Opera nazionale Balilla e l'educazione fascista* (Florence: La Nuova Italia, 1984), 32–33; Tracy H. Koon, *Believe, Obey, Fight: Political Socialization of Youth in Fascist Italy, 1922–1943* (Chapel Hill: University of North Carolina, 1985); Charnitzky, *Fascismo e scuola*, 326–67; La Rovere and Bongiovanni, *Storia dei Guf*, 24–36; Ornella Stellavato, "La nascita dell'Opera nazionale Balilla," *Mondo contemporaneo* 2 (2009): 5–81; Alessio Ponzio, *La palestra del littorio: L'Accademia della Farnesina; Un esperimento di pedagogia totalitaria nell'Italia fascista* (Milan: FrancoAngeli, 2009); and more recently, Alessio Ponzio, *Shaping the New Man: Youth Training Regimes in Fascist Italy and Nazi Germany* (Madison: University of Wisconsin Press, 2015).

71. Zapponi, "Il partito della gioventù," 571.

72. Emilio Gentile, *Fascismo: Storia e interpretazione* (Rome: Laterza, 2002), 253.

73. Zapponi, "Il partito della gioventù," 599.

74. See Ponzio, *La palestra del littorio*.

75. Betti, *L'Opera nazionale Balilla e l'educazione fascista*, 129.

76. Camillo Barbarito, *Lo sport fascista e la razza* (Turin: G. B. Paravia, 1937), 18–20; Maria Canella and Sergio Giuntini, eds., *Sport e fascismo* (Milan: FrancoAngeli, 2009), and in particular Salvatore Finocchiaro, "L'educazione fisica, lo sport scolastico e giovanile durante il regime fascista," 119–32, in that volume.

77. Emilio Gentile, *The Italian Road to Totalitarianism* (London: Frank Cass, 2004).

78. Betti, *L'Opera nazionale Balilla e l'educazione fascista*; Koon, *Believe, Obey, Fight*.

79. Victoria De Grazia, *Consenso e cultura di massa nell'Italia fascista: L'organizzazione del dopolavoro* (Rome: Laterza, 1981), 33; Elena Vigilante, *L'Opera nazionale dopolavoro: Tempo libero dei lavoratori, assistenza e regime fascista, 1925–1943* (Bologna: Il Mulino, 2014).

80. De Grazia, *Consenso e cultura di massa nell'Italia fascista*, 33.

81. De Grazia, *Consenso e cultura di massa nell'Italia fascista*, 42.

82. De Grazia, *Consenso e cultura di massa nell'Italia fascista*, 207.

83. De Grazia, *Consenso e cultura di massa nell'Italia fascista*, 47.

84. Vigilante, *L'Opera nazionale dopolavoro*, 115–45.

Chapter 3. Intellectuals and Artists in the 1920s

1. See Emilio Gentile, *The Origins of Fascist Ideology, 1918–1925* (New York: Enigma Books, 2012), 255–56, 264–67, 271; Emilio Gentile, "Bottai e il fascismo," in

Il mito dello stato nuovo: Dal radicalismo nazionale al fascismo (Rome: Laterza, 1999), 211–36; Niccolò Zapponi, "Il partito della gioventù: Le organizzazioni giovanili del fascismo, 1926–1943," *Storia contemporanea* 13, nos. 4–5 (1982): 569–633; Monica Galfré, *Giuseppe Bottai: Un intellettuale fascista* (Florence: Giunti, 2000), 4, who notes: "the now-dated definitions of the 'critical' or 'contradictory' fascist echoed widely, and the image of Bottai as a 'stranger to the regime' is still deeply rooted."

2. Zapponi, "Il partito della gioventù," 578.

3. The argument for seeing Bottai as a moderate fascist may be found in Luisa Mangoni, *L'interventismo della cultura: Intellettuali e riviste del fascismo* (Rome/Bari: Laterza, 1974), 65–80. The image of Bottai as a *sui generis* fascist was introduced by Giordano Bruno Guerri, *Giuseppe Bottai, un fascista critico* (Milan: Feltrinelli, 1976); see also Loreto Di Nucci, "Giuseppe Bottai," in *Dizionario del fascismo*, ed. Victoria De Grazia and Sergio Luzzatto (Turin: Einaudi, 2005), 1:194–98.

4. Giuseppe Bottai, "L'equivoco antifascista (Il Fascismo nel suo fondamento dottrinario): Conferenza tenuta all'Augusteum in Roma il 27 marzo 1924," *Critica fascista* 2, no. 7 (April 1, 1924): 395–99.

5. Alessandra Tarquini, *Il Gentile dei fascisti: Gentiliani e antigentiliani nel regime fascista* (Bologna: Il Mulino, 2009), 69–86.

6. On Pellizzi see Gentile, *The Origins of Fascist Ideology, 1918–1925*, 287–90, 338–44; Roberta Suzzi Valli, "Il 'fascismo integrale' di Camillo Pellizzi," *Annali della Fondazione Ugo Spirito* 7 (1995): 243–84; Roberta Suzzi Valli, "Il fascio italiano a Londra: L'attività politica di Camillo Pellizzi," *Storia contemporanea* 25, no. 6 (1995): 957–1001; Gisella Longo and Francesco Perfetti, *L'Istituto nazionale fascista di cultura: Gli intellettuali tra partito e regime* (Rome: Pellicani, 2000), in which the final section is entirely dedicated to Pellizzi; Danilo Breschi and Gisella Longo, *Camillo Pellizzi: La ricerca delle élites tra politica e sociologia (1896–1979)* (Soveria Mannelli (CZ): Rubbettino, 2004).

7. Camillo Pellizzi, *Problemi e realtà del fascismo* (Florence: Vallecchi, 1924), 11.

8. Pellizzi, *Problemi e realtà del fascismo*, 159–61.

9. See Gentile, *The Origins of Fascist Ideology*, 223–28, 230–53.

10. On Malaparte see Mangoni, *L'interventismo della cultura*, 92–96, 98–99, 103–9, 179–81; Luisa Mangoni, "Il fascismo," in *Letteratura Italiana*, vol. 1: *Il letterato e le istituzioni* (Turin: Einaudi, 1982), 525–30; Giuseppe Pardini, *Curzio Malaparte: Biografia politica* (Milan: Luni, 1998); Giuseppe Parlato, *La sinistra fascista: Storia di un progetto mancato* (Bologna: Il Mulino, 2000), 31–33; Marino Biondi, *Scrittori e miti totalitari: Malaparte, Pratolini, Silone* (Florence: Polistampa, 2002); Sergio Luzzatto, "Curzio Malaparte," in De Grazia and Luzzatto, *Dizionario del fascismo*, 2:78–81.

11. Curzio Suckert, *L'Europa vivente: Teoria storica del sindacalismo nazionale* (Florence: La Voce, 1923), 19.

12. Suckert, *L'Europa vivente*, 24.

13. Giuseppe Parlato, ed., "Ardengo Soffici: Miei rapporti con Mussolini," *Storia contemporanea* 25, no. 5 (1994): 746. See also Ardengo Soffici, "Prefazione," in Suckert, *L'Europa vivente*, xiv; Michele Ciliberto, "Le idee di Soffici," in *Ardengo Soffici: Un*

bilancio critico; Atti del convegno di Florence 16–17 ottobre 1987, ed. Marino Biondi (Florence: Festina Lente, 1990), 65–77.

14. Anna Scarantino, *"L'Impero": Un quotidiano "reazionario-futurista" degli anni venti* (Rome: Bonacci, 1981).

15. Quoted in Tarquini, *Il Gentile dei fascisti*, 60.

16. See Francesco Perfetti, *Fascismo monarchico: I paladini della monarchia assoluta fra integralismo e dissidenza* (Rome: Bonacci, 1988); Yvon De Begnac, *Taccuini mussoliniani*, ed. Francesco Perfetti (Bologna: Il Mulino, 1990), 146–53.

17. See Perfetti, *Fascismo monarchico*, 213–57. Volt was the pseudonym of Vincenzo Fani Ciotti, another radical fascist, who in his *Programma della destra fascista* (Program of the fascist right) highlighted three main ideas for fascist doctrine— Nation, Expansion, and Hierarchy—and maintained that the movement founded by Mussolini naturally situated itself to the right in the history of political thought. In the book he explained that history had demonstrated the failure of the attempt to repudiate authority and tradition, and "put man in the place of God at the altar." Fascism, according to Volt, would respond to the "great heresy of the nineteenth century"—that is, "the freedom of conscience." Vincenzo Fani Ciotti, *Programma della destra fascista* (Florence: La Voce, 1924), 50, 147, 153. See also Tarquini, *Il Gentile dei fascisti*, 74–77, 93–96.

18. La Direzione, "Per Giovanni Gentile," *Levana: Rassegna trimestrale di filosofia dell'educazione e di politica scolastica* 1, no. 4 (October 1922): 369.

19. Ugo Spirito, "Il concetto di libertà e i diritti dell'opposizione," *Critica fascista* 2, no. 12 (June 15, 1924): 502–5.

20. Ernesto Codignola, "La nostra crisi politica," *La nuova scuola italiana* 1, no. 40 (June 29, 1924): 529–30.

21. Ernesto Codignola, "Lo sviluppo del fascismo," *L'educazione politica* 3, no. 7 (July 1925): 315–20; Giuseppe Parlato, ed., "Il carteggio Bottai-Spirito (1924–1932)," *Annali della Fondazione Ugo Spirito* 6 (1994): 116.

22. Quoted in Giovanni Belardelli, *Il ventennio degli intellettuali: Cultura, politica, ideologia nell'Italia fascista* (Rome: Laterza, 2005), 112, and see 97–140. See also Giovanni Belardelli, *Il mito della "Nuova Italia": Gioacchino Volpe tra guerra e fascismo* (Rome: Edizioni Lavoro, 1988); Roberto Bonuglia, ed., *Gioacchino Volpe tra passato e presente* (Rome: Aracne, 2007); Eugenio Di Rienzo, *La storia e l'azione: Vita politica di Gioacchino Volpe* (Florence: Le Lettere, 2008).

23. Giovanni Gentile, "Revisione," *L'educazione politica* 4, no. 1 (January 1926): 1–5. On this article, see the observations in Parlato, "Il carteggio Bottai-Spirito (1924–1932)," 116ff. For Volpe's opinion on liberal Italy, also see S. Lupo, "Croce, Volpe e l'Italia liberale," *Storica* 1 (1995): 11–36.

24. Ardengo Soffici, "Gerarchia," *Gerarchia* 1, no. 9 (September 1922): 504–7. Also see Laura Malvano, "La politique artistique dans un régime totalitaire," in *Art et fascisme: Totalitarisme et résistance au totalitarisme dans les arts en Italie, Allemagne et France des années 30 à la défaite de l'Axe; Actes*, ed. Pierre Milza and Fanette Roche-Pézard (Brussels: Éditions Complexe, 1989), 159.

25. Alighiero Ciattini, "Coscienza nazionale e cultura," *Critica fascista* 1, no. 8 (October 1, 1923): 155; Lorenzo Giusso, "Letteratura fascista," *Critica fascista* 4, no. 13 (July 1, 1926): 247.

26. Richard A. Etlin, *Modernism in Italian Architecture, 1890–1940* (Cambridge, MA: MIT Press, 1991), 379.

27. For example, Philip Cannistraro, *La fabbrica del consenso: Fascismo e mass media* (Rome: Laterza, 1975), 57; and Marla Stone, *The Patron State: Art and Politics in Fascist Italy* (Princeton: Princeton University Press, 1998), 5.

28. Walter L. Adamson, "Avant-Garde Modernism and Italian Fascism: Cultural Politics in the Era of Mussolini," *Journal of Modern Italian Studies* 6, no. 2 (January 1, 2001): 234.

29. Cannistraro, *La fabbrica del consenso*, 43; Etlin, *Modernism in Italian Architecture*, 380; Jeffrey T. Schnapp, "Epic Demonstrations: Fascist Modernity and the 1932 Exhibition of the Fascist Revolution," in *Fascism, Aesthetics, and Culture*, ed. Richard Joseph Golsan (Hanover, NH: University Press of New England, 1992), 3.

30. Ardengo Soffici, "Atto d'accusa," *Critica fascista* 4, no. 20 (October 15, 1926); Filippo Tommaso Marinetti, "L'arte fascista futurista," *Critica fascista* 4, no. 20 (October 15, 1926): 3; Mino Maccari, "Arte fascista," *Critica fascista* 4, no. 21 (November 1, 1926): 396ff.; Massimo Bontempelli, "Arte fascista," *Critica fascista* 4, no. 21 (November 1, 1926): 416; Antonio Pagano, "Arte, fascismo e popolo," *Critica fascista* 4, no. 21 (November 1, 1926): 436.

31. Antonio Aniante, "Opinioni sull'arte fascista, Arte di Stato," *Critica fascista* 5, no. 2 (January 15, 1927): 23.

32. "Resultanze dell'inchiesta sull'arte fascista," *Critica fascista* 5, no. 4 (February 15, 1927): 61–64; see also Margherita Sarfatti, "Arte, fascismo e antiretorica," *Critica fascista* 5, no. 5 (March 1, 1927): 82.

33. Mario Sironi, "Manifesto della pittura murale, in 'La Colonna,'" in *Scritti editi e inediti*, ed. Ettore Camesasca and Claudia Gian Ferrari (Milan: Feltrinelli, 1980), 155–57.

34. Note Gramsci's interest in the magazine: Antonio Gramsci, *Note sul Machiavelli, sulla politica e sullo stato moderno* (Turin: Giulio Einaudi, 1966), 319; G. Manacorda, *Letteratura e cultura del periodo fascista* (Milan: Principato Editore, 1974), 7; Mangoni, *L'interventismo della cultura*, 155–59; Mangoni, "Il fascismo," 534–35; Alberto Asor Rosa, "Il fascismo: Il regime (1926–1943)," in *Storia d'Italia*, 4: *Dall'unità a oggi* (Turin: Einaudi, 1975), part 2, 1500–1506; Luciano Troisio, *Le riviste di Strapaese e Stracittà: Il Selvaggio, l'Italiano, "900"* (Treviso: Canova, 1975); Walter L. Adamson, "The Culture of Italian Fascism and the Fascist Crisis of Modernity: The Case of Il Selvaggio," *Journal of Contemporary History* 30, no. 4 (1995): 555–75; Adamson, "Avant-Garde Modernism and Italian Fascism," 230–48.

35. Mino Maccari, "Una pietra sopra!" *Il Selvaggio* 3, no. 2 (March 1, 1926): 1.

36. Asor Rosa, "Il fascismo: Il regime (1926–1943)," 1502.

37. "Gazzettino ufficiale di Strapaese," *Il Selvaggio* 4, no. 16 (September 16, 1927): 1.

38. Manacorda, *Letteratura e cultura del periodo fascista*, 8.

39. Cf. Asor Rosa, "Il fascismo: Il regime (1926–1943)," 1507–14; Mangoni, "Il fascismo," 530–33; Adamson, "Avant-Garde Modernism and Italian Fascism," 230–48.

40. Manacorda, *Letteratura e cultura del periodo fascista*, 9. See also the magazine's manifesto: *900* 1 (1926): 1.

41. Manacorda, *Letteratura e cultura del periodo fascista*, 102.

42. Manacorda, *Letteratura e cultura del periodo fascista*, 103.

43. Manacorda, *Letteratura e cultura del periodo fascista*, 105.

44. Mangoni, "Il fascismo," 533.

45. Giovanni Gentile, "La filosofia del fascismo," *Educazione fascista* 6, no. 11 (November 1928): 641–43.

46. Francesco Formigari, "Ancora cultura e fascismo," *Critica fascista* 4, no. 4 (April 1926): 219.

47. Aldo Bertelè, "La dottrina fascista di Giovanni Gentile," *Critica fascista* 8, no. 7 (April 1, 1930): 134–35. See also Agostino Nasti, "Educazione politica e fascismo," *Critica fascista* 8, no. 8 (April 15, 1929): 167; D. Rende, "Libertà ed autorità," *Critica fascista* 7, no. 16 (August 15, 1929): 316–17; Umberto Gabbi, "Il fascismo nella scuola e nell'università," *Critica fascista* 10, no. 21 (November 1, 1932): 413–16.

48. Ernesto Codignola, *Il rinnovamento spirituale dei giovani* (Milan: A. Mondadori, 1933).

49. Ernesto Codignola, "Dieci anni di educazione fascista," *Critica fascista* 11, no. 5 (March 1, 1933): 98–100.

50. See Paolo Simoncelli, *Cantimori, Gentile e la Normale di Pisa: Profili e documenti* (Milan: FrancoAngeli, 1994); Roberto Pertici, "Mazzinianesimo, fascismo, comunismo: L'itinerario politico di Delio Cantimori (1919–1943)," *Cromohs* 2 (1997): 1–128; Leandro Perini, *Delio Cantimori: Un profilo* (Rome: Edizioni di storia e letteratura, 2004); Gennaro Sasso, *Delio Cantimori: Filosofia e storiografia* (Pisa: Edizioni della Normale, 2005).

51. Delio Cantimori, "Recensione di Ernesto Codignola, *Il rinnovamento spirituale dei giovani*," in *Politica e storia contemporanea: Scritti, 1927–1942*, ed. Luisa Mangoni (Turin: Einaudi, 1991), 194.

52. Cantimori, "Recensione di Ernesto Codignola," 194.

53. G. Gamberini, "Fede e competenza," *Critica fascista* 8, no. 15 (August 1, 1930): 283–84.

Chapter 4. The Ideology of the Totalitarian State

1. Sergio Luzzatto, "The Political Culture of Fascist Italy," *Contemporary European History* 8, no. 2 (July 1999): 322.

2. See Jeffrey T. Schnapp, *Staging Fascism: 18 BL and the Theater of Masses for Masses* (Stanford, CA: Stanford University Press, 1996); David D. Roberts, *The Totalitarian Experiment in Twentieth Century Europe: Understanding the Poverty of Great Politics* (London: Routledge, 2006); David D. Roberts, "How Not to Think about Fascism and Ideology, Intellectual Antecedents and Historical Meaning," *Journal of Contemporary History* 35, no. 2 (2000): 185–211; and David D. Roberts, "Myth, Style,

Substance and the Totalitarian Dynamic in Fascist Italy," *Contemporary European History* 16, no. 1 (2007): 1–36.

3. Karl Mannheim, *Ideology and Utopia* (London: Routledge, 2013), 49–62.

4. Mannheim, *Ideology and Utopia*, 112. Among the vast literature, see Leon Bailey, *Critical Theory and the Sociology of Knowledge: A Comparative Study in the Theory of Ideology* (New York: Lang, 1994); Carmelina Chiara Canta, *Ricostruire la società: Teoria del mutamento sociale in Karl Mannheim* (Milan: FrancoAngeli, 2006).

5. Mannheim, *Ideology and Utopia*, 119. For a review article, see Kathleen Knight, "Transformations of the Concept of Ideology in the Twentieth Century," *American Political Science Review* 100, no. 4 (November 2006): 619–26. See also the classic work by Daniel Bell, *The End of Ideology: On the Exhaustion of Political Ideas in the Fifties* (Cambridge, MA: Harvard University Press, 2000), 395. For some scholars, such as John B. Thompson, *Ideology and Modern Culture: Critical Social Theory in the Era of Mass Communication* (Stanford: Stanford University Press, 1991), ideologies are symbolic forms, and linguistic and cultural products, to which a group assigns meaning in creating relations of domination. According to Michael Freeden, *Ideologies and Political Theory: A Conceptual Approach* (Oxford: Oxford University Press, 1998), however, ideologies must be studied as political philosophies, identifying the concepts that shape political discourse. For J. M. Balkin, *Cultural Software: A Theory of Ideology* (New Haven: Yale University Press, 2003), they are systems of knowledge derived from the evolution of cultural competencies, while according to Andrew Heywood, *Political Ideologies: An Introduction* (London-Basingstoke: Palgrave Macmillan, 1992), ideology is a form of political thought. For an examination of the crisis of the concept of ideology in postmodern culture, see Terry Eagleton, *Ideology: An Introduction* (London: Verso, 2007).

6. Zeev Sternhell, "Fascist Ideology," in *Fascism: A Reader's Guide: Analyses, Interpretations, Bibliography*, ed. Walter Laqueur (Aldershot: Wildwood House, 1976).

7. Emilio Gentile, *Fascismo: Storia e interpretazione* (Rome: Laterza, 2002), 78.

8. Ernst Cassirer, *The Myth of the State* (New Haven: Yale University Press, 2013). For a synthesis of work on the relationship between political myth and Western philosophy, see Federico D'Agostino, *Dialectics of the Rational and the Irrational in the Process of Social Change: A Theoretical Analysis* (Berkeley: University of California, 1976); Roberto Esposito, "Mito," in *Nove pensieri sulla politica* (Bologna: Il Mulino, 1993), 113–36; Nico Di Napoli, *Mito politico e teoria razionale* (Naples: Loffredo, 1995).

9. Émile Durkheim and Joseph Ward Swain, *The Elementary Forms of the Religious Life* (London: G. Allen & Unwin, 1915).

10. See Piero Melograni, "The Cult of the Duce in Mussolini's Italy," *Journal of Contemporary History* 11, no. 4 (1976): 221–37; Renzo De Felice and Luigi Goglia, *Mussolini: Il mito* (Rome/Bari: Laterza, 1983); Emilio Gentile, *Il mito dello stato nuovo: Dal radicalismo nazionale al fascismo* (Rome: Laterza, 1999), 105–38; Pierre Milza, *Mussolini* (Rome: La biblioteca di Republica, 2000); Alessandro Campi, *Mussolini*

(Bologna: Il Mulino, 2001), especially chap. 1, in which he discusses works that see the myth of Mussolini as one of many expressions of fascist propaganda; Simonetta Falasca Zamponi, *Lo spettacolo del fascismo* (Soveria Mannelli (CZ): Rubbettino, 2003); Didier Musiedlak, *Mussolini* (Paris: Presses de Sciences Po, 2005), especially 409–12 on "the creation of the myth"; Gentile, *Fascismo: Storia e interpretazione*, 113–46. Musiedlak, *Mussolini*, is available in Italian translation as *Mussolini* (Florence: Le Lettere, 2009).

11. Henri Béraud, *Ce que j'ai vu à Rome* (Paris: Les Éditions de France, 1929), 39–41.

12. Gentile, *Fascismo: Storia e interpretazione*, 127.

13. Gabriele Pedullà, *Parole al potere: Discorsi politici italiani* (Milan: BUR Rizzoli, 2011), lx; Falasca Zamponi, *Lo spettacolo del fascismo*, 18, 137.

14. Quoted in Gentile, *Fascismo: Storia e interpretazione*, 128.

15. See Campi, *Mussolini*, 15.

16. Gentile, *Fascismo: Storia e interpretazione*, 131. For other examples, see Teresa Maria Mazzatosta, Claudio Volpi, and Benito Mussolini, *L'Italietta fascista: Lettere al potere, 1936–1943* (Bologna: Cappelli, 1980), 39; Alberto Vacca and Mario Avagliano, *Duce! tu sei un Dio! Mussolini e il suo mito nelle lettere degli Italiani* (Milan: Baldini & Castoldi, 2013).

17. Gianni Bertone, *I figli d'Italia si chiaman Balilla: Come e cosa insegnava la scuola fascista* (Rimini/Florence: Guaraldi, 1975), 64.

18. Gentile, *Fascismo: Storia e interpretazione*, 132.

19. Giovanni Gentile, "Il fascismo e la Sicilia," in *Opere complete di Giovanni Gentile*, vol. 45: *Politica e cultura I*, ed. Hervé A. Cavallera (Florence: Le Lettere, 1990), 60.

20. Giovanni Gentile, "Discorso inaugurale dell'Istituto nazionale fascista di cultura," in *Opere complete*, 45: *Politica e cultura I*, 258.

21. Gentile, "Discorso inaugurale dell'Istituto nazionale fascista di cultura," 260.

22. Gentile, "Discorso inaugurale dell'Istituto nazionale fascista di cultura," 260.

23. Giovanni Gentile, "Il programma," in *Opere complete*, 45: *Politica e cultura I*, 286.

24. Giovanni Gentile, "Dopo la fondazione dell'Impero," in *Opere complete*, 45: *Politica e cultura II*, ed. Hervé A. Cavallera (Florence: Le Lettere, 1990), 141–57.

25. Giuseppe Bottai, *Diario 1935–1944* (Milan: Rizzoli, 1982), 246–47.

26. Musiedlak, *Mussolini*, 284–88.

27. Gentile, *Fascismo: Storia e interpretazione*, 136.

28. See Daniele Marchesini, *La scuola dei gerarchi: Mistica fascista, storia, problemi, istituzioni* (Milan: Feltrinelli Economica, 1976); Emilio Gentile, *The Sacralization of Politics in Fascist Italy* (Cambridge, MA: Harvard University Press, 1996), 138; Tomaso Carini and Marcello Veneziani, *Niccolò Giani e la scuola di mistica fascista: 1930–1945* (Milan: Mursia, 2009).

29. N. Giani, "La mistica come dottrina del fascismo," *Dottrina fascista* 2, no. 6 (April 1937): 291.

30. C. E. Ferri, "Ortodossia fascista," *Dottrina fascista* 1, no. 1 (September 1937): 20–21.

31. Benito Mussolini, *Opera omnia*, vol. 21, ed. Edoardo Susmel and Duilio Susmel (Florence: La Fenice, 1954), 425.

32. Giovanni Gentile, Benito Mussolini, and Gioacchino Volpe, "Idee fondamentali," in *La dottrina del fascismo: Con una "Storia del movimento fascista" di Gioacchino Volpe* (Rome: Istituto della Enciclopedia italiana, 1934), 1.

33. Gentile, Mussolini, and Volpe, "Idee fondamentali," 1.

34. Giovanni Gentile, *Opere complete di Giovanni Gentile*, vol. 4: *I fondamenti della filosofia del diritto* (Florence: Sansoni, 1961), 108–14. See in particular Sasso, *Le due Italie di Giovanni Gentile*, 263–316, for reflections on the different editions of Gentile's text. See also Lo Schiavo and Gentile, *La filosofia politica di Giovanni Gentile*, 182–93; Faucci, *La filosofia politica di Croce e di Gentile*, 113–25; Valitutti, *Il diritto secondo Gentile. Il pensiero di Giovanni Gentile*, 873–83; Marini, "Aspetti sistematici della 'Filosofia del diritto' di Gentile," 462–83; Punzo, "I fondamenti della filosofia del diritto di Giovanni Gentile," 375; Amato, *L'etica oltre lo Stato*; Pinazzi, *Attualismo e problema giuridico.*

35. Paolo Ungari, *Alfredo Rocco e l'ideologia giuridica del fascismo* (Brescia: Morcelliana, 1963); Rocco D'Alfonso and Arturo Colombo, *Costruire lo Stato forte: Politica, diritto, economia in Alfredo Rocco* (Milan: FrancoAngeli, 2004); Saverio Battente, *Alfredo Rocco: Dal nazionalismo al fascismo, 1907–1935* (Milan: FrancoAngeli, 2005), 372; Alfredo Rocco and Giuliano Vassalli, *Alfredo Rocco: Discorsi parlamentari* (Bologna: Il Mulino, 2005); Emilio Gentile, Fulco Lanchester, and Alessandra Tarquini, eds., *Alfredo Rocco: Dalla crisi del parlamentarismo alla costruzione dello Stato nuovo* (Rome: Carocci, 2010).

36. Alfredo Rocco, "Che cosa è il nazionalismo," in *Scritti e discorsi politici di Alfredo Rocco*, 1: *La formazione dello Stato fascista, 1925–1934* (Milan: Giuffrè, 1938), 69–89.

37. The modern nature of Rocco's thought was first underscored in Ungari, *Alfredo Rocco e l'ideologia giuridica del fascismo.* It was also observed by Saverio Battente, *Alfredo Rocco verso la rivoluzione nazionale: Nazionalismo giuridico economico e modernizzazione, 1907–1922* (Siena: Copinfax, 2001), 51.

38. Alfredo Rocco, "Il fascismo verso il nazionalismo," in *Scritti e discorsi politici di Alfredo Rocco*, 2: *La lotta contro la reazione antinazionale, 1919–1924* (Milan: Giuffrè, 1938), 693.

39. Fulco Lanchester, "Alfredo Rocco e le origini dello Stato totale," in Gentile, Tarquini, and Lanchester, *Alfredo Rocco*, 15–39.

40. Alfredo Rocco, "La dottrina politica del fascismo," in *Scritti e discorsi politici di Alfredo Rocco*, 3: *La formazione dello Stato fascista, 1925–1934* (Milan: Giuffrè, 1938), 1093–1115, quotation on 1097, Mussolini's approval on 1115.

41. Rocco, "La dottrina politica del fascismo," 1107.

42. Francesco Perfetti, "Introduzione," in Sergio Panunzio, *Il fondamento giuridico del fascismo* (Rome: Bonacci, 1987); Francesco Perfetti, *Il sindacalismo fascista*

(Rome: Bonacci, 1988); Ferdinando Cordova, *Le origini dei sindacati fascisti, 1918–1926* (Scandicci [Florence]: La Nuova Italia, 1990), 247; Susanna Nistri De Angelis and Gian Biagio Furiozzi, *Sergio Panunzio: Quarant'anni di sindacalismo* (Florence: CET, 1990); Paolo Ridola, "Sulla fondazione teorica della 'dottrina dello Stato': I giuspubblicisti della Facoltà romana di Scienze politiche dalla istituzione della Facoltà al 1943," in *Passato e presente delle facoltà di scienze politiche*, ed. Fulco Lanchester (Milan: Giuffrè, 2003), 128–38; A. James Gregor, *Mussolini's Intellectuals: Fascist Social and Political Thought* (Princeton, NJ: Princeton University Press, 2005), 140–64; Francesco Perfetti, *Lo stato fascista: Le basi sindacali e corporative* (Florence: Le Lettere, 2010), 343–435.

43. Sergio Panunzio, *Lo Stato fascista* (Bologna: L. Cappelli Editore, 1925), 170.

44. Sergio Panunzio, *Il sentimento dello stato* (Rome: Libreria del Littorio, 1929), 27.

45. Quoted in Emilio Gentile, "La facoltà di scienze politiche," in Lanchester, *Passato e presente delle facoltà di scienze politiche*, 71.

46. Quoted in Gentile, "La facoltà di scienze politiche," 197.

47. Quoted in Gentile, "La facoltà di scienze politiche," 197.

48. Quoted in Gentile, "La facoltà di scienze politiche," 181.

49. Sergio Panunzio, *Teoria generale dello Stato fascista: Appunti di lezioni* (Padua: CEDAM, 1937), viii.

50. See Vincenzo Zangara, *Il Partito e lo Stato* (Catania: Studio editoriale moderno, 1935); Gaspare Ambrosini, *Il partito fascista e lo Stato* (Rome: Istituto Nazionale Fascista di Cultura, 1934); for a review of works on the nature of the PNF, see Panunzio, *Teoria generale dello Stato fascista*, 177ff.

51. Among various works, see "Carlo Costamagna," in *Repertorio biografico dei senatori dell'Italia fascista*, ed. Emilio Gentile and Emilia Campochiaro (Naples: Bibliopolis, 2003), vol. 2 (C–D); Marco Cupellaro, "Carlo Costamagna," in *Dizionario biografico degli Italiani* (Rome: Istituto della Enciclopedia italiana, 1981), 25:276; Mario Sbriccoli, "Carlo Costamagna," in *Dizionario del fascismo*, ed. Victoria De Grazia and Sergio Luzzatto (Turin: Einaudi, 2005), 1:367; Monica Toraldo di Francia, "Per un corporativismo senza 'Corporazioni': 'Lo Stato' di Carlo Costamagna," *Quaderni fiorentini: Per la storia del pensiero giuridico moderno* 18 (1989): 267–327; Fulco Lanchester, "Dottrina e politica nell'università italiana: Carlo Costamagna e il primo concorso di diritto corporativo," in *Momenti e figure nel diritto costituzionale in Italia e in Germania* (Milan: Giuffrè, 1994), 93–119; L. Galantini, "Il fascismo radicale di Carlo Costamagna," *Annali della Fondazione Ugo Spirito* 11 (1999): 89–104; M. Benvenuti, "Il pensiero giuridico di Carlo Costamagna," *Nomos* 10, nos. 1–2 (2005): 17–102; Alessandra Tarquini, *Il Gentile dei fascisti: Gentiliani e antigentiliani nel regime fascista* (Bologna: Il Mulino, 2009), 256–68.

52. Carlo Costamagna, "L'Istituto fascista di cultura," *Lo Stato* 6, nos. 8–9 (September 1935): 604; Carlo Costamagna, "Nascita dell'Istituto Nazionale di Cultura Fascista," *Lo Stato* 8, no. 1 (January 1937): 51–52; Carlo Costamagna, "Orientamenti culturali," *Lo Stato* 6, no. 6 (June 1935): 435; Carlo Costamagna, "Aggiornare l'Enciclopedia italiana," *Lo Stato* 9, no. 10 (October 1938): 547.

53. See Carlo Costamagna, *Storia e dottrina del fascismo* (Turin: UTET, 1938), 29.

54. Costamagna, *Storia e dottrina del fascismo*, 29.

55. Quoted in A. James Gregor, *The Ideology of Fascism: The Rationale of Totalitarianism* (New York: Free Press, 1969).

56. Luisa Mangoni, *L'interventismo della cultura: Intellettuali e riviste del fascismo* (Rome/Bari: Laterza, 1974), 48; and see Palmiro Togliatti, *Sul fascismo* (Rome: GLF Ed. Laterza, 2004), 146. In 1975 Philip Cannistraro made a similar argument, commenting on Mussolini's first statements about art and culture and asserting that the fascists had no program of cultural politics and thus delegated the management of cultural institutions to the nationalists. See Philip Cannistraro, *La fabbrica del consenso: Fascismo e mass media* (Rome: Laterza, 1975), 43. See also Giuseppe Parlato, "Nazionalismo e fascismo," in *Nazione e anti-nazione: Il movimento nazionalista dalla guerra di Libia al fascismo*, vol. 2 (Rome: Viella, 2016), 239–44.

57. Franco Gaeta, *Il nazionalismo italiano* (Rome: Laterza, 1981), 248–49.

58. Renzo De Felice, *Mussolini il fascista: L'organizzazione dello Stato fascista, 1925–1929* (Turin: G. Einaudi, 1968), 163.

59. De Felice, *Mussolini il fascista*, 164.

60. Renzo De Felice, *Mussolini il duce*, part 1: *Gli anni del consenso, 1929–1936* (Turin: Einaudi, 1974), 35.

61. De Felice, *Mussolini il duce*, part 1, 37.

62. Ungari, *Alfredo Rocco e l'ideologia giuridica del fascismo*, 18.

63. Emilio Gentile, *The Origins of Fascist Ideology 1918–1925* (New York: Enigma Books, 2012), 280.

64. Gentile, *The Origins of Fascist Ideology*, 326.

65. In 1975 Manlio Di Lalla also examined the jurist's and the philosopher's thought during the First World War, forming a similar hypothesis and highlighting the profound differences between their political ideas. Manlio Di Lalla, *Vita di Giovanni Gentile* (Florence: Sansoni, 1975), 287; see also Augusto Del Noce, *Giovanni Gentile: Per una interpretazione filosofica della storia contemporanea* (Bologna: Il Mulino, 1990), 359–60; Giovanni Gentile and Francesco Perfetti, *Discorsi parlamentari* (Bologna: Il Mulino, 2004), 32, but also 49–50; Francesco Perfetti, *Il movimento nazionalista in Italia (1903–1914)* (Rome: Bonacci, 1984).

66. Gentile, *The Origins of Fascist Ideology*, 332.

67. Emilio Gentile, *La Grande Italia: The Myth of the Nation in the Twentieth Century*, tr. Suzanne Dingee and Jennifer Pudney (Madison: University of Wisconsin Press, 2009), 158.

68. Camillo Pellizzi, "Lo Stato e la Nazione," *L'educazione politica* 4, no. 6 (June 1926): 317–20.

69. Camillo Pellizzi, "Rinascimento politico," *L'educazione politica* 4, no. 7 (July 1926): 389–92; also cf. C. Licitra, "Dalla Nazione allo Stato," *L'educazione politica* 4, no. 8 (August 1926): 415–19; C. Licitra, "Dalla Nazione allo Stato II," *L'educazione politica* 4, no. 9 (September 1926): 471–77.

70. Carlo Costamagna, "Nazione," in *Dizionario di politica*, ed. Partito nazionale fascista (Rome: Istituto della Enciclopedia italiana, 1940), vol. 3 (M–Q): 263.

71. See Andrea Giardina and André Vauchez, *Il mito di Roma: Da Carlo Magno a Mussolini* (Rome/Bari: Editori Laterza, 2000), including their reflections on the distance between the myth of Rome in fascist culture and actual Roman history; Vittorio Vidotto, "La capitale del fascismo," in *Rome capitale*, ed. Vittorio Vidotto (Rome/Bari: Laterza, 2002), 379–414; Luca Scuccimarra, "Romanità, culto della," in *Dizionario del fascismo*, ed. Victoria De Grazia and Sergio Luzzatto (Turin: Einaudi, 2005), 2:539–54; Giovanni Belardelli, *Il ventennio degli intellettuali: Cultura, politica, ideologia nell'Italia fascista* (Rome: Laterza, 2005), 206–29; Emilio Gentile, *Fascismo di pietra* (Rome: Laterza, 2007), 43. For a consideration of the *fascio littorio* as political symbol, see Luca Scuccimarra, "Il fascio littorio," in *Simboli della politica*, ed. Francesco Benigno and Luca Scuccimarra (Rome: Viella, 2010), 23–44.

72. Luciano Canfora, "Classicismo e fascismo," in *Matrici culturali del fascismo: Seminari promossi dal Consiglio regionale pugliese e dall'Ateneo barese nel trentennale della liberazione* (Bari: Università di Bari, Facoltà di lettere e filosofia, 1977), 85. Also see Luciano Canfora, *Ideologie del classicismo* (Turin: Einaudi, 1980), 247–70, especially the criticism of the concept of equality in fascist journalism; Paola S. Salvatori, "Fascismo e Romanità," *Studi storici* 55, no. 1 (2014): 227–39.

73. Giardina and Vauchez, *Il mito di Roma*, 239.

74. Gentile, *Fascismo di pietra*, 46–48.

75. Giardina and Vauchez, *Il mito di Roma*, 220–21; Gentile, *Fascismo di pietra*, 52.

76. Giardina and Vauchez, *Il mito di Roma*, 224–27; Gentile, *Fascismo di pietra*, 62.

77. Giardina and Vauchez, *Il mito di Roma*, 225; Gentile, *Fascismo di pietra*, 62; Gentile, *The Sacralization of Politics in Fascist Italy*, 43.

78. Gentile, *The Sacralization of Politics in Fascist Italy*, 44–45.

79. Gentile, *The Sacralization of Politics in Fascist Italy*, 50–52; Giardina and Vauchez, *Il mito di Roma*, 229.

80. Gentile, *Fascismo di pietra*, 72.

81. Gentile, *Fascismo di pietra*, 82. See also Paolo Nicoloso, *Mussolini architetto: Propaganda e paesaggio urbano nell'Italia fascista* (Turin: Einaudi, 2008), 34–81; Joshua Arthurs, *Excavating Modernity: The Roman Past in Fascist Italy* (Ithaca, NY: Cornell University Press, 2012); Aristotle Kallis, "The 'Third Rome' of Fascism: Demolitions and the Search for a New Urban Syntax," *Journal of Modern History* 84, no. 1 (March 2012): 40–79.

82. Mariella Cagnetta, *Antichisti e impero fascista* (Bari: Dedalo Libri, 1979), 39.

83. Cagnetta, *Antichisti e impero fascista*, 40.

84. Cagnetta, *Antichisti e impero fascista*, 54.

85. Cagnetta, *Antichisti e impero fascista*, 143; Gentile, *The Sacralization of Politics in Fascist Italy*, 76. See also Aristotle Kallis, "'Framing' Romanità: The Celebrations for the Bimillenario Augusteo and the Augusteo–Ara Pacis Project," *Journal of Contemporary History* 46, no. 4 (2011): 809–31.

86. See Renzo De Felice, *Mussolini il duce*, part 2: *Lo stato totalitario, 1936–1940* (Turin: Einaudi, 1981), 100; Giuseppe Parlato, *La sinistra fascista: Storia di un progetto mancato* (Bologna: Il Mulino, 2000), 107–22; George L. Mosse, *The Image of Man: The Creation of Modern Masculinity* (New York: Oxford University Press, 1996); Roberta Suzzi Valli, "The Myth of Squadrismo in the Fascist Regime," *Journal of Contemporary History* 35, no. 2 (2000): 131–50; Gentile, *Fascismo: Storia e interpretazione*, 235–65; Lorenzo Benadusi, *Il nemico dell'uomo nuovo: L'omosessualità nell'esperimento totalitario fascista* (Milan: Feltrinelli, 2005); Luca La Rovere, "Rifare gli italiani: L'esperimento di creazione dell'uomo nuovo nel regime fascista," *Annali di storia dell'educazione e delle istituzioni scolastiche* 9 (2002): 51–77; Ornella Stellavato, "La nascita dell'Opera nazionale Balilla," *Mondo contemporaneo* 2 (2009): 5–81.

87. Benadusi, *Il nemico dell'uomo nuovo*.

88. Benito Mussolini, *Opera omnia*, vol. 34, 2nd reprint, ed. Edoardo Susmel (Florence: LaFenice, 1967), 117.

89. De Felice, *Mussolini il duce*, part 2: *Lo stato totalitario, 1936–1940*, 100.

90. De Felice, *Mussolini il duce*, part 2, 96.

91. De Felice, *Mussolini il duce*, part 2, 101. Also see the 1939 special issue of the magazine *Antieuropa* edited by A. Gravelli and devoted to the polemic against *lei*; and Marie-Anne Matard, "L'anti-lei: Utopie linguistique ou projet totalitaire?" *Mélanges de l'École française de Rome* 2 (1998): 971–1010.

92. De Felice, *Mussolini il duce*, part 2, 101; see also Mosse, *The Image of Man*, 154–80; Gentile, *Fascismo: Storia e interpretazione*, 239.

93. Gianpasquale Santomassimo, *La terza via fascista: Il mito del corporativismo* (Rome: Carocci, 2006), 11; see also Giuseppe Parlato, *Il convegno italo-francese di studi corporativi (1935): Con il testo integrale degli atti* (Rome: Fondazione Ugo Spirito, 1990); Alessio Gagliardi, *Il corporativismo fascista* (Rome: Laterza, 2010); Maurizio Cau, "Un nuovo ordine tra stato e società: Recenti ricerche sul corporativismo," *Storica* 16, no. 48 (October 2010): 135–63.

94. See Renzo De Felice, "Ugo Spirito e la politica fra le due guerre," in *Il pensiero di Ugo Spirito*, vol. 2 (Rome: Istituto della Enciclopedia italiana, 1990), 255. See also Franco Tamassia, ed., *L'opera di Ugo Spirito: Bibliografia* (Rome: Fondazione Ugo Spirito, 1986). For a collection of studies on Ugo Spirito, see Giovanni Dessì, *Ugo Spirito: Filosofia e rivoluzione* (Milan: Luni, 1999); and, more recently, see Danilo Breschi, *Spirito del Novecento: Il secolo di Ugo Spirito dal fascismo alla contestazione* (Soveria Mannelli [CZ]: Rubbettino, 2010).

95. Ugo Spirito, *I fondamenti dell'economia corporativa* (Milan: Treves, 1932), 28.

96. Spirito, *I fondamenti dell'economia corporativa*, 41.

97. Alberto Asor Rosa, "Una polemica corporativa," in *Il fascismo: Il regime (1926–1943)* (Turin: Einaudi, 1975), 1489–95; Luigi Punzo, "L'esperienza di 'nuovi studi di diritto, economia e politica,'" in *Il pensiero di Ugo Spirito*, 2:367–78; Luigi Punzo, *La soluzione corporativa dell'attualismo di Ugo Spirito* (Naples: Edizioni Scientifiche Italiane, 1984), 21–22; Dessì, *Ugo Spirito*, 50–53.

98. Dessì, *Ugo Spirito*, 70.

99. Ugo Spirito, "Individuo e Stato nella concezione corporativa," in *Atti del secondo convegno di studi sindacali e corporativi, Ferrara, 5–8 maggio 1932*, vol. 1 (Rome: Tipografia del Senato, 1932), 188.

100. Spirito, "Individuo e Stato nella concezione corporativa," 189.

101. Perfetti, *Lo stato fascista*, 413–43.

102. Perfetti, *Lo stato fascista*, 422. For the debates that followed the convention, see Ugo Spirito, "Risposta alle obiezioni," *Nuovi studi di diritto, economia e politica* 5, no. 2 (May 1932): 94–99; De Felice, *Mussolini il duce*, part 1, 9–18; Francesco Perfetti, "Ugo Spirito e la concezione della corporazione proprietaria al convegno di studi sindacali e corporativi di Ferrara del 1932," *Critica storica* 25, no. 2 (1988): 202–43; Giuseppe Parlato, "Ugo Spirito e il sindacalismo fascista (1932–1942)," in *Il pensiero di Ugo Spirito*, vol. 1 (Rome: Istituto della Enciclopedia italiana, 1990), 79–124; Dessì, *Ugo Spirito*, 64–86.

103. Cau, "Un nuovo ordine tra stato e società," 152, quoting Pietro Costa, *Civitas: Storia della cittadinanza in Europa* 4: *L'età dei totalitarismi e della democrazia* (Rome: Laterza, 2001), 259.

104. Cau, "Un nuovo ordine tra stato e società," 153.

105. Zeev Sternhell, "Modernity and Its Enemies: From the Revolt against the Enlightenment to the Undermining of Democracy," in *The Intellectual Revolt against Democracy 1870–1945: International Conference in Memory of Jacob L. Talmon* (Jerusalem: Israel Academy of Sciences and Humanities, 1996), 7–32; Maurizio Serra, *La ferita della modernità: Intellettuali, totalitarismo e immagine del nemico* (Bologna: Il Mulino, 1992); Niccolò Zapponi, *La modernità deviante* (Bologna: Il Mulino, 1992); Belardelli, *Il ventennio degli intellettuali*, 237–59; Antonino De Francesco, *Mito e storiografia della "Grande Rivoluzione": La rivoluzione francese nella cultura politica italiana del '900* (Naples: Guida, 2006), 107–235.

106. De Felice, *Mussolini il duce*, part 1, 36, 232, 780; Eugenio Garin, *Cronache di filosofia italiana: 1900–1943* (Bari: Laterza, 1966), 148; Tullio Gregory, Marta Fattori, and Nicola Siciliani de Cumis, eds., *Filosofi, universita, regime: La scuola di filosofia di Roma negli anni trenta; Mostra storico-documentaria* (Rome/Naples: Istituto di filosofia della Sapienza Istituto italiano per gli studi filosofici, 1985), 91–95; Tarquini, *Il Gentile dei fascisti*, 201–11.

107. G. Silvano Spinetti, *L'Europa verso la rivoluzione* (Rome: Edizioni di Novissima, 1936), 11.

108. Niccolò Zapponi, ed., "Il ricordo di Babele: Note sull'idea di modernità," *Storia contemporanea* 21, no. 6 (1990): 997–1046.

109. G. Lumbroso, "Quel che rimane del 1789," *Critica fascista* 5, no. 8 (April 15, 1927): 144–45.

110. Antonio Pagano, "Origini e fattori della rivoluzione fascista," in *Dottrina e politica fascista* (Perugia: La Nuova Italia, 1930), 28.

111. Pagano, "Origini e fattori della rivoluzione fascista," 29.

112. Panunzio, *Lo Stato fascista*, 25.

113. Sergio Panunzio, *Rivoluzione e costituzione (Problemi costituzionali della rivoluzione)* (Milan: Treves, 1933), 86.

114. George L. Mosse, "Fascism and the French Revolution," *Journal of Contemporary History* 24, no. 1 (1989): 6.

115. Mosse, "Fascism and the French Revolution," 7.

116. Gentile, *The Sacralization of Politics in Fascist Italy*, 3.

Chapter 5. Cultural Politics in the 1930s

1. See Renzo De Felice, *Mussolini il duce*, part 1: *Gli anni del consenso, 1929–1936* (Turin: Einaudi, 1974), 127, 189–91, 288, 311. Also see Roberto Pertici, "Balbino Giuliano," in *Dizionario biografico degli Italiani* (Rome: Istituto della Enciclopedia italiana, 1981), 56:770–76. See also Alessandra Tarquini, *Il Gentile dei fascisti: Gentiliani e antigentiliani nel regime fascista* (Bologna: Il Mulino, 2009), 301–14.

2. See "Il Consiglio dei ministri e il Gran Consiglio si riuniscono oggi sotto la presidenza del Capo del Governo," *Il popolo d'Italia* 17, no. 66 (March 18, 1930): 1; "La seduta del Gran Consiglio," *Il popolo d'Italia* 17, no. 67 (March 19, 1930): 1. See also Benito Mussolini, *Opera omnia*, vol. 24, ed. Edoardo Susmel (Florence: La Fenice, 1954), 205.

3. Tarquini, *Il Gentile dei fascisti*, 305.

4. Tarquini, *Il Gentile dei fascisti*, 305.

5. De Felice, *Mussolini il duce*, part 1, 189.

6. Michel Ostenc, *La scuola italiana durante il fascismo* (Rome/Bari: Laterza, 1981), 203; Jürgen Charnitzky, *Fascismo e scuola: La politica scolastica del regime (1922–1943)* (Florence: La Nuova Italia, 1994), 426–30; Tarquini, *Il Gentile dei fascisti*, 308.

7. For a detailed and clear analysis of the textbooks, see Mariella Colin, *"Les enfants de Mussolini": Littérature, livres, lectures d'enfance et de jeunesse; De la grande guerre à la chute du régime* (Caen: Presses universitaires de Caen, 2010), 190–212.

8. Charnitzky, *Fascismo e scuola*, 319.

9. Charnitzky, *Fascismo e scuola*, 320. See also Giorgio Boatti, *Preferirei di no: Le storie dei dodici professori che si opposero a Mussolini* (Turin: Einaudi, 2001); Helmut Goetz, *Il giuramento rifiutato: I docenti universitari e il regime fascista* (Florence: La Nuova Italia, 2000). On Gentile's role, see Gennaro Sasso, *Filosofia e idealismo*, vol. 2: *Giovanni Gentile* (Naples: Bibliopolis, 1995), 11–52.

10. Charnitzky, *Fascismo e scuola*, 324.

11. L. Lo Bianco, "Francesco Ercole," in *Dizionario biografico degli Italiani* (Rome: Istituto della Enciclopedia italiana, 1993), 43:132–34; Charnitzky, *Fascismo e scuola*, 432–37.

12. Tarquini, *Il Gentile dei fascisti*, 309.

13. Tarquini, *Il Gentile dei fascisti*, 309.

14. Benito Mussolini, *Opera omnia*, vol. 42, ed. Duilio Susmel and Edoardo Susmel (Florence: La Fenice, 1979), 59.

15. Ostenc, *La scuola italiana durante il fascismo*, 127.

16. Tarquini, *Il Gentile dei fascisti*, 310; see also Cesare Maria de Vecchi di Val Cismon and Sandro Setta, *Tra Papa, Duce e Re: Il conflitto tra Chiesa cattolica e Stato fascista nel Diario 1930–1931 del primo ambasciatore del Regno d'Italia presso la Santa Sede* (Rome: Jouvence, 1998), 12; E. Santarelli, "Cesare Maria De Vecchi," in *Dizionario biografico degli Italiani* (Rome: Istituto della Enciclopedia italiana, 1991), 39:522–31; Sandro Setta, "Cesare Maria de Vecchi di Val Cismon," *Storia contemporanea* 24, no. 6 (1993): 1057–1113.

17. Cesare Maria De Vecchi, *Bonifica fascista della cultura* (Milan: Mondadori, 1937).

18. Ostenc, *La scuola italiana durante il fascismo*, 214–27.

19. Giovanni Gentile, "La tradizione italiana," in *Opere complete di Giovanni Gentile*, 48: *Frammenti di estetica di teoria della storia*, part 2, ed. Hervé A. Cavallera (Florence: Le Lettere, 1992), 97–118. See also Vittorio Vidotto, "La capitale del fascismo," in *Roma capitale*, ed. Vittorio Vidotto (Rome/Bari: Laterza, 2002), 394.

20. The incident was reconstructed by Paolo Simoncelli in *Cantimori, Gentile e la Normale di Pisa: Profili e documenti* (Milan: FrancoAngeli, 1994), 61–75; Paolo Simoncelli, *La Normale di Pisa tensioni e consenso 1928–1938: Appendice 1944–1949* (Milan: FrancoAngeli, 1998).

21. Istituto nazionale fascista di cultura, "Ordinamento dell'Istituto nazionale di cultura fascista," *Civiltà fascista* 4, nos. 1–2 (February 1937): 102ff.

22. Quoted in Tarquini, *Il Gentile dei fascisti*, 327–28.

23. Tarquini, *Il Gentile dei fascisti*, 328.

24. Beyond the essays cited in chapter 2, for further reading on the topic of young people and youth organizations under the fascist regime, see Maria Cristina Giuntella, "I gruppi universitari fascisti nel primo decennio del regime fascista," *Movimento di liberazione in Italia* 24, no. 107 (1972): 3–38; also appearing in Maria Cristina Giuntella, *Autonomia e nazionalizzazione dell'università: Il fascismo e l'inquadramento degli atenei* (Rome: Studium, 1992), 125–70; Ugoberto Alfassio Grimaldi and Marina Addis Saba, eds., *Cultura a passo romano: Storia e strategie dei Littoriali della cultura e dell'arte* (Milan: Feltrinelli, 1983); Ruth Ben-Ghiat, "Gruppi universitari fascisti," in *Dizionario del fascismo*, ed. Victoria De Grazia and Sergio Luzzatto (Turin: Einaudi, 2005), 1:640–42.

25. Charnitzky, *Fascismo e scuola*, 361.

26. Quoted in Charnitzky, *Fascismo e scuola*, 362.

27. Niccolò Zapponi, "Il partito della gioventù: Le organizzazioni giovanili del fascismo, 1926–1943," *Storia contemporanea* 13, nos. 4–5 (1982): 569–633, especially 572.

28. Emilio Gentile, *Fascismo: Storia e interpretazione* (Rome: Laterza, 2002), 193–97; Luca La Rovere and Bruno Bongiovanni, *Storia dei Guf: Organizzazione, politica e miti della gioventù universitaria fascista 1919–1943* (Turin: Bollati Boringhieri, 2003), 220–27; Alessio Ponzio, *La palestra del Littorio: L'Accademia della Farnesina, un esperimento di pedagogia totalitaria nell'Italia fascista* (Milan: FrancoAngeli, 2009), 127.

29. Quoted in Zapponi, "Il partito della gioventù," 572.

30. La Rovere and Bongiovanni, *Storia dei Guf*, 303.

31. La Rovere and Bongiovanni, *Storia dei Guf*, 303–7.

32. See Emilio Gentile, *The Italian Road to Totalitarianism* (London: Frank Cass, 2004); Emilio Gentile, *Storia del Partito fascista, 1919–1922: Movimento e milizia* (Rome: Laterza, 1989).

33. See La Rovere and Bongiovanni, *Storia dei Guf*, 265.

34. Charnitzky, *Fascismo e scuola*, 381; cf. Tracy H. Koon, *Believe, Obey, Fight: Political Socialization of Youth in Fascist Italy, 1922–1943* (Chapel Hill: University of North Carolina, 1985), 203.

35. Ruth Ben-Ghiat, *Fascist Modernities: Italy, 1922–1945* (Berkeley: University of California Press, 2009), 13–14.

36. Domenico Carella, *Fascismo prima, fascismo dopo* (Rome: A. Armando, 1973), 126.

37. Zapponi, "Il partito della gioventù," 573. As has been observed, "all of those who lived through and believed in fascism emerged from a traumatic experience: in order to explain their positions in the regime, they would have required a clarity that some people never attain, and a courage that they did not possess, because it was not even clear to them whether they were the victims or the guilty parties." Grimaldi and Addis Saba, *Cultura a passo romano*, 14. On young people's difficulties during the transition to postfascism, see Luca La Rovere, *L'eredità del fascismo: Gli intellettuali, i giovani e la transizione al postfascismo, 1943–1948* (Turin: Bollati Boringheri, 2008).

38. Denise Detragiache, "Le fascisme féminin, de San Sepolcro à l'affaire Matteotti (1919–1925)," *Revue d'histoire moderne et contemporaine (1954–)* 30, no. 3 (1983): 366–400; Maria Fraddosio, "The Fallen Hero: The Myth of Mussolini and Fascist Women in the Italian Social Republic (1943–5)," *Journal of Contemporary History* 31, no. 1 (1996): 99–124; Perry R. Willson and Patrizia Marangon, *Italiane biografia del Novecento* (Bari: Laterza, 2011); Stefania Bartoloni, *Il fascismo e le donne nella "Rassegna femminile italiana": 1925–1930* (Rome: Biblink, 2012); Perry Willson, "Fasciste della prima e della seconda ora," in *Di generazione in generazione: Le italiane dall'unità ad oggi*, ed. Maria Teresa Mori et al. (Rome: Viella, 2015), 183–206; Lorenzo Benadusi, "Storia del fascismo e questioni di genere," *Studi Storici* 55, no. 1 (2014): 183–95.

39. Fraddosio, "The Fallen Hero," 101.

40. Fraddosio, "The Fallen Hero," 101.

41. Marina Addis Saba, "Littoriali al femminile," in Grimaldi and Addis Saba, *Cultura a passo romano*, 144–64.

42. Victoria De Grazia, *Le donne nel regime fascista* (Venice: Marsilio, 2001), 18.

43. Detragiache, "Le fascisme féminin, de San Sepolcro à l'affaire Matteotti (1919–1925)," 378; cf. Bartoloni, *Il fascismo e le donne nella "Rassegna femminile italiana*," 24–28.

44. De Grazia, *Le donne nel regime fascista*, 61.

45. De Grazia, *Le donne nel regime fascista*, 55.

46. Detragiache, "Le fascisme féminin, de San Sepolcro à l'affaire Matteotti (1919–1925)," 385.

47. Detragiache, "Le fascisme féminin, de San Sepolcro à l'affaire Matteotti (1919–1925)," 396.

48. De Grazia, *Le donne nel regime fascista*, 97.

49. De Grazia, *Le donne nel regime fascista*, 101.

50. De Grazia, *Le donne nel regime fascista*, 79.

51. Fraddosio, "The Fallen Hero," 101–3.

52. Willson, "Fasciste della prima e della seconda ora," 193; Willson and Marangon, *Italiane biografia del Novecento*, 149–61.

53. Philip Cannistraro, *La fabbrica del consenso: Fascismo e mass media* (Rome: Laterza, 1975); Renzo De Felice, *Mussolini il duce*, part 2: *Lo stato totalitario, 1936–1940* (Turin: Einaudi, 1981), 181–87; Nicola Tranfaglia, Paolo Murialdi, and Massimo Legnani, *La stampa italiana nell'età fascista* (Rome/Bari: Laterza, 1980); Patrizia Ferrara and Marina Giannetto, *Il Ministero della cultura popolare, il Ministero delle poste e telegrafi* (Bologna: Il Mulino, 1992).

54. Tranfaglia, Murialdi, and Legnani, *La stampa italiana nell'età fascista*, 48–51.

55. Tranfaglia, Murialdi, and Legnani, *La stampa italiana nell'età fascista*, 48–51. See also De Felice, *Mussolini il duce*, part 2, 183; Romano Canosa, *La voce del duce: L'agenzia Stefani; L'arma segreta di Mussolini* (Milan: Mondadori, 2002), 20.

56. Tranfaglia, Murialdi, and Legnani, *La stampa italiana nell'età fascista*, 104.

57. Ferrara and Giannetto, *Il Ministero della cultura popolare, il Ministero delle poste e telegrafi*, 27.

58. Cannistraro, *La fabbrica del consenso*, 80.

59. Pierluigi Allotti, *Giornalisti di regime: La stampa italiana tra fascismo e antifascismo* (Rome: Carocci, 2012), 55.

60. Allotti, *Giornalisti di regime*, 58.

61. Allotti, *Giornalisti di regime*, 91.

62. See Giovanni Sedita, *Gli intellettuali di Mussolini: La cultura finanziata dal fascismo* (Florence: Le Lettere, 2010), 38.

63. Sedita, *Gli intellettuali di Mussolini*, 127.

64. Gian Piero Brunetta, *Cinema italiano tra le due guerre: Fascismo e politica cinematografica* (Milan: Mursia, 1975), 33; Mino Argentieri, *L'occhio del regime: Informazione e propaganda nel cinema del fascismo* (Florence: Vallecchi, 1979); Ernesto G. Laura, *Le stagioni dell'aquila: Storia dell'Istituto Luce* (Rome: Ente dello spettacolo, 2000); Vito Zagarrio, *Cinema e fascismo: Film, modelli, immaginari* (Venice: Marsilio, 2004); for an exploration of the historiographic debate over film under fascism, see Ermanno Taviani, "Il cinema e la propaganda fascista," *Studi storici* 55, no. 1 (2014): 241–56; Daniela Calanca, *Bianco e nero: L'Istituto nazionale Luce e l'immaginario del fascismo (1924–1940)* (Bologna: Bononia University Press, 2016).

65. Brunetta, *Cinema italiano tra le due guerre*, 38.

66. Brunetta, *Cinema italiano tra le due guerre*, 38.

67. Brunetta, *Cinema italiano tra le due guerre*, 43.

68. Alfonso Venturini, *La politica cinematografica del regime fascista* (Rome: Carocci, 2015), 42.

69. Venturini, *La politica cinematografica del regime fascista*, 50. See also Ruth Ben-Ghiat, *Italian Fascism's Empire Cinema* (Bloomington: Indiana University Press, 2015).

70. Maurizio Zinni, "L'impero sul grande schermo: Il cinema di finzione fascista e la conquista coloniale (1936–1942)," *Mondo contemporaneo* 3 (2011): 5–38.

71. Zinni, "L'impero sul grande schermo," 23.

72. Fiamma Nicolodi, *Musica e musicisti nel ventennio fascista* (Fiesole: Discanto, 1984), 35–66; Harvey Sachs, *Music in Fascist Italy* (New York: Norton, 1988); Marco Gervasoni, *Le armi di Orfeo: Musica, mitologie nazionali e religioni politiche nell'Europa del Novecento* (Florence: La Nuova Italia, 2002), 123; Stefano Biguzzi, *L'orchestra del duce: Mussolini, la musica e il mito del capo* (Turin: UTET Libreria, 2003); Lorenzo Santoro, *Musica e politica nell'Italia unita: Dall'illuminismo alla repubblica dei partiti* (Venice: Marsilio, 2013), 35–66.

73. Gervasoni, *Le armi di Orfeo*, 126.

74. Biguzzi, *L'orchestra del Duce*, 59–74.

75. Nicola Badolato and Anna Scalfaro, "L'educazione musicale nella scuola italiana dall'unità a oggi," *Musica docta: Rivista digitale di pedagogia e didattica della musica* 3 (2013): 87–99, https://musicadocta.unibo.it/article/view/4022.

76. Badolato and Scalfaro, "L'educazione musicale nella scuola italiana dall'unità a oggi."

77. Biguzzi, *L'orchestra del Duce*, 63.

78. Biguzzi, *L'orchestra del Duce*, 64.

79. Biguzzi, *L'orchestra del Duce*, 64.

80. Gervasoni, *Le armi di Orfeo*, 135; Biguzzi, *L'orchestra del duce*, 88–112; Nicolodi, *Musica e musicisti nel ventennio fascista*, 235–74, in particular the pages on Casella.

81. Emanuela Scarpellini, *Organizzazione teatrale e politica del teatro nell'Italia fascista* (Florence: Nuova Italia, 1989), 107.

82. Gianfranco Pedullà, *Il teatro italiano nel tempo del fascismo* (Bologna: Il Mulino, 1994), 204–11.

83. Scarpellini, *Organizzazione teatrale e politica del teatro nell'Italia fascista*, 109.

84. Scarpellini, *Organizzazione teatrale e politica del teatro nell'Italia fascista*, 110.

85. Jeffrey T. Schnapp, *Staging Fascism: 18 BL and the Theater of Masses for Masses* (Stanford, CA: Stanford University Press, 1996), 17; and see also Victoria De Grazia, *Consenso e cultura di massa nell'Italia fascista: L'organizzazione del dopolavoro* (Rome: Laterza, 1981), 184–90.

86. Franco Monteleone, *La radio italiana nel periodo fascista: Studi e documenti, 1922–1945* (Venice: Marsilio, 1976); Alberto Monticone and Luigi Parola, *Il fascismo al microfono: Radio e politica in Italia (1924–1945)* (Rome: Edizioni Studium, 1978); Gianni Isola, *Abbassa la tua radio, per favore: Storia dell' ascolto radiofonico nell' Italia fascista* (Florence: La Nuova Italia, 1990); Franco Monteleone, *Storia della radio e della televisione in Italia* (Venice: Marsilio, 2003).

87. Isola, *Abbassa la tua radio, per favore*, 115; Monteleone, *La radio italiana nel periodo fascista*, 96–110.

88. Isola, *Abbassa la tua radio, per favore*, 115–41.

89. Sara Zambotti, *La scuola sintonizzata: Pratiche di ascolto e immaginario tecnologico nei programmi dell'Ente radio rurale (1933–1940)* (Turin: Trauben, 2007).

90. Isola, *Abbassa la tua radio, per favore*, 103.

91. Monteleone, *La radio italiana nel periodo fascista*, 136.

92. Isola, *Abbassa la tua radio, per favore*, 177.

93. Monteleone, *La radio italiana nel periodo fascista*, 125.

94. Monteleone, *La radio italiana nel periodo fascista*, 131.

95. Isola, *Abbassa la tua radio, per favore*, 25.

96. Giuseppe Bottai, "Appunti sui rapporti fra lingua e rivoluzione," *L'Orto* 4, no. 3 (1934): 3; Fabio Foresti, "Proposte interpretative e di ricerca su lingua e fascismo: La politica linguistica," in *Credere, obbedire, combattere: Il regime linguistico nel ventennio*, ed. Fabio Foresti (Bologna: Pendragon, 2003), 32.

97. Foresti, "Proposte interpretative e di ricerca su lingua e fascismo," 39–40.

98. Bruno Migliorini, *Lingua contemporanea* (Florence: Sansoni, 1938), 28.

99. Gabriella Klein, *La politica linguistica del fascismo* (Bologna: Il Mulino, 1986), 56.

100. Quoted in Klein, *La politica linguistica del fascismo*, 73.

101. Foresti, "Proposte interpretative e di ricerca su lingua e fascismo," 60; Klein, *La politica linguistica del fascismo*, 93.

102. Klein, *La politica linguistica del fascismo*, 107. See also Patrizia Dogliani, "Lingua/dialetti," in *Dizionario del fascismo*, ed. Victoria De Grazia and Sergio Luzzatto (Turin: Einaudi, 2005), 2:53–56.

103. See Foresti, *Credere, obbedire, combattere*, 51, for comments by linguists; Sergio Raffaelli, *Le parole proibite: Purismo di stato e regolamentazione della pubblicità in Italia, 1812–1945* (Bologna: Il Mulino, 1983), 156–59.

104. Raffaelli, *Le parole proibite*, 155.

105. Claudio Marazzini, *L'ordine delle parole: Storia di vocabolari italiani* (Bologna: Il Mulino, 2009), 386; Raffaelli, *Le parole proibite*, 200.

106. Foresti, *Credere, obbedire, combattere*, 61; Klein, *La politica linguistica del fascismo*, 124–36.

107. Raffaelli, *Le parole proibite*, 203, 225.

Chapter 6. Intellectuals and Artists in the 1930s

1. Eugenio Garin, "La filosofia italiana di fronte al fascismo," in *Tendenze della filosofia italiana nell'età del fascismo*, ed. Ornella Pompeo Faracovi (Livorno: Belforte, 1985), 18, but this opinion was also expressed in Eugenio Garin, *Cronache di filosofia italiana: 1900–1943* (Bari: Laterza, 1966).

2. Renato Moro, *La formazione della classe dirigente cattolica (1929–1937)* (Bologna: Il Mulino, 1979), 41; Luisa Mangoni, *L'interventismo della cultura: Intellettuali e riviste del fascismo* (Rome/Bari: Laterza, 1974), 246–49; Luisa Mangoni, "Aspetti

della cultura cattolica sotto il fascismo: La rivista 'Il Frontespizio,'" in *Modernismo, fascismo, comunismo: Aspetti e figure della cultura e della politica dei cattolici nel '900*, ed. Giuseppe Rossini (Bologna: Il Mulino, 1972), 363–417; this interpretation was reaffirmed by Guido Verucci, *Idealisti all'indice: Croce, Gentile e la condanna del Sant'Uffizio* (Rome/Bari: Laterza, 2006), 80.

3. Domenico Montalto, "La libertà e i giovani," *Critica fascista* 7, no. 16 (August 15, 1929): 312–13.

4. Mario Carli and G. A. Fanelli, *Antologia degli scrittori fascisti* (Florence: Bemporad, 1931). Giuseppe Attilio Fanelli, *Contra Gentiles: Mistificazioni dell'idealismo attuale nella rivoluzione fascista* (Rome: Società degli autori ed editori, 1933), 13.

5. Fanelli, *Contra Gentiles*, 20. For the editors' debates over the criteria for compiling the anthology and other aspects of the volume's creation, see Francesco Perfetti, *Fascismo monarchico: I paladini della monarchia assoluta fra integralismo e dissidenza* (Rome: Bonacci, 1988), 266–76; Anna Scarantino, *"L'Impero": Un quotidiano "reazionario-futurista" degli anni venti* (Rome: Bonacci, 1981), 133–36.

6. Carli and Fanelli, *Antologia degli scrittori fascisti*, viii.

7. Carli and Fanelli, *Antologia degli scrittori fascisti*, ix.

8. Besides the compilers of the work and Mussolini, the most prominent authors were Giacomo Acerbo, Gino Arias, Italo Balbo, Emilio Bodrero, Massimo Bontempelli, Giuseppe Bottai, Antonio Bruers, Giuseppe Brunati, Franco Ciarlantini, Francesco Coppola, Enrico Corradini, Carlo Costamagna, Ugo D'Andrea, Gabriele D'Annunzio, Luigi Federzoni, Roberto Forges Davanzati, Balbino Giuliano, Giovanni Giuriati, Asvero Gravelli, Ezio Maria Gray, Telesio Interlandi, Leo Longanesi, Curzio Malaparte, Maurizio Maraviglia, Filippo Tommaso Marinetti, Arturo Marpicati, Arnaldo Mussolini, Angelo Oliviero Olivetti, Paolo Orano, Sergio Panunzio, Giorgio Pini, Giovanni Preziosi, Alfredo Rocco, Nino Serventi, Emilio Settimelli, Ardengo Soffici, Bruno Spampanato, and Vincenzo Zangara.

9. Carli and Fanelli, *Antologia degli scrittori fascisti*, viii.

10. Gherardo Casini, "Esortazione ad una letteratura," *Critica fascista* 10, no. 18 (September 15, 1932): 344.

11. Gherardo Casini, "Per una letteratura: Appello al coraggio," *Critica fascista* 10, no. 20 (October 15, 1932): 384.

12. Ugo Ojetti, "Italianità e modernità (Lettera di Ojetti e risposta di Bottai)," *Critica fascista* 10, no. 20 (October 15, 1932): 392.

13. Ruth Ben-Ghiat, *Fascist Modernities: Italy, 1922–1945* (Berkeley: University of California Press, 2009), 46. Ghiat believes that the attempt to create a modern literature failed; the argument of the present book is the opposite.

14. On novels of the fascist era, and in particular on the works of Barbaro, Emanuelli and Moravia, see Ben-Ghiat, *Fascist Modernities*, 55–64.

15. See Diano Brocchi, ed., *Antologia de "L'Universale"* (Pisa: Giardini, 1961); Paolo Buchignani, *Un fascismo impossibile: L'eresia di Berto Ricci nella cultura del Ventennio* (Bologna: Il Mulino, 1994); Mangoni, *L'interventismo della cultura*, 218–29; Alberto

Asor Rosa, "Lo Stato democratico e i partiti politici," in *Letteratura italiana*, vol. 1: *Il letterato e le istituzioni* (Turin: Einaudi, 1982), 551–55; Alberto Asor Rosa, "Il fascismo: Il regime (1926–1943)," in *Storia d'Italia*, 4: *Dall'unità a oggi* (Turin: Einaudi, 1975), part 2, 1505, 1567–1572; Alessandra Tarquini, *Il Gentile dei fascisti: Gentiliani e antigentiliani nel regime fascista* (Bologna: Il Mulino, 2009), 180–89.

16. Buchignani, *Un fascismo impossibile*, 40.

17. Berto Ricci, *Scrittore italiano* (Rome: Critica Fascista, 1931), 9.

18. Ricci, *Scrittore italiano*, 9.

19. Ricci, *Scrittore italiano*, 73.

20. Ricci, *Scrittore italiano*, 103.

21. Ricci, *Scrittore italiano*, 16.

22. Asor Rosa, "Lo Stato democratico e i partiti politici," 552.

23. Berto Ricci, "Risposta alla Santità di Papa Pio XI sull'ultima Enciclica," in "Il duello col Papa: Contestazioni all'ultima Enciclica," *L'Universale* 1, no. 7 bis (July 11, 1931). On the subject of universal fascism, which was particularly important to the culture of young fascists, see Marco Cuzzi, *L'internazionale delle camicie nere: I CAUR, Comitati d'azione per l'universalità di Roma, 1933–1939* (Milan: Mursia, 2005).

24. See Domenico Carella, *Fascismo prima, fascismo dopo* (Rome: A. Armando, 1973), 127. On the magazine see Garin, *Cronache di filosofia italiana: 1900–1943*, 465–69; Renzo De Felice, *Mussolini il duce*, part 1: *Gli anni del consenso, 1929–1936* (Turin: Einaudi, 1974), 104; Mangoni, *L'interventismo della cultura*, 229, 236, 294; Pasquale Voza, "Il problema del realismo negli anni trenta: 'Il Saggiatore,' 'Il Cantiere,'" *Lavoro critico* 21–22 (1981): 65–105; Giuseppe Carlo Marino, *L'autarchia della cultura: intellettuali e fascismo negli anni trenta* (Rome: Editori Riuniti, 1983), 25–31; Mario Sechi, *Il mito della nuova cultura: Giovani, realismo e politica negli anni trenta* (Manduria: Lacaita, 1984), 65ff.; A. R. Longo, "Individuo e critica della democrazia nella cultura politica italiana degli anni trenta," *Democrazia e diritto* 1 (1997): 270–96; Ben-Ghiat, *Fascist Modernities*, chapter 4; Tarquini, *Il Gentile dei fascisti*, 171–80.

25. Domenico Carella, "La concretezza del mio oggi," *Il Saggiatore* 1, f. 1, nos. 1–2 (April 1930): 3–8; and, in the same issue, G. Granata, "Dei giovani," *Il Saggiatore* 1, f. 1, nos. 1–2 (April 1930): 9.

26. "Risposte all'inchiesta sulla nuova generazione," *Il Saggiatore* 3, f. 19, no. 1 (March 1932): 3. See also Luisa Mangoni, "Il fascismo," in *Letteratura italiana*, vol. 1: *Il letterato e le istituzioni* (Turin: Einaudi, 1982), 540ff.

27. "Conclusioni all'inchiesta sulla nuova generazione," *Il Saggiatore* 3, no. 11 (January 1933): 437–64. The most prominent authors who participated in the debate were Francesco Orestano, Paolo Orano, Julius Evola, Antonino Anile, Giuseppe Bottai, Agostino Gemelli, Margherita Sarfatti, Adriano Tilgher, Ernesto Codignola, and Filippo Tommaso Marinetti. Most intellectuals—minus the idealists, who were not consulted because the authors thought they represented an outdated culture—denied that there was a profound divide between the generations. In fact, the authors interviewed reaffirmed the contributions of each generation since the beginning of fascism and the birth of a new culture.

28. "Conclusioni all'inchiesta sulla nuova generazione," 443.

29. "Conclusioni all'inchiesta sulla nuova generazione," 450.

30. Among the many contributions to the debate begun in "Il Saggiatore," see Giuseppe Bottai, "Atteggiamenti e orientamenti della nuova generazione," *Critica fascista* 10, no. 19 (October 1, 1932): 363–65.

31. Domenico Carella, "Cultura e mentalità del dopoguerra," *Critica fascista* 3, no, 20 (April 2, 1932): 51–56.

32. "Contributo per una nuova cultura," *Il Saggiatore* 4, nos. 6–8 (October 1933): 243–381.

33. See Luigi Fallacara, ed., *Il Frontespizio: 1929–1938* (San Giovanni Valdarno/Rome: Landi, 1961); Piero Bargellini, *Vita senza miracoli* (Brescia: La Scuola, 1964); Vittorio Vettori, *Giovanni Papini* (Turin: Borla, 1967); Mangoni, *L'interventismo della cultura*, 256–83; Mangoni, "Aspetti della cultura cattolica sotto il fascismo," 363–417; Moro, *La formazione della classe dirigente cattolica*, 142; F. Mazzariol, "I maggiori protagonisti del Frontespizio," *Studium* 77, no. 5 (1981): 545–63; Piero Bargellini, Carlo Bo, and Lorenzo Bedeschi, *Il tempo de "Il frontespizio": Carteggio Bargellini—Bo, 1930–1943* (Milan: Camunia, 1989).

34. Giovanni Papini and Domenico Giuliotti, eds., *Dizionario dell'Omo salvatico* (Florence: Vallecchi, 1923), 10. On Papini and Giuliotti's contributions, cf. Renato Moro, "La religione e la 'nuova epoca': Cattolicesimo e modernità tra le due guerre mondiali," in *Il modernismo tra cristianità e secolarizzazione: Atti del Convegno internazionale di Urbino, 1–4 ottobre 1997*, ed. Alfonso Botti and Rocco Cerrato (Urbino: QuattroVenti, 2000), 535ff.

35. Moro, "La religione e la 'nuova epoca,'" 542.

36. Antonio Baldini and Giuseppe De Luca, *Carteggio: 1929–1961*, ed. Emilio Giordano (Rome: Edizioni di storia e letteratura, 1992), 16.

37. I. Speranza, "Intelligenza e sentimento," *Il Frontespizio* 7, no. 4 (April 1935): 6.

38. Garin, *Cronache di filosofia italiana: 1900–1943*, 451; Garin, "La filosofia italiana di fronte al fascismo," 17–40; see also Garin's introduction to Giovanni Gentile and Eugenio Garin, *Opere filosofiche* (Milan: Garzanti, 1991).

39. Franco Restaino, *La filosofia contemporanea 4*, vol. 10 of *Storia della filosofia*, ed. Nicola Abbagnano (Milan: TEA, 1995), 212–16.

40. Francesco Orestano, *Il nuovo realismo* (Milan: Fratelli Bocca, 1939), 4.

41. Carmelo Ottaviano, *Il pensiero di Francesco Orestano* (Palermo: Industrie Riunite Editori Siciliani, 1933); Garin, *Cronache di filosofia italiana: 1900–1943*, 137–51; Tarquini, *Il Gentile dei fascisti*, 216–30. Regarding the Italian Philosophical Society during the years of the fascist regime, see M. Portale, "L'Archivio di Filosofia: Organo della Società Filosofica Italiana," in *Idealismo e anti-idealismo nella filosofia italiana del Novecento* (Milan: FrancoAngeli, 2005), 211–15; E. Castelli Gattinara, "L'Avventura filosofica italiana," *Quaderni della Biblioteca filosofica di Turin*, 1970, 3–9.

42. Universitá di Roma, Instituto di Studi Filosofici, *Archivio di filosofia* 1, no. 1 (January–March 1933): 120.

43. "Discorso del Presidente S. E. Francesco Orestano Accademico d'Italia," in *Atti VIIIo Congresso nazionale di filosofia, Roma, 24–28 ottobre 1933* (Rome: Società filosofica italiana, 1934), 9.

44. Francesco Orestano, *Nuovi princìpi* (Palermo: Biblioteca di Filosofia e Scienza, 1925), 50.

45. "Relazione di S. E. Orestano," in *Atti VIIIo Congresso nazionale di filosofia: Roma, 24–28 ottobre 1933*, 18. See also Maurizio Torrini, "Scienza e filosofia negli anni '30," *Ricerche di matematica* 40 (1990): 35–56.

46. *Atti VIIIo Congresso nazionale di filosofia: Roma, 24–28 ottobre 1933*, 25.

47. Michele Federico Sciacca, "I congressi contro l'idealismo," *Giornale critico della filosofia italiana* 17, no. 4 (1936): 121.

48. Orestano, *Il nuovo realismo*, 4.

49. Orestano, *Il nuovo realismo*, 15.

50. Julius Evola, *Saggi sull'idealismo magico* (Todi/Rome: Atanòr, 1925), 12. See also Francesco Cassata, *A destra del fascismo: Profilo politico di Julius Evola* (Turin: Bollati Boringhieri, 2003); Francesco Germinario, *Razza del sangue, razza dello spirito: Julius Evola, l'antisemitismo e il nazionalsocialismo (1930–43)* (Turin: Bollati Boringhieri, 2001). See also Francesco Germinario, "Julius Evola," in *Dizionario del fascismo*, ed. Victoria De Grazia and Sergio Luzzatto (Turin: Einaudi, 2005), 1:497–98; Antimo Negri, *Julius Evola e la filosofia* (Milan: Spirali, 1988); Marco Rossi, ed., "'Lo Stato democratico' e l'antifascismo antidemocratico di Julius Evola," *Storia contemporanea* 20, no. 1 (1989): 5–43; Marco Rossi, "L'avanguardia che si fa tradizione: L'itinerario culturale di Julius Evola dal primo dopoguerra alla metà degli anni trenta," *Storia contemporanea* 22, no. 6 (1991): 1039–90; Marco Rossi, "Julius Evola e la Lega teosofica indipendente di Roma," *Storia contemporanea* 25, no. 1 (1994): 39–55.

51. Julius Evola, "Il fascismo quale volontà d'impero e il cristianesimo," *Critica fascista* 5, no. 24 (December 15, 1927): 463–64.

52. Evola, "Il fascismo quale volontà d'impero e il cristianesimo," 464.

53. Julius Evola, "'Cultura,' stile di vita e stile fascista," *Vita nova* 8, no. 1 (January 1932): 3–7.

54. Julius Evola, "Di chi è precursore Hegel?" *La vita italiana* 22, no. 251 (February 15, 1934): 169–81. See also the contributions of Giovanni Preziosi, "Hegel precursore, che fregatura!" *La vita italiana* 22, no. 250 (January 15, 1934): 107; Giovanni Preziosi, "Gioco di bussolotti," *La vita italiana* 22, no. 253 (April 15, 1934): 488; Giovanni Preziosi, "A fil di logica," *La vita italiana* 22, no. 254 (May 15, 1934): 627.

55. Julius Evola, "Il superamento dell'idealismo," in *Diorama, problemi dello spirito nell'etica fascista: Antologia della pagina speciale di "Regime Fascista" diretta da Julius Evola*, ed. Marco Tarchi (Rome: Ed. Europa, 1974), 211; see also Julius Evola, "La ricostruzione dell'idea di Stato," *Lo Stato* 5, no. 2 (February 1934): 113–33.

56. See Augusto Guzzo, *Armando Carlini* (Turin: Edizioni di "Filosofia," 1960), with a biographical note by Vittorio Sainati; Vittorio Sainati, *Armando Carlini* (Turin: Edizioni di "Filosofia," 1961); Garin, *Cronache di filosofia italiana: 1900–1943*, 411 and

passim; Garin, "La filosofia italiana di fronte al fascismo," 17; Corrado Dollo, *Momenti e problemi dello spiritualismo: Varisco, Carabellese, Carlini, Le Senne* (Padua: CEDAM, 1967); regarding contacts with Mussolini, see Yvon De Begnac and Francesco Perfetti, eds., *Taccuini mussoliniani* (Bologna: Il Mulino, 1990), 377 and passim; Vittorio Sainati, "Armando Carlini e Ugo Spirito: Una concordia (fortemente) discors [*sic*]," *Annali della Fondazione Ugo Spirito* 6 (1994): 189–98; Pietro Prini, *La filosofia cattolica italiana del Novecento* (Rome: Laterza, 1996), 117–27; Michele Ciliberto, "La filosofia tra Pisa e Florence," in *Le città filosofiche: Per una geografia della cultura filosofica del Novecento*, ed. Pietro Rossi and Carlo Augusto Viano (Bologna: Il Mulino, 2004), 223–29.

57. Armando Carlini, "Fascistizziamo le università!" *Vita nova* 4, no. 9 (September 1928): 719–20.

58. Armando Carlini, *Orientamenti della filosofia contemporanea* (Rome: Critica fascista, 1931), 13.

59. Carlini, *Orientamenti della filosofia contemporanea*, 30.

60. Carlini, *Orientamenti della filosofia contemporanea*, 79.

61. Armando Carlini, *Alla ricerca di me stesso (esame critico del mio pensiero)* (Florence: Sansoni, 1951), 39.

62. Armando Carlini, *Filosofia e religione nel pensiero di Mussolini* (Rome: Istituto nazionale fascista di cultura, 1934), 7. See also Garin, "La filosofia italiana di fronte al fascismo," 15–36, especially the observations on 16.

63. Carlini, *Filosofia e religione nel pensiero di Mussolini*, 9.

64. Carlini, *Filosofia e religione nel pensiero di Mussolini*, 20. For a more detailed analysis, see Tarquini, *Il Gentile dei fascisti*, 290–300.

65. Carlini, *Filosofia e religione nel pensiero di Mussolini*, 20.

66. Armando Carlini, "La concezione della vita nel fascismo," *Critica fascista* 17, no. 3 (December 1, 1938): 46–47.

67. This opinion can also be found in Robert Solomon Wistrich, "Fascism and the Jews of Italy," in *Fascist Antisemitism and the Italian Jews*, ed. Robert Solomon Wistrich and Sergio Della Pergola (Jerusalem: Hebrew University of Jerusalem, Avraham Harman Institute of Contemporary Jewry, Vidal Sassoon International Center for the Study of Antisemitism, 1995), 13–18. See also David Bidussa, *Il mito del bravo italiano* (Milan: Il Saggiatore, 1994); Mario Toscano, "Fascismo, razzismo, antisemitismo: Osservazioni per un bilancio storiografico," in *Ebraismo e antisemitismo in Italia: Dal 1848 alla guerra dei sei giorni* (Milan: FrancoAngeli, 2003), 208–43; a historiographic balance is also found in Valeria Galimi, "Politica della razza, antisemitismo, Shoah," *Studi storici* 55, no. 1 (2014): 169–81.

68. See Giorgio Israel and Pietro Nastasi, *Scienza e razza nell'Italia fascista* (Bologna: Il Mulino, 1998), 11–33; Roberto Maiocchi, *Scienza italiana e razzismo fascista* (Scandicci [Florence]: La Nuova Italia, 1999), 7–29; a different interpretation appears in Francesco Germinario, *Fascismo e antisemitismo: Progetto razziale e ideologia totalitaria* (Rome: Laterza, 2009), 77–98, and Marie Anne Matard-Bonucci, *L'Italia fascista e la persecuzione degli ebrei* (Bologna: Il Mulino, 2008).

69. Israel and Nastasi, *Scienza e razza nell'Italia fascista*, 111; and Francesco Cassata, *Il fascismo razionale: Corrado Gini fra scienza e politica* (Rome: Carocci, 2006). Maiocchi, *Scienza italiana e razzismo fascista*, 38, emphasizes how many scientists changed their minds after this speech and adapted their research based on the new guidelines. See also Aaron Gillette, *Racial Theories in Fascist Italy* (London: Routledge, 2002), 45–47.

70. Anna Treves, *Le nascite e la politica nell'Italia del Novecento* (Milan: LED, 2001), 16.

71. Nicola Pende, *Bonifica umana razionale e biologia politica* (Bologna: Cappelli, 1933), 12; Maiocchi, *Scienza italiana e razzismo fascista*, 46–57; Israel and Nastasi, *Scienza e razza nell'Italia fascista*, 136–41.

72. Pende, *Bonifica umana razionale e biologia politica*, 38–39.

73. Pende, *Bonifica umana razionale e biologia politica*, 231.

74. Pende, *Bonifica umana razionale e biologia politica*, 239.

75. Luigi Goglia, "Il colore del razzismo fascista," in *Leggi del 1938 e cultura del razzismo: Storia, memoria, rimozione*, ed. Marina Beer, Anna Foa, and Isabella Iannuzzi (Rome: Viella, 2010), 38; on the legislation, see Michael A. Livingston, *The Fascists and the Jews of Italy: Mussolini's Race Laws, 1938–1943* (Cambridge: Cambridge University Press, 2014).

76. See also Francesco Cassata, *"La difesa della razza": Politica, ideologia e immagine del razzismo fascista* (Turin: Einaudi, 2008), 59.

77. Israel and Nastasi, *Scienza e razza nell'Italia fascista*, 225; Cassata, *"La difesa della razza,"* 56–166.

78. Roberto Finzi, *L'università italiana e le leggi antiebraiche* (Rome: Editori Riuniti, 1997), 29–39; Valeria Galimi and Giovanna Procacci, *"Per la difesa della razza": L'applicazione delle leggi antiebraiche nelle università italiane* (Milan: UNICOPLI, 2009); Angelo Ventura, "La persecuzione fascista contro gli ebrei nell'università italiana," in *Il fascismo e gli ebrei: Il razzismo antisemita nell'ideologia e nella politica del regime* (Rome: Donizelli, 2013). On the censorship of Jewish authors, see Giorgio Fabre, *L'elenco: Censura fascista, editoria e autori ebrei* (Turin: S. Zamorani, 1998); Annalisa Capristo, *L'espulsione degli ebrei dalle accademie italiane* (Turin: S. Zamorani, 2002).

79. Giorgio Israel, "L'espulsione dei professori ebrei dalle facoltà scientifiche," in Beer, Foa, and Iannuzzi, *Leggi del 1938 e cultura del razzismo*, 46; Gabriele Turi, "Ruolo e destino degli intellettuali nella politica razziale del fascismo," in *La legislazione antiebraica in Italia e in Europa: Atti del convegno nel cinquantenario delle leggi razziali (Roma, 17–18 ottobre 1988)* (Rome: Camera dei deputati, 1989), 95–121.

80. Maiocchi, *Scienza italiana e razzismo fascista*, 213–14; Germinario, *Fascismo e antisemitismo*, 36–38.

81. Leone Franzì, *Fase attuale del razzismo tedesco* (Rome: Istituto nazionale di cultura fascista, 1939), 41.

82. Franzì, *Fase attuale del razzismo tedesco*, 41.

83. Franzì, *Fase attuale del razzismo tedesco*, 54.

84. Franzì, *Fase attuale del razzismo tedesco*, 55.

85. Germinario, *Fascismo e antisemitismo*, 18.

86. Rosella Faraone, *Giovanni Gentile e la questione ebraica* (Soveria Mannelli (CZ): Rubbettino, 2003). For the story of Paul Oskar Kristeller, see Paolo Simoncelli, *Cantimori, Gentile e la Normale di Pisa: Profili e documenti* (Milan: FrancoAngeli, 1994), 81–88.

87. Faraone, *Giovanni Gentile e la questione ebraica*, 98; compare Gennaro Sasso, "Gentile e il nazionalsocialismo: Appunti e documenti," *La Cultura* 23, no. 1 (1995): 5–22; see also the discussion in Giovanni Rota, "Il filosofo Gentile e le leggi razziali," *Rivista di storia della filosofia (1984–)* 62, no. 2 (2007): 265–300; Gennaro Sasso, "Gentiliana et Cantimoriana," *La cultura* 47, no. 2 (2009): 187–246.

88. Finzi, *L'università italiana e le leggi antiebraiche*, 39–51; Fabre, *L'elenco*, 117–18, 142, 367, 385.

89. Riccardo Mariani, *Fascismo e "città nuove"* (Milan: Feltrinelli, 1976); Giorgio Ciucci, *Gli architetti e il fascismo: Architettura e città, 1922–1944* (Turin: Einaudi, 1989); Giuseppe Pagano and Cesare De Seta, eds., *Architettura e città durante il fascismo* (Rome-Bari: Laterza, 1990); Richard A. Etlin, *Modernism in Italian Architecture, 1890–1940* (Cambridge, MA: MIT Press, 1991); Paolo Nicoloso, *Mussolini architetto: Propaganda e paesaggio urbano nell'Italia fascista* (Turin: Einaudi, 2008); Paolo Nicoloso, "Urbanistica," in De Grazia and Luzzatto, *Dizionario del fascismo*, 2:769–74.

90. Ciucci, *Gli architetti e il fascismo*, xx.

91. Ciucci, *Gli architetti e il fascismo*.

92. Etlin, *Modernism in Italian Architecture, 1890–1940*, 234.

93. Quoted in Ciucci, *Gli architetti e il fascismo*, 386.

94. Mariani, *Fascismo e "città nuove,"* 130.

95. Mariani, *Fascismo e "città nuove,"* 437.

96. Emilio Gentile, *Fascismo di pietra* (Rome: Laterza, 2007), 166; Etlin, *Modernism in Italian Architecture, 1890–1940*; Marla Stone, "Staging Fascism: The Exhibition of the Fascist Revolution," *Journal of Contemporary History* 28, no. 2 (1993): 215–43; Jeffrey T. Schnapp, *Anno X: La mostra della rivoluzione fascista del 1932* (Pisa: Istituti editoriali e poligrafici internazionali, 2003).

97. Margherita Sarfatti, "Architettura, arte e simbolo alla Mostra del fascismo," in Schnapp, *Anno X*, 69–72. A description of the exhibition halls can be found in on 51–60. See also the chapter by Claudio Fogu, "L'immaginario storico fascista e la Mostra della Rivoluzione," 131–54.

98. Gentile, *Fascismo di pietra*, 166.

99. Emily Braun, "Expressionism as Fascist Aesthetic," *Journal of Contemporary History* 31, no. 2 (1996): 273–92; Emily Braun, "Mario Sironi: Art and Politics in Fascist Italy 1919–1945" (PhD dissertation, New York University, Graduate School of Arts and Science, 1991); Emily Braun, "Pittura e scultura," in De Grazia and Luzzatto, *Dizionario del fascismo*, 2:386–90; Monica Cioli, *Il fascismo e la sua arte: Dottrina e istituzioni tra futurismo e Novecento* (Florence: Olschki, 2011), 35–58.

100. Mario Sironi, "Manifesto della pittura murale, in 'La Colonna,'" in *Scritti editi e inediti*, ed. Ettore Camesasca and Claudia Gian Ferrari (Milan: Feltrinelli, 1980), 155–57.

101. Mariani, *Fascismo e "città nuove,"* 195–200.

102. Mariani, *Fascismo e "città nuove,"* 87.

103. Mariani, *Fascismo e "città nuove,"* 249–65; see also Aristotle A. Kallis, *The Third Rome, 1922–1943: The Making of the Fascist Capital* (New York: Palgrave Macmillan, 2014).

104. Gentile, *Fascismo di pietra*, 184.

105. Ciucci, *Gli architetti e il fascismo*, 177.

106. Gentile, *Fascismo di pietra*, 164.

107. Enrico Guidoni, "L'E42, città della rappresentazione: Il progetto urbanistico e le polemiche sull'architettura," in *E 42: Utopia e scenario del regime*, vol. 2, ed. Maurizio Calvesi and Enrico Guidoni (Venice: Cataloghi Marsilio, 1987), 45.

108. Guidoni, "L'E42, città della rappresentazione," 189.

109. Gentile, *Fascismo di pietra*, 184.

110. Quoted in Etlin, *Modernism in Italian Architecture, 1890–1940*, 491.

111. Etlin, *Modernism in Italian Architecture, 1890–1940*, 491.

Chapter 7. Cultural Politics and Intellectuals in the 1940s

1. Renzo De Felice, *Mussolini il duce*, part 2: *Lo stato totalitario, 1936–1940* (Turin: Einaudi, 1981), 117–30. For a deeper examination, see Alessandra Tarquini, *Il Gentile dei fascisti: Gentiliani e antigentiliani nel regime fascista* (Bologna: Il Mulino, 2009), 330–44.

2. Annibale Orani, *La Carta della scuola con annesso grafico-guida* (Rome: A. Signorelli, 1941), 3.

3. Orani, *La carta della scuola con annesso grafico-guida*, 4.

4. Teresa Maria Mazzatosta, *Il regime fascista tra educazione e propaganda (1935–1943)* (Bologna: Cappelli, 1978), 92.

5. Orani, *La carta della scuola con annesso grafico-guida*, 5.

6. Quoted in Tarquini, *Il Gentile dei fascisti*, 338.

7. Giuseppe Bottai, "La Carta della scuola e la sua etica," *Critica fascista* 17, no. 9 (March 1, 1939): 130–31.

8. Ministero dell'educazione nazionale and Direzione generale dell'Ordine superiore classico, *Dalla riforma Gentile alla Carta della scuola* (Florence: Vallecchi, 1941): xvi.

9. Luigi Volpicelli, *Scuola e lavoro* (Rome: Signorelli, 1941), 163.

10. Luigi Volpicelli, *Commento alla Carta della scuola* (Rome: Istituto nazionale di cultura fascista, 1940), 52.

11. See also Rita Pelagatti, *Bibliografia della Carta della scuola*, vol. 1 (Rome: Edizione di istruzione tecnica, 1940).

12. P. Orano, "Educazione fascista," in *Scuola fascista: La Carta della scuola e sua interpretazione*, ed. Carlo Magi-Spinetti (Rome: Editrice Pinciana, 1939), 165.

13. Armando Carlini, *Verso la nuova scuola* (Florence: G. C. Sansoni, 1941), 242; Armando Carlini, "Aspetti della Carta," *Critica fascista* 17, no. 9 (March 1, 1939): 131–33.

14. Luisa Mangoni, *"Primato" 1940-1943: Antologia* (Bari: De Donato, 1977); Luisa Mangoni, *L'interventismo della cultura: Intellettuali e riviste del fascismo* (Rome/ Bari: Laterza, 1974), 347–66; Luisa Mangoni, "Il fascismo," in *Letteratura Italiana*, vol. 1: *Il letterato e le istituzioni* (Turin: Einaudi, 1982), 521–48; A. Cicchetti and Alberto Asor Rosa, "Roma," in *Letteratura italiana*, vol. 3: *L'età contemporanea* (Turin: Einaudi, 1989); Mirella Serri, *I redenti: Gli intellettuali che vissero due volte, 1938-1948* (Milan: Corbaccio, 2005); Vito Zagarrio, *"Primato": Arte, cultura, cinema del fascismo attraverso una rivista esemplare* (Rome: Edizioni di storia e letteratura, 2007).

15. C. Morandi, "Le università e la cultura," *Primato* 2, no. 4 (February 15, 1941): 6.

16. L. Russo, "Le università e la cultura," *Primato* 2, no. 4 (February 15, 1941): 7.

17. Luigi Volpicelli, "Le università e la cultura," *Primato* 2, no. 6 (March 15, 1941): 6.

18. Danilo Breschi and Gisella Longo, *Camillo Pellizzi: La ricerca delle élites tra politica e sociologia (1896-1979)* (Soveria Mannelli (CZ): Rubbettino, 2004), 146–65.

19. Camillo Pellizzi, "Le università e la cultura," *Primato* 2, no. 5 (March 1, 1941): 4.

20. Regarding Pellizzi's activities during the 1940s, see Gisella Longo, ed., "Il primo convegno dei gruppi scientifici dell'Istituto nazionale di cultura fascista sull' 'Idea di Europa' (23–24 novembre 1942)," *Annali della Fondazione Ugo Spirito* 5 (1994): 127–88; and Breschi and Longo, *Camillo Pellizzi*, 133–95, which is entirely focused on this subject.

21. Carlo Ghisalberti, "Per una storia del 'Dizionario di Politica' (1940)," *Clio* 26 (1990): 671–97; Alessia Pedio, *La cultura del totalitarismo imperfetto: Il Dizionario di politica del Partito nazionale fascista (1940)* (Milan: Ed. Unicopli, 2000), 104–10.

22. Antonino Pagliaro, *Il Fascismo: Commento alla dottrina* (Rome: Libreria di scienze e lettere, 1933), x. Translated into Spanish: Antonino Pagliaro, *El Fascismo: Comentario a su doctrina* (Bilbao: Editorial Vizcaína, 1938).

23. On the PNF's Office of Research and Legislation, see Emilio Gentile, *The Italian Road to Totalitarianism* (London: Frank Cass, 2004), 256–69.

24. Antonino Pagliaro, "Il Dizionario di politica del Pnf," *Civiltà fascista: Rivista mensile* 7, no. 1 (January 1940): 33. The same concept was expressed by Guido Mancini, who introduced the *Dizionario* to Mussolini.

25. Ferdinando Mezzasoma, "Premessa," in *Dizionario di politica*, ed. Partito nazionale fascista (Rome: Istituto della Enciclopedia italiana, 1940), I.

26. Franco Polato, *Bibliografia degli scritti di e su Felice Battaglia* (Bologna: CLUEB, 1989); Franco Polato, "Felice Battaglia," in *Dizionario biografico degli italiani* (Rome: Istituto della Enciclopedia italiana, 1988), 34:311–14. See also Nicola Matteucci and Alberto Pasquinelli, eds., *Il pensiero di Felice Battaglia: Atti del Seminario promosso dal Dipartimento di Filosofia di Bologna (29-30 ottobre 1987)* (Bologna: CLUEB, 1989); Gabriele Turi, *Il fascismo e il consenso degli intellettuali* (Bologna: Il

Mulino, 1980), 86–92, 125–27; Gabriele Turi, *Giovanni Gentile: Una biografia* (Florence: Giunti, 1995), 428, 456.

27. Turi, *Il fascismo e il consenso degli intellettuali*, 91.

28. Felice Battaglia, *Scritti di teoria dello Stato* (Milan: Giuffrè, 1939), 23.

29. Battaglia, *Scritti di teoria dello Stato*, v.

30. Felice Battaglia, "Dichiarazione dei diritti," in *Dizionario di politica*, ed. Partito nazionale fascista (Rome: Istituto della Enciclopedia italiana, 1940), vol. 1 (A–D): 782.

31. Felice Battaglia, "Illuminismo," in *Dizionario di politica*, vol. 2 (E–L): 471.

32. Felice Battaglia, "Rousseau," in *Dizionario di politica*, vol. 4 (R–Z): 157.

33. Felice Battaglia, "Sorel," in *Dizionario di politica*, vol. 4 (R–Z): 315.

34. Felice Battaglia, "Pisacane," in *Dizionario di politica*, vol. 3 (M–Q): 431.

35. Carlo Curcio, "Fascismo e università," *Lo Stato* 1, no. 1 (February 1930): 60–62.

36. Carlo Curcio, "Tendenze nuove della dottrina tedesca: C. Schmitt," *Lo Stato* 1, no. 4 (August 1930): 484.

37. Carlo Curcio, "Contenuto, funzioni ed aspetti politici del Partito nazionale fascista," *Lo Stato* 5, no. 3 (March 1934): 161–71.

38. Carlo Curcio, "Contenuto, funzioni ed aspetti politici del Partito nazionale fascista," 161–71.

39. These articles were then collected in a single volume, with an introduction on modern myths and a conclusion dealing with utopia: Carlo Curcio, *Miti della politica: Tre saggi sulla democrazia, sul socialismo e sul liberalismo con una introduzione intorno ai miti moderni ed una conclusione sull' utopia* (Rome: Cremonese, 1940). See also Carlo Curcio, "Considerazioni sulla presente civiltà," *Lo Stato* 9, no. 2 (February 1938): 65–76.

40. Giacomo Perticone and Carlo Curcio, "Partito," in *Dizionario di politica*, vol. 3 (M–Q): 381.

Conclusion

1. Benito Mussolini, *Opera omnia*, vol. 34, 2nd reprint, ed. Edoardo Susmel (Florence: LaFenice, 1967), 117.

INDEX

900 (magazine), 69–70. *See also*
  Novecento group

academic freedom: abolition under
  fascist regime, 104–5, 106, 164; fascist
  opposition to, 40, 41
Accademia d'arte drammatica and
  cinecittà, 27
Acerbo, Giacomo, 201n8
Action Party (Partito d'azione), 8
activism, as foundation of fascism, 8,
  11
Adamson, Walter, 66, 177n90
African colonies: racist laws in,
  145; Roman history and fascist
  policies in, 93. *See also* Ethiopia,
  occupation of
Alessandrini, Goffredo, 120
Alfano, Franco, 121, 123
Alfieri, Dino, 116, 123
alienation, fascism as response to,
  20–21
Allmayer, Vito Fazio, 63
Allotti, Pierluigi, 117
Alto Adige Institute, 126
amateur theater companies, 123
Amicucci, Ermanno, 117

Aniante, Antonio (Antonio Rapisarda),
  67
anthropological revolution, fascist
  vision of, 95, 165. *See also* new
  (fascist) man
anthropologists, fascist, 144–46
antihumanist worldview, 99
antirationalist ideology: and architecture, 150; and fascism, 37
anti-Semitism, fascist intellectuals and,
  118, 143, 146–48
architecture, fascist, 4, 54, 149–51, 166;
  E42 district, Rome, 94, 152–54;
  maximalist design in, 154
Arditi, 35–36
Arendt, Hannah, 25
Arias, Gino, 48, 201n8
art, fascist: aesthetic pluralism of, 66,
  167; debate about, 65–68; mural
  paintings, 151–52; subordination to
  politics, 66–67, 131–32
artists, fascist, 66–68, 151–52, 166, 167;
  loyalty of, 66, 68, 121; secret subsidies
  granted to, 118
Asor Rosa, Alberto, 13–15, 22, 97, 133
Augustus, celebration of bimillennium
  of, 94

Croce, Benedetto: on contemporary relevance of history, 5; and cultural tradition of fascism, 60; on education, 41; on fascism, 7, 32, 33; influence on Bobbio, 8; influence on Garin, 9, 10; influence on Marxist scholars, 13

cults: fascist, Mosse on, 21, 22; first politician to employ, 36. *See also* myth(s)

Cultura e fascismo (collection of essays), 27–28

cultural politics: National Fascist Party and, 3, 4; use of term, 4. *See also* fascist culture

cultural studies, approach to fascism, 29–30

culture: Bobbio on, 8–9; history of, Marxist scholars on, 12; modern anthropology on, 21; National Fascist Party on, 3; totalitarianism and understanding of, 3, 24, 72. *See also* culture and politics; fascist culture

Culture and Art Tournaments, 111

culture and politics, fascism and merging of, 168, 169; Cantimori on, 72; Codignola on, 71, 72; Gentile (Emilio) on, 31; Gentile (Giovanni) on, 70–71, 72; Pellizzi on, 159

Curcio, Carlo, 160, 162–63

D'Andrea, Ugo, 201n8

D'Annunzio, Gabriele, 36, 201n8

Davanzati, Roberto Forges, 125, 201n8

De Chirico, Giorgio, 66, 69, 151

De Crecchio, Luigi, 133

De Felice, Renzo, 23–24, 32, 33, 87–88, 95, 96, 175n60

De Grazia, Victoria, 56, 58, 113

Del Debbio, Enrico, 4, 54

Deledda, Grazia, 52

Del Noce, Augusto, 11–12, 19, 42

De Luca, Giuseppe, 136

Del Vecchio, Giorgio, 137, 162

De Marchi, Luigi, 52

democracy: ancient world's rejection of, 90; debates about meaning of, 74; fascism defined in opposition to, 36, 100; as mimetic force, Pellizzi on, 61; Nietzsche's rejection of, 90, 99

demographic campaign, fascist, 115, 144

demography, organicist theory of, 143

Demorazza, 146

Depero, Fortunato, 66

De Pirro, Nicola, 122

De Renzi, Mario, 151

De Sarlo, Francesco, 104

De Vecchi di Val Cismon, Cesare Maria, 106, 157; and education reform, 50, 106; vs. Gentile (Giovanni), 106–7; as minister of education, 50, 106, 109

dialects, limits on use of, 126

Di Lalla, Manilo, 191n65

Directorate General for Demography and Race (Demorazza), 146

Directorate General of Music and Theater, 121, 122

Dizionario di politica (Dictionary of politics), 89, 159–63

doctrine, fascist: inability to produce, 73. *See also* fascist ideology

Donati, Ines, 114

Dottrina fascista (magazine), 79

Ducati, Pericle, 92

Durkheim, Émile, 75

E42 (Esposizione del '42) district, Rome, 94, 152–54, 166

education policy, fascist, 39–41, 164–65; in 1920s, 40–41, 50–53; in 1930s, 103–7; in 1940s, 155–59; Bottai and, 50, 155–59; and consolidated textbook, 52, 104, 105; De Vecchi and, 50, 106; Fedele and, 50, 51; Gentile (Giovanni) and, 41, 44–46, 48, 50,

www.ingramcontent.com/pod-product-compliance
Lightning Source LLC
Chambersburg PA
CBHW031546260326
41914CB00002B/295